"Then **Tress** Said to **Troy...**"

The Best Ohio State Football Stories Ever Told

Jeff Snook

TRIUMPH
B O O K S

table of
contents

foreword

I want to begin by telling you a story about something that happened to me recently. I was sitting in my home in California when a young man in his late twenties brought several items over for me to sign for his dad, who was a huge Buckeyes fan.

As we sat talking, he asked if I owned a pair of gold pants—the kind you get when you play on an Ohio State football team that beats "that team up north." I pulled out two pairs and handed them to him. We sat and visited for about 45 minutes as I told him one story after another about the good old days—earning those gold pants, Woody Hayes, the day I received my varsity O jacket, more Woody, the 1968 national championship season, playing in front of all those great fans in the Horseshoe, our captains' breakfasts, even more Woody, and anything and everything about being a Buckeye.

He sat the whole time holding my gold pants and staring at them as if he were a five-year-old boy on Christmas morning. Truthfully, I wondered if I was ever going to get them back!

I guess my point is Ohio State's glorious history is made up of some wonderful stories, from the players, coaches, and all the team personnel that have been fortunate enough to be a part of the more than 115 years of Buckeyes football.

There are literally millions of them—and it takes more than 45 minutes to tell them all.

Let me take you back to the very first day I arrived on The Ohio State University campus as a young freshman during the fall of 1967. I was checking into my dormitory, Smith Hall, and a slender young man was in the elevator with me and had the most discouraging, depressing look on his face.

I asked him what was wrong.

"I just got cut from the marching band for the very last time," he told me. "It had been a goal of mine my whole life to make that marching band."

That planted a seed in my mind that there must be something very special about this marching band at Ohio State.

Another time, a trumpet player roomed next door, and he used to tell stories about how the band members' performances were reviewed on film, just like that of football players, and if they screwed up, they were thrown into the Olentangy River on Monday afternoons following our Saturday games.

Before my first game as a Buckeye, the season opener in 1968 at Ohio Stadium against Southern Methodist, I walked out promptly that day at 12:10 PM, as Woody had written the time on his big blackboard for quarterbacks and centers to enter the field. I looked around and saw just how large this place was. I stood there in awe of the stadium. My goodness, you feel so small during a moment like that.

Just then, Jan Fetters, the Ohio State head cheerleader, who was from my hometown of Lancaster, Ohio, came over to greet me and to wish me luck in that day's game. I had to say that relaxed me a little. When we finally came out as a team, like many players will say, I don't remember my feet touching the ground. It was euphoric. It was an out-of-body experience. To hear the roar of the crowd and to hear that great marching band playing "Across the Field," it was one of the greatest experiences of my life.

When I was a freshman, one of my biggest goals for the future had been to earn a Varsity O lettermen's jacket. And once it happened, I'll never forget that day: following our huge win over the school up north in '68, we had our annual team banquet the following Monday, and I received my first Varsity O lettermen's jacket.

I couldn't wait to wear it to class the next day.

I was coming out of class at Haggerty Hall, all proud in my new jacket. I saw some of my teammates down this hill, and they were all wearing their jackets. We were all pumped, sporting our lettermen's jackets. I headed down to see them, and as I got to the bottom of this small slope, my feet fell out from under me and I went flying, landing smack down on my hind end, looking straight up at the sky. Now here I am, supposed to be an athlete with good balance, and I cannot even stay on my feet running down a tiny hill as dozens of students walk by!

*   *   *

You cannot write a book about Ohio State football without having Wayne Woodrow Hayes dominate the content. I could tell you hundreds of stories about my beloved coach, and there are several in a chapter that details the man, his compassion, his drive to graduate his players, his motivational skills, his life, and his legacy.

Most of the time, I truly loved the ol' man.

When he recruited me, Woody promised me I would make lifelong friends and share lasting memories with my teammates and receive "a great, great education." Woody did not lie. We forged a strong bond, not only by winning two national championships, two Big Ten championships, one co–Big Ten championship, and 27 games, losing only two, but by living in a dorm together, toiling through two-a-day practices together, running the six-minute mile together, going to study table together, participating in snowball fights outside Denny Hall, and crossing the Oval together on our way to classes.

I will never forget when I went back to Ohio Stadium for the first time after my playing days were done. I saw that band come down the ramp and march onto the field, and the drum major touched his head to the ground behind him as the crowd was cheering. The next thing I knew, tears were rolling down my face. That was such an emotional experience for me—and it still is.

I sometimes remember that poor kid at my dorm who got cut from the marching band. He was right, there is something pretty special about the Best Damn Band in the Land. And I discovered that about the rest of The Ohio State University.

It is just hard to put into words what Ohio State means to me. I am a product of Ohio State, and I am proud to say that three times I walked across the stage to get degrees (bachelor's, master's, and doctorate). And I am a product of many of these stories that you will read here, from the many men who played before me, with me, and long after I left campus.

We all have much in common, starting with the fact that we were once, and always will be, Buckeyes.

It is safe to say that for most all of us, these stories help us relive the best times of our lives. This book gives you the chance to experience them as we did. Enjoy.

Go Bucks!

—Rex Kern

Rex Kern, one of the greatest quarterbacks in Ohio State history, led the Buckeyes to a 27–2 record in three seasons, including the consensus national championship in 1968. He was an All-American in 1969 and a team captain in '70. He is a member of the OSU and Rose Bowl Halls of Fame. He will be inducted into the College Football Hall of Fame in the summer of 2008.

acknowledgments

I want to thank all of those Buckeyes players and coaches who contributed stories for this book, especially Rex Kern, one of Ohio State's greatest players of yesteryear and one of its finest ambassadors of today.

I firmly believe that by telling the stories of Buckeyes football history, we can preserve them for future generations.

When it comes to philanthropy, most Ohioans know there was none better than Woody Hayes. He didn't care about making money, he cared about making others' lives better. As the saying goes, "Life is not about what you do, it is about what you do for others." Ohio State's legendary coach demonstrated that, as you will read in the chapter about his career.

Woody's favorite line was "You cannot pay back, so pay forward." Thus, I want to encourage all Buckeyes to follow that credo of Coach Hayes's to help make others' lives better.

The following are a few causes with which I am very familiar:

- The Arthur G. James Cancer Hospital. Ohio State's cancer research and treatment hospital is among the country's finest, and I have witnessed firsthand its excellent care and treatment. It is likely that you know someone who has been diagnosed with cancer in the past year. For instance, two of Ohio State's assistant coaches, Joe Daniels and Jim Bollman, were diagnosed with cancer before the start of the 2006 season. For more information, call (614) 293-3744 or go to www.jamesline.com/waystogive.
- Your local hospice organization, which provides care and comfort for terminally ill patients. To find a hospice in your Ohio community, call the Ohio Hospice center at (800) 776-9513 or go to www.OHPCO.org.
- The American Diabetes Association. More than 21 million Americans have diabetes. Hayes had it for most of his life. Two-time All-American defensive back Jack Tatum

(1968–1970) recently had his lower left leg amputated as a result of this disease. For more information, call (800) DIABETES or go to www.diabetes.org.

introduction

It is just another quiet Saturday morning inside the ROTC Building on Neil Avenue on the north end of The Ohio State University campus. Outside the sky is overcast and the temperature is in the low 40s as thousands of football fans scurry about, clad in scarlet and gray sweaters and coats.

It is 11:00 AM, November 18, 2006.

The number-one-ranked Buckeyes will battle number-two-ranked Michigan in a few hours at Ohio Stadium, just a few hundred yards away. It has been billed as the Game of the Century, and for good reason. Both teams are undefeated for the first time since 1973.

"Crazy outside, isn't it?" one ROTC student asks another. "Man, this is going to be some football game."

The other adds, "And some celebration afterward, right?"

They both laugh as one of them motions to a visitor.

"Hey, you want to see the room that was Coach Hayes's office?" he asks. "Follow me down the hall. This is it."

He waved for me to come inside. "This is our conference room now," he said, "but this was Woody's office."

A rectangular-shaped room with wood-paneled walls just off the main hallway, Woody Hayes used it as his office from the time he was fired as Ohio State's legendary football coach on December 30, 1978, until his death on March 12, 1987.

For more than eight years, this is where he segued into a forced retirement, if you will. He spent his days here, writing letters, talking to former presidents and players, and holding court with anybody who wanted—or didn't want—to hear a lecture on military history, politics, society's current problems, and, very rarely, football.

Yes, if these walls could talk, they would tell one hell of a story. Plenty of them. These days, the only remnant of Woody's life in this room is a small framed photo on the wall. He is pictured in his black navy dress uniform, standing on the deck of his ship. His hair is dark, and his face is young. He is smiling, and the sun is shining.

The bronzed caption reads: "Lt. Wayne Woodrow Hayes, USNR, Captain—USS Rinehart (DE 196), Pacific Theater, September 1945."

The picture was taken less than six years before he arrived at Ohio State as a thirty-something football coach ready to make his mark on the college football world. That is the only sign that a legend once occupied this room. His desk and chair have been long gone. The plaques, game balls, and pictures have long been removed, except for this one.

On this day, there are a few snacks and soft drinks arranged neatly on a table. There is a big-screen, high-definition television in the corner of the room, tuned to a college football pregame show. Suddenly, Woody's image flashes on the giant TV screen, next to former Michigan coach Bo Schembechler's, his former protégé and 10-year rival who died just 24 hours earlier.

Schembechler, after being granted permission from then–Ohio State president Edward Jennings, had visited this room on the day of Woody's funeral. He wanted to see where his mentor, then intense rival, and subsequently, good friend had worked following his coaching career. He sat down at Woody's desk that day and noticed a manuscript he had started, what would be another in a string of books he had written. One of the chapters was titled "Bo."

Bo picked it up, read Woody's words about himself, and sat there in Woody's chair and cried.

Almost 20 years later, being in this room at this moment with their images on television suddenly is very eerie.

"Woody and Bo are now together," the announcer claims, "and they will be looking down today on Ohio Stadium, watching this game and arguing just like old days."

*   *   *

Four hours and 20 minutes later, the clouds have disappeared and the skies have cleared, but it is colder now and the wind is blowing stronger.

I am standing on the sidelines of Ohio Stadium, next to hundreds of former Buckeyes players as the Best Damn Band in the Land puts its finishing touches on Script Ohio.

Suddenly I notice that at the top of the small *o*, a trumpet player sobs as tears stream down his cheek. After the sousaphone player dots the *i*, igniting a thunderous roar from the record crowd of 105,708 fans, the poor guy cries so hard that he is literally convulsing.

Leaning over to Jerry Rudzinski, a former OSU linebacker, I have to shout to be heard above the crowd's roar: "He must be a senior and this is his final Script Ohio." Jerry nods and smiles.

When the band finishes singing the "Buckeye Battle Cry" and marches off the field, it is a noticeable relief to many band members and yet an obvious sadness to many.

"When we came down the ramp, I looked around me and I could tell who the seniors were," a sophomore drummer said. "They were the ones who had tears running down their faces. You know, you only get to do this so many times in your lifetime.

"And when you know it is your final time..."

The baby-faced drummer couldn't finish. He, too, started to choke up. He knew his time was coming.

A few moments later, the Buckeyes seniors are introduced one-by-one until quarterback Troy Smith, the final player in line, digs in his heels, runs through the man-made tunnel of former players, and lands in Jim Tressel's arms. The player and coach hug tightly for a moment, and the crowd erupts again.

For the next three and a half hours, the state of Ohio is captivated, either in person or via television, from where the rest of the nation will watch.

The Buckeyes and Wolverines, comprising the greatest rivalry in college athletics, battle in a game for the ages. It was billed as the Game of the Century, and by the end, it has lived up to the season-long hype.

Every year, the Game is big.

This time, it is *humongous*.

When it is finally finished, after 81 points scored and 900 yards gained, the Buckeyes cling to a 42–39 victory, and thousands of Ohio State fans swarm the field of the giant Horseshoe. Many dig up chunks of the cold, moist turf for souvenirs. Some hoist players on their shoulders. Thousands of photo flashes from all decks of the massive stadium fill the sky like lightning bugs.

By the time these heroes and their fans finish singing the final note of "Carmen Ohio," with Tressel in the middle of it all, his arms spread wide forming the O-HI-O sign, every Buckeyes player and fan is either crying with joy or smiling with satisfaction.

"Does it get any better than this?" one OSU student asks another. "I could die now and be very happy. I am already in heaven anyway!"

If you are a Buckeye, there really isn't a better way to describe this scene, on this day. An undefeated season, a team ranked number one from start to finish. A win over rival Michigan, which also happened to enter the game undefeated. Played in perfect weather—football weather. At Ohio Stadium.

Yes, for a true Buckeye, these moments are indeed heaven on earth.

From above, Woody and Bo had to be watching, many sportswriters wrote that day.

And at the end of the game, only one of them was smiling.

The right one.

*   *   *

If I am asked, "What does Ohio State football mean to you?" all I have to do is think of that scene and tell you that it was a perfect day.

I could narrow it down this way: there are 365 days in a year, including 12 of them on average on which Ohio State plays a football game. Only six of those are played in Ohio Stadium. But only one of them—every other year—is against Michigan. And most importantly, it was a *win*.

When you throw in that those two teams were undefeated and vying for not only the Big Ten championship, but also a shot at a national championship, well, this day was *nirvana* in a Buckeye's life.

In the winter of 2003, I approached Jim Tressel about writing a book on the Buckeyes' recently concluded national championship season. After all, it had been 34 long years since Ohio State had captured college football's ultimate prize, and most of us were residing above cloud nine for a few months. I figured, what would be better for Buckeyes fans than to read about that improbable 14–0 season all over again, especially from the viewpoint of the man who created and shaped it all?

Plus, most Ohio State fans don't know enough about their coach. They know he is the son of a legendary coach. That he played quarterback at Baldwin-Wallace in Berea, Ohio, and that he is a devoted family man and a Christian. They know he is a winner. They know he can coach. And they know he can beat Michigan, as he promised he would on the day he was hired.

Instead, in his typical "it's not about me" fashion, Jim suggested a book on Ohio State's football tradition, based on letters that adorned the team's meeting room. Soon after he had accepted the job in January 2001, he had asked former OSU players to write short letters to current players, reminding them of Ohio State's tradition and putting into words what it meant to them to be a Buckeye.

Soon the walls of the large meeting room at the Woody Hayes Athletic Center on Olentangy River Road were covered with these framed letters. There were hundreds of them, dating back to Buckeyes who played in the 1930s. They came from all the greatest, from Rex Kern to John Hicks to Brian Baschnagel. They came from Heisman Trophy–winners Archie Griffin and Hopalong Cassady. And they came from backup players, those who practiced and toiled in obscurity but earned varsity letters. They all had one thing in common: they knew what it meant to be a Buckeye. Hence, we put their words into chapters, publishing the book *What It Means to Be a Buckeye.*

"It is about Ohio State's tradition and how rich and important that is to people," Tressel said. "It is not about me. This is not my program. It belongs to the players. The current players and the past players. Our responsibility is to make them proud of what we are trying to do. We all love this program, and we all love Ohio State."

For a true Buckeye, the love of Ohio State has to do with more than football. I mean, really, football is just a game, even if it is a game which angers us on some days and makes us ecstatic and proud on others. More importantly, it's everything that surrounds the game that matters as well. And it is everything that the game gives us.

Consider that as you grow older, through all the births, marriages, deaths, accomplishments, disappointments, and joys, you soon realize that time passes much too quickly. But when you come to Ohio Stadium on a Saturday in the fall, and you witness the marching band methodically stepping down the north ramp, time stands still. When you see Script Ohio as goose bumps stick out on the back of your neck as if you have a case of the measles, time stands still. And when you sing "Carmen Ohio," knowing all the words without glancing at the JumboTron, time stands still. It's as if that certain day in that giant old stadium surrounded by thousands of people you never met, but with whom you have so much in common, somehow recaptures your youth and summarizes your journey.

And it has meaning. As Woody himself would say, "You're damned right it has meaning. Yes, sir. It damn sure does. Don't let the skeptics tell you it doesn't."

Ohio State fans are all a part of something special that most people in the other 49 states aren't. If you grew up in Ohio, attended Ohio State, graduated from Ohio State, or simply rooted for Ohio State, you know what it is.

As a sportswriter covering college football for more than 25 years, I have been to most of the other major college stadiums on fall Saturdays. I have seen the Tigers touch Howard's Rock at Clemson, watched the Gators enter the Swamp in Gainesville, heard the War Chant in Tallahassee, witnessed the Hurricanes enter the Orange Bowl through the white smoke, the War Eagle fly majestically in Auburn, Mike the Tiger in Baton Rouge, Touchdown Jesus at South Bend, the Big Red Sea in Lincoln, the Sooner Schooner in Norman, and many others. They are all great traditions, making college football the best sport this country has, in my opinion.

Their traditions have roots reaching back to the late 1800s. The players aren't traded. And when alumni and fans move, they don't switch allegiances. They are Cornhuskers, Sooners, Wolverines, and Seminoles for *life*.

But if you are from Ohio, or you are a Buckeye, none of those traditions surpass what was created between High Street and the Olentangy River and nurtured over the past 100-plus years.

Game day in Columbus, Ohio, is unique.

Few stadiums compare to Ohio Stadium. The combination of its tradition, size, and shape is unmatched. And now that it has been renovated, yet still maintaining its Roman-like appearance, nothing comes close.

TBDBITL? I am telling you, I have seen all the others. Some bands, like Purdue's, Alabama's, Texas's, and USC's are pretty good. They are all tied for second. I know of no other place where band members are revered like celebrities. Where else do more than 10,000 fans show up to watch and listen to the skull session before every home game? Where else do band members sign autographs? Where else is a sousaphone player cheered as if he just scored the winning touchdown in the final quarter of the season's most important game?

Fight songs? You can have Notre Dame's "Victory March" and Michigan's "The Victors," but give me "Across the Field" and "Buckeye Battle Cry."

Alma maters? Please. Most students at other universities don't know the titles, let alone the words, of theirs. When Buckeyes hear those chimes signify the beginning of "Carmen Ohio," they know nothing Rogers and Hammerstein created compares.

"One thing is for sure," Tressel explained, "as the years go by, those things mean more to you and the passing of time brings everything into perspective. That's why 'Carmen Ohio' means so much to people. When we are singing it after each game, I look into that crowd of scarlet and gray and I see tears running down faces. Ohio State is important to them. Ohio State is important to us. I love the words…"

Oh come let's sing Ohio's praise,
And songs to Alma Mater raise.
While our hearts rebounding thrill,
With joy which death alone can still.
Summer's heat or winter's cold,

The seasons pass, the years will roll,
Time and change will surely show,
How firm thy friendship O-HI-O.

It must be said that the roots of the Ohio State traditions reach deeper than the songs, the band, and the football games.

If you are a Buckeyes fan who never attended OSU, take a walk across campus some day. See your reflection in Mirror Lake, sit on the Oval and watch the students walk by. See the giant statue of William Oxley Thompson in front of the library. Visit Harley's Rock just steps away from High Street, south of Woodruff Avenue. Listen to those chimes from Orton Hall. Check your watch by that giant clock on University Hall. Skip a rock across the Olentangy.

Yes, The Ohio State University is more than football, but what brings us back no matter where we live is the game.

Maybe it is our connection to the past, somehow making us feel young as we grow old. As I said, when we watch from the seats at Ohio Stadium, time seems to stand still. So hopefully, while you read this book of short stories, time will stand still for you. And I hope you find a greater insight into what drives our love and passion for Ohio State football.

I consider it a trip down memory lane, or in this case, Woody Hayes Drive. So here goes...

—Jeff Snook

chapter 1

A Name Known Throughout the College Football World

An Ohio buckeye tree stands in full bloom. This tree produces the lucky nut from which the team took its name.

Tigers, Lions, Bears, and other four-legged creatures dot the college football landscape, but there is only one school and one state that belongs to the Buckeyes.

What's in a Name?

"The Buckeyes."

The Ohio State University first fielded a football team in 1890, which was 20 years after the birth of the university, but the term *Buckeyes* was not officially adopted by the university's athletic council until 1950.

Not that it ever needed to be.

The term was firmly established by 1900, and most records indicate that it had probably been used with some frequency to refer to Ohio State and its athletic teams since before the turn of the century, according to the school's archives.

As most Ohioans know, the buckeye (*Aesculus glabra*) is a tree native to Ohio and particularly common in the Ohio River Valley. The tree's shiny, dark brown nuts with lighter tan patches resemble the eye of a deer.

What you may not have known is that pioneers carved the soft wood from buckeye trees into troughs, platters, and even cradles. Before the days of plastic, buckeye wood was often used to fashion artificial limbs. The nuts, inedible, are attractive, and folk wisdom had it that carrying one in one's pocket brings good luck and wards off rheumatism.

However, that rarely worked for a Tennessean named John Harold Cooper, especially when the winds of November blew cold. Not that he had rheumatism, just a severe case of Can't-Beat-Michiganism.

On the negative side, the wood does not burn well, the bark has an unpleasant odor, and the bitter nut meat is mildly poisonous. Still, the tree has grit. It grows where others cannot, is difficult to kill, and adapts to its circumstances.

Daniel Drake once gave a detailed speech on behalf of the buckeye tree at a public function in Cincinnati in 1833.

"In all our woods there is not a tree so hard to kill as the buckeye," he said. "The deepest girdling does not deaden it, and even after it is cut down and worked up into the side of a cabin it will send out young branches, denoting to all the world that buckeyes are not easily conquered, and could with difficulty be destroyed."

More than a century and a half later, a football coach named Earle Bruce stood at a podium in downtown Dallas, Texas, and used similar words to educate Southerners.

"For all you Texans who do not know what a Buckeye is, let me tell you," Bruce started, about to coach his team in the 1987 Cotton Bowl. "A Buckeye is the toughest thing you'll ever come across. A Buckeye is indestructible. You cannot crack a Buckeye. You cannot smash a Buckeye. The only way for you ever to get rid of a Buckeye is by burning it."

With that, he walked off the stage and within days, led his team to victory over a team from Texas A&M University.

According to the OSU archives, the first recorded use of the term referring to a resident of the area was in 1788—15 years before Ohio became a state. Colonel Ebenezer Sproat led the legal delegation at the first court session of the Northwest Territory, held in an area that is now Marietta.

The Indians in attendance greeted him with shouts of "Hetuck, Hetuck" (Indian word for buckeye), because they were impressed by his 6'4" stature. He proudly carried the buckeye nickname for the rest of his life, and it gradually spread to his companions and to other local white settlers.

By the 1830s, writers were commonly referring to locals as Buckeyes.

It was the presidential election of 1840 when William Henry Harrison made the term well-known. Harrison adopted the buckeye tree and its nuts as his campaign symbols. At the Whig convention, Harrison delegates carried buckeye canes decorated with strings of buckeye beads. As time passed, the buckeye became unmistakably linked with Ohio, and its citizens became known as Buckeyes.

Legendary football coach Woody Hayes once told a recruit, "You can go become a tiger, a bear, a lion, or any other animal that is a mascot at schools across this country, but there is only one place in this world you can become a Buckeye. Are you ready to be a Buckeye?"

Today, the tree's five-fingered leaflet, along with the nut, are sometimes used as symbols for The Ohio State University Alumni Association logo.

The Buckeye leaf decals placed on OSU players' helmets as rewards for successful individual plays and team goals—a tradition Hayes started in 1968—makes an Ohio State football helmet more recognizable than any in college football.

No Buckeyes player receives a single leaf following a loss.

"Why should he?" Hayes once said. "Winning a football game is the ultimate goal in the ultimate game."

From May 3, 1890, when Ohio State University defeated Ohio Wesleyan 20–14 in the first football game in school history, and for the next 116 years, there have been 787 days in which the Buckeyes were victorious on the football field.

And every one of them has been celebrated throughout the great state of Ohio.

chapter 2

The First Superstar

Ohio Stadium, built in 1922 and called the "House That Harley Built," was constructed in the aftermath of Chic Harley's (inset) statewide celebrity.

Way back then, he was a tiny man,

with a big heart and blazing speed,

but what Chic Harley owns now is a

legacy unlike any other Buckeye.

The Buckeyes' First Superstar

On November 18, 2006, just a few hours before the latest "Game of the Century," the classic showdown of Ohio State versus Michigan, I ambled over to High Street, just south of Woodruff Avenue.

A huge rock rests just a few feet off of the sidewalk.

"Harley's Rock."

It is adorned with a rectangular plaque, inscribed with these words:

SITE OF OHIO FIELD (1903–21) WHERE CHARLES W. "CHIC" HARLEY, ALL-AMERICAN HALFBACK IN 1916–17–19 PERFORMED THOSE FEATS WHICH MADE HIM AN OHIO STATE FOOTBALL LEGEND AND SPARKED THE PUBLIC ENTHUSIASM WHICH LED TO THE CONSTRUCTION OF OHIO STADIUM.

As hundreds of people walked up and down High Street, anticipating the upcoming game, few noticed Harley's Rock or took the time to read the inscription.

A parking garage now stands where Chic once thrilled the masses. As I stood there, watching those fans pass by, I felt a tremendous amount of guilt. In my four years of college, I had never noticed Harley's Rock. Not once. I had never once thought of Chic and the tradition he helped create.

Like many other students, perhaps I felt shame for paying more attention to what was located on the other side of High Street in those days.

"You know, I didn't even know it existed, either, until my dad told me about it a few years ago," Rob Harley, Chic's great, great nephew who played for the Buckeyes from 2003 to 2005, said recently. "We visited it together when Dad came up for a golf outing one day. I stood there, just trying to picture what the campus looked like at that spot back then when Chic played.

"It was a surreal thing for us, because that area is just teeming with activity now."

You wonder why Chic Harley was such an important figure in Ohio State football history?

Let me take you back in time…

The seven charter members of the Western Conference in 1896 were Illinois, Michigan, Chicago, Wisconsin, Minnesota, Northwestern, and Purdue. Four years later, Indiana and Iowa joined. (Michigan State joined in 1953, and Penn State became the 11th member in 1993.)

Ohio State was invited to join the conference in 1913, and, for the record, the Buckeyes lost their first conference game 7–6 to Indiana on November 1 that year.

Until that time, Ohio State's schedule consisted mostly of smaller Ohio colleges (with the exception of Michigan), such as Wooster, Otterbein, Denison, Kenyon, Oberlin, and Ohio Wesleyan. And when the Buckeyes beat them, as they did with consistency after 1898, they were declared the Ohio College Champions.

Once Ohio State joined the Western Conference, its football schedule gradually changed to include teams from neighboring states. And with that, so spread the school's recognition as a burgeoning football power.

By the time the 1916 season rolled around, 26 years after its birth, Ohio State had produced some excellent seasons (9–0–1 in 1899, 8–1–1 in 1900, and 8–1 in 1906). OSU's home field, first labeled University Field and later Ohio Field, was attracting more and more fans with each season. During most games, 5,000, 6,000, or even 7,000 fans would show up to watch Ohio State play the likes of Oberlin, Case, or Ohio Wesleyan.

Then a tiny sophomore who was born in Chicago and had moved to Columbus, where he played high school football, single-handedly transformed a curious but interesting athletic event into the most popular pastime in town.

To put it bluntly, Chic Harley made Ohio State football games into one tough ticket.

Standing about 5'9" and weighing only 155 pounds, he was virtually untouchable in the open field. He was faster than any other player who played the game at the time and possessed the moves and cutting ability of many of today's best running backs.

Harley was not one-dimensional, either. There is little doubt that he was the greatest runner of his time, but he also could pass and kick with the best, and he was a great defensive back. He lettered in football, track, baseball, and basketball at Ohio State.

"If you never saw him run with a football, we can't describe it to you," Bob Hooey of the *Ohio State Journal* once wrote. "It wasn't like Thorpe or Grange or Harmon or anyone else. It was kind of a cross between music and cannon fire, and it brought your heart up under your ears. In the hardest-fought gridiron battles, Harley usually would get away and score the winning touchdown."

After trouncing Oberlin 128–0, which remains the largest margin of victory in OSU history, the Buckeyes stunned Illinois 7–6 in a road game in which Harley scrambled for the tying touchdown and then kicked the extra point for the victory.

By the time Wisconsin arrived at Ohio Field the next week for homecoming, news of Harley's exploits had spread around campus. He was fast becoming Ohio's first real football hero, and cozy Ohio Field was overwhelmed with fans wanting to see what all the talk was about. The $2 tickets were being scalped for 10 times that amount (sound familiar?).

More than 12,000 fans, by far the largest crowd thus far, watched the game in which Harley starred again as the Buckeyes beat the Badgers 14–13. He continued to run and kick and lead Ohio State to a perfect 7–0 season and its first Western Conference championship.

Chic followed it up with another spectacular season in 1917 as Ohio State rolled to an 8–0–1 record and another conference championship. The only blemish was a scoreless tie at Auburn. Many of OSU's best players, including Harley, missed an abbreviated 1918 season (only six games were played) because they were serving in the armed services during World War I.

By 1919, almost all of Ohio State's best players, especially Harley, had returned to campus. It was a perfect season. Almost. The Buckeyes beat Michigan for the first time, by a 13–3 score, thanks to Harley's touchdown and four interceptions.

The win over Michigan at Ann Arbor, in front of 28,000 fans, was the first after 13 losses and two ties to the school that would become OSU's most bitter rival.

The victory was monumental for Ohio State.

Following the game, the legendary Michigan coach Fielding Yost congratulated the Buckeyes in their locker room, pointing to Harley and stating, "And you, Mister Harley, I believe, are one of the finest little machines I have ever seen."

That season, Ohio Field was swollen with fans, and university leaders started to talk about the need for a newer, larger place for their beloved Buckeyes to play. The next step was to find the proper location. Athletics director L.W. St. Johns, Thomas French, head of the Department of Engineering; and William Oxley Thompson, OSU's president at the time, organized the fund-raising drive to build a new stadium.

The 1920 season was a landmark for two reasons: Ohio State earned a first-ever berth in the Rose Bowl, resulting in a 28–0 loss to California, and the university spent the year raising money for a new stadium. In one year, it had raised $1.3 million in private donations from all over Ohio.

They faced two immediate decisions: where and how big.

They picked a 15-acre spot just east of the Olentangy River and south of Woodruff Avenue. Groundbreaking took place August 3, 1921.

Fortunately, St. John, French, and Thompson, with a large thanks to Harley, had fallen in love with Ohio State football and realized its potential benefits for the university in terms of national recognition. They also believed an extracurricular athletic event such as football had the potential to draw alumni back to campus and students closer together.

Today, their love of athletics and of Ohio State is symbolized by the French Field House, which adjoins St. John Arena, and the William Oxley Thompson Library, located on the west end of the Oval.

Ohio Stadium opened in time for the 1922 season and was dedicated October 21 in front of 71,138 fans during a 19–0 loss to Michigan.

Today it is one of the country's most recognized athletic venues of any kind, hosting more than 105,000 fans on any given Saturday. It was recently renovated for $194 million, or 150 times its original cost.

Today Chic Harley's name and number 47 are framed on the north façade of Ohio Stadium, along with the school's Heisman Trophy winners. Harley was the school's first three-time All-American, and he surely would have been OSU's first Heisman Trophy winner, if not for the fact that the award was a good 16 years from being created.

One thing is certain: Harley was Ohio State's first football legend.

Ohio Stadium probably would have been built sooner or later anyway, but his talent ignited the sport's popularity as the Buckeyes' subsequent success pushed the groundbreaking for the massive structure.

During a home game in 1949, the Ohio State marching band opened the Os in their famous Script Ohio one day to honor Harley with a Script Chic.

"That's the urban legend—that Chic was destined to come to Ohio State, because all you had to do was close the ends of the two Cs in his name to write Ohio," Rob Harley said. "He actually was ready to go to Michigan, but he stayed in Columbus, went to Ohio State, and the rest is history."

During the 1954 game at Illinois, Harley was ill but attended the game and watched from the press box. Woody Hayes was a history buff of not only politics and world wars, but of Ohio State athletics. He knew well about Chic's contribution to the game, to Ohio State, and to the stadium he came to call home.

"Woody was always very emotional in giving a pregame speech," said Dr. Erwin Thal, a team manager from 1954 to 1957. "He knew Chic Harley was at the game that day, and he told the team, 'We are going to win this one for Chic. Go out there and play for Chic!'

"At the end of the game [a 40–7 victory], Jim Parker went over to the referee and grabbed the game ball out of his hands and took it to Chic Harley in the locker room."

Harley, Ohio State's first inductee into the College Football Hall of Fame (1951), died April 21, 1974, following a long illness. The pallbearers at his funeral were Buckeyes starters Archie Griffin, Kurt Schumacher, Arnie Jones, Neal Colzie, Steve Myers, and Pete Cusick.

"It was really an honor to be a pallbearer for the greatest player in Ohio State history," Griffin said. "Chic put Ohio State football on the map."

Chic is buried at Union Cemetery just east of Olentangy River Road and north of Ackerman Road. When he died, he didn't have much money, but he had been so popular, his former teammates chipped in to pay for a six-foot headstone at his gravesite.

James Thurber's poem about Chic is inscribed on the face of the headstone:

> The years of football playing reach back a long, long way,
> And the heroes are a hundred who have worn the red and
>   gray;
> You can name the brilliant players from the year the game
>   began,
> You can say that someone's plunging was the best you
>   ever saw—
> You can claim the boys now playing stage a game without
>   a flaw—
> But admit there was no splendor in all the bright array
> Like the glory of the going when Chic Harley got away.

Honoring the Legend

When Ohio State honored Harley's career a few years ago by adding Chic's name to the stadium's Ring of Honor, it was announced that his number 47 would be retired also, once linebacker A.J. Hawk was finished wearing it in 2005.

Rob Harley was proud to see his great, great uncle's name on that concrete façade.

"To see the Harley name up on the stadium, that will remind me every time I come back," Rob said. "That's a great honor for Chic to have.

"Every Christmas, my grandpa would bring up the stories of what Chic had done. He's a big part of our family and a great tradition to carry on. One of the big things for me is to go over to the Buckeye Hall of Fame Café and see that he was a four-sport letterman in basketball, track, baseball, and football. That's unbelievable to me. For one man to have the ability to do that, that is amazing. It's unfortunate we don't have film of that. He must have been amazing.

"All we have are the newspaper clippings. That was a time when the newspaper writers were like poets. Those were the leather-helmet days. I read in one of our game programs that the last game of his senior year they started wearing numbers. He wore 47 in only *one* game."

Jim Tressel, a stickler for having his players learn about Ohio State's rich football history, has ensured today's Buckeyes know about Chic Harley. A small plaque is mounted above the exit of the Buckeyes' locker room at Ohio Stadium. It contains a quote from Chic himself: "We are heart and soul for this stadium, the fellows who know what it is to go in there and fight with all that's in us for Ohio State and her glory."

On the way out of the locker room before each game, every Buckeye touches that plaque.

"He's the one that made the legend possible," Tressel said. "It is appropriate that we honor him."

To the left of the plaque is a large framed lithograph Rob Harley illustrated. It pictures Ohio Stadium, showing Chic's retired number 47 on the north façade.

An image of Chic's face peers through the clouds above, as if he is looking down upon the field, watching his alma mater play the game he made popular in the stadium he helped build.

chapter 3

A Legend in His Own Time

William Henry Harrison "Tippy" Dye, a star quarterback who also excelled in basketball and baseball at OSU in the 1930s, visits the press box at Ohio Stadium before the 2006 game between top-ranked Ohio State and number two Michigan.

From beating Michigan on an annual basis, to owning the first three pairs of gold pants, to coaching basketball, Tippy Dye has led a championship life.

William Henry Harrison "Tippy" Dye was one of the greatest collegiate athletes of the 1930s, one of the most successful collegiate basketball coaches of the 1940s and '50s, and a very effective athletics administrator in the '60s and '70s.

It is true to say he is an American sports legend.

Dye entered The Ohio State University as a freshman in 1933, becoming a star for the Buckeyes on the football and baseball fields and on the basketball court over the next three seasons.

He led Ohio State to three consecutive wins over Michigan in football from 1934 to 1936, although he started only the game against the Wolverines in his senior season. He earned three pairs of gold pants during the first three years of the tradition started by coach Francis Schmidt.

After he received a degree in education, Dye entered the coaching ranks in football and basketball. He was an assistant coach under Paul Brown on the Buckeyes' first national championship team in 1942. He later became Ohio State's head basketball coach from 1947 to 1950, coaching one Big Ten championship team, before leaving for the same position at the University of Washington, where he coached the Huskies to the Final Four in 1953.

Dye was named athletics director at the University of Nebraska in 1962, where he hired football coach Bob Devaney, who built the Cornhuskers into a national power. He left to become athletics director at Northwestern in 1967 and retired in 1974. He and his wife, Mary, moved to Port Charlotte, Florida, where they lived for 23 years until moving to California. Mary died in 2001.

Dye has been inducted into the Halls of Fame at Ohio State and Washington.

Dye, who turned 92 on April 1, 2006, lives with his daughter and son-in-law in Camptonville, California. He still roots for the Buckeyes and returned to Ohio Stadium for the 2006 victory over Michigan.

His longevity and prominence place him in elite company—Dye would be the only man ever to know the first and the last Heisman Trophy winners, as well as many in between. He was a part of the 1935 Ohio State team that beat the University of Chicago 20–13, the season in which Chicago's Jay Berwanger won the award in its inaugural year.

Seventy-one years later, he met Troy Smith only two weeks before Smith became Ohio State's first quarterback to win the Heisman.

* * *

People have always written that I was named after President William Henry Harrison, but that really is not true. I was named after a great uncle of mine, who was named after the president. And they called me "Tippy" right away, from my earliest memories. That's the only name I ever knew.

I grew up in Pomeroy, Ohio, right down on the river. I have to admit that I wasn't really interested in Ohio State, because Athens, Ohio, was closer, and my brother and my sister went to Ohio U. So I may have ended up there, too, until my Mary went to Ohio State. I was dating Mary Russell, and she was headed to Ohio State, so I wanted to follow her.

When I got there, I later joined a fraternity, Phi Delta Theta, and made many lifelong friends that way.

As far as previous Ohio State players, I had met "Chic" Harley once but didn't know him well. I did know they called Ohio Stadium "the house that Harley built." I knew Pete Stinchcomb, who had played with him [1917–1920], and he had plenty of good stories about Ohio State from that period. Pete was a great, great player as well.

My first coach, Sam Willaman, didn't think I was big enough to play college football. I was 5'7" and 135 pounds, and I never got much bigger. I may have got up to 138 or 140 pounds, but that was about it. Fortunately, a new coach came in during my sophomore year, and I loved him. Francis Schmidt was ahead of his time, let me tell you. He knew the game of football.

I played quarterback with the number 50, and I can't honestly tell you how I got that number. I really have no idea. Anyway, in 1934 we played Western Reserve, and that is where Willaman went to coach after he left Ohio State. I ran a punt back on him, and I [like] to think that he changed his mind about me not being big enough.

Schmidt ran a very open type of offense, which later led to the T formation. You know that we had over 300 plays that we ran out of seven different formations? I loved that offense. There were a lot of lateral passes on many plays, where the man running the ball would lateral back to a man following him. That is one reason we scored so many points. Sid Gillman was one of the assistant coaches for Schmidt, and he took all of that offense to the West Coast when he got into pro football.

As a sophomore and a junior, I split time at quarterback with Stan Pincura, who was a year ahead of me. We won the conference one year [1935] and came within a few points of winning it the other two [1934 and 1936]. We had three great years.

That game against Notre Dame in 1935 is one people always talked about. We were the top two teams in the country and had never played before. We got ahead of them 13–0, and they scored right before the third quarter ended. But they were experimenting with a new rule back then: if you left the game in a certain quarter, you could not return until that quarter was over.

Well, Schmidt took some of our key players out in the fourth quarter, I don't know why really...maybe he thought we were going to win the game anyway. But Notre Dame came back and won it 18–13, and he was criticized quite a bit after that. That was a hard one to lose for us.

We did beat Michigan in my three years, and they never scored a point on us. The scores were 34–0, 38–0, and 21–0. Gerald Ford was on that 1934 team. I ran one punt back 60-some yards for one touchdown and then ran another one back but got caught at the 4-yard line. Oh well, we scored on the next play.

We always felt strongly about wanting to beat Michigan, of course, but I really don't think we wanted to beat them more than any other team. We just wanted to beat every team that we played in those days. We hated to lose.

I got three pairs of gold pants in the first three years the tradition was started. But I gave them to my son, and somebody *stole them from him. It was, and is, a great tradition, which Schmidt started and deserves all the credit for.*

I had read in the newspaper that I was the first and last quarterback to beat Michigan three times [until Troy Smith, 2004–2006], but I did not start those games in my sophomore and junior years. Stan Pincura did because he was a year older, but I played quite a bit in all of them.

By the time my career was finished, I became very close with Schmidt. I think he considered me as his son. I can't tell you all the stories about Francis, but he was a great cusser. He cussed all the time. I think that was his second language. He didn't mean anything bad by it, but that's just the way he coached. One time, the athletics director, L.W. St. John, came by and told him there would be women visiting practice one day and to make sure his language would be all right for them.

I really felt that I was a better basketball player than a football player. I was second-team All-American in my senior year. And I played wherever they wanted me to play on the baseball team, from shortstop to second base to third base. I earned nine varsity letters, and I think I am the only one to do that at Ohio State.

I knew Jesse Owens, too. I didn't get to see him compete much because I was playing baseball and he was in track and we were always on different fields at the same time.

When I coached the basketball team at Ohio State [1947–1950], in that first season we had four players back from a team that had won the conference the previous year, and we had a great many returning service people that had been in the war coming back. We also had three or four freshmen that came in. We had enough personnel for sure, but nobody got along with anybody. I have to say, I had an awful time that first year.

Then things got much better, and we grew together as a team. We had won the Big Ten in 1950 but lost in the tournament by one point to City College on their home court at Madison Square Garden. They won the NIT tournament that same year. They were a good team, but not quite as good as we were that year.

Why did I leave for Washington in 1951? Not that I ever wanted to leave my alma mater, but I knew that I wanted to be an athletics director someday. We ended up winning the Pacific Conference that first year in basketball, so my teams won two different conferences in consecutive seasons.

But back to Ohio State. When I went into the OSU Hall of Fame, Woody Hayes was the speaker that day. I knew him well and counted him as a good friend. He had arrived when I was leaving.

The university invited me back for the game against Michigan [in 2006], and I have to say it was a great time for me. They really took care of me. The athletics director, Gene Smith, had the thing well-organized. I went to the Senior Tackle inside the Woody Hayes Facility. Coach Tressel came over and introduced himself and then introduced me to Troy Smith and the entire team. It was a thrill for me. I was very happy to see him win the Heisman Trophy.

Saturday before the game they took me to the press box, and then I went down to one of the suites and watched the game. I sat next to Bill Willis—I was on the coaching staff when Bill played the year we won our first national championship, in 1942. We had quite a good visit and, of course, we beat Michigan that day.

The stadium has changed a great deal over the years, that's for sure. We don't have the track around the field anymore, and the south end is completely different. They added so many seats.

I still have great feelings for Ohio State, naturally. You always have feelings for your alma mater. That feeling never leaves you, no matter how old you are—and I should know, because I am older than most.

chapter 4

The First National Championship

Tackle Bill Willis was a star on Coach Paul Brown's 1942 national championship team, the first in Buckeyes history.

Paul Brown's teams were 18–8–1 in his three seasons, winning Ohio State's first-ever national championship, in 1942. He then received his navy commission following the '43 season and was named head coach of the Great Lakes football team. The following season, the Buckeyes, who would go on to win all nine games, defeated Great Lakes 26–6 in Brown's return to Ohio Stadium.

Seven years later, Brown wanted to return as Ohio State's head coach, but the job went to a little-known coach named Woody Hayes.

In the three seasons during the height of America's involvement in World War II, 1942–1944, Ohio State played against a few non-collegiate teams. For example, the Buckeyes, coached by Paul Brown, beat Fort Knox 59–0 to open the '42 season and beat the Iowa Seahawks 41–12 to close it for a 9–1 record and the school's first national championship.

To open the next season, the Seahawks upset Ohio State 28–13, and Great Lakes beat the Buckeyes 13–6 two weeks later. In 1944 the Buckeyes earned revenge by whipping Great Lakes 26–6 in the final game ever played against a non-university football team.

Through those times, Charlie Ream, James Langhurst, and John T. White did something unheard of in today's game of football.

Ream was a main contributor to Ohio State's outstanding teams from 1934 to 1937, which finished with a 25–7 record and never allowed a point to Michigan, beating the Wolverines by scores of 34–0, 38–0, 21–0, and 21–0.

Then, five years after he graduated, he played *against* the Buckeyes.

"The strangest thing happened to me when I played with the Iowa Seahawks in 1942," Ream said. "I was in the service, and Ohio State was on their schedule. Here I was, playing my alma mater—now that was awful strange to me. Still, it was a thrill to go back to Columbus to play them, but I remember they wouldn't let me in the Ohio State locker room.

"That '42 team was a great one. Anyway, they whipped us pretty badly that day. I remember one of our linebackers would look at me and say, 'Who ran by me that time?' That Ohio State team wasn't big, but boy were they fast."

Langhurst, who was the MVP of the 1938 Buckeyes and the captain of the '40 team during his senior season, also was a part of that Iowa Pre-Flight team. He rushed for 108 yards against his alma mater that day.

Don't You Recognize Me?

Early in his first season of 1941 as head coach of the Buckeyes, Paul Brown wasn't a highly recognizable face around Columbus. Before his first game, a 12–7 win over Don Faurot's Missouri team, he was stopped at the gate at Ohio Stadium.

"You cannot come in here, sir, without a ticket," the guard told him.

"I don't have a ticket," the coach explained. "I am Paul Brown."

"Is that right? Well, I am President Roosevelt," the guard replied. "But you still cannot come in."

After the Buckeyes upset Southern California 33–0 the next week and rolled to a 6–1–1 record that season, most everyone knew Paul Brown's face.

White Experienced Rivalry Full-Circle

White, known as "J.T." to his teammates, had a football career like no other.

First of all, he was an end for the 1942 Buckeyes, which defeated Michigan 21–7 at Ohio Stadium and were later declared national champions. White's brother Paul was a superb running back on that Wolverines team.

"I still cherish the pair of gold pants we received for beating Michigan," White told author Don Steinberg for the book *Expanding Your Horizons*.

White spent the next three years serving in the military during World War II. He then attended Michigan, of all schools, on the G.I. Bill. Remarkably, he started at center for the 1947 national championship Wolverines, which beat the Buckeyes 21–0 in Ann Arbor.

So not only did White play for both the Buckeyes and the Wolverines, he also played for national championship teams at two different universities.

"I am sure that no other player has ever played for two universities who were national champions," he told Steinberg.

White, who later became a longtime assistant coach under Joe Paterno at Penn State, died in 2005.

Which Way Is the Wind Blowing?

Two-time All-American Warren Amling (1944–1946), who died in 2001, loved to tell the story about being a captain and being confused during the coin toss before the 1945 game against Illinois at Ohio Stadium.

*   *   *

Coach [Carroll] Widdoes instructed me, "If we win the toss, defend the north goal, since the wind is blowing from the north. If we lose the toss and the Illini take the north goal, we will receive."

Then, as it does now, the wind in the stadium played tricks on you. Just before the toss, I looked at the flag, and it was blowing the opposite way. We won the toss, and I said we would defend the south goal, so Illinois chose to receive. As I jogged off, I glanced up at the flag and the wind had changed directions again!

Coach Widdoes asked, "What did we get?"

"Neither," I replied.

Thank goodness Coach was an understanding man. Fortunately, we beat Illinois, my home-state team, 27–2 that day.

Calling Dr. Horvath...

While at Ohio State, not only did Les Horvath become the school's first Heisman Trophy winner, earning the award in 1944, but he was already a gifted student in dental school.

"There was nothing average about that man's smarts," said teammate Bob Brugge. "He was the smartest guy playing football. It is no wonder he later became such a great dentist. I remember Les was going to dental school at the time, and I kept getting my teeth knocked out while playing football.

Les Horvath, a dental student at the time, became the first Buckeye to win the Heisman Trophy in 1944.

"Les would fix them for me. I would go see him, and he would fill my cavities with gold fillings. I would say, 'Les, I can't afford those fillings. How can I pay you?'

"He said, 'Don't worry, this one's on the school.'"

...And Dr. Steinberg

Don Steinberg is one of the most accomplished men ever to play football at Ohio State. Following his career as a Buckeye (1942–1945), he became a distinguished surgeon and also wrote the aforementioned book, *Expanding Your Horizons,* about the school's first national championship team.

During his senior season, Steinberg was in medical school in the Army Student Training Program and was part of the football team.

"I was assigned to deliver babies of poor patients in their homes," Steinberg said. "I carried two large satchels to football practice each day, and when I received notice to deliver a baby, I would change into my army uniform and catch a street car down on High Street to get to the expect[ing] mother's home.

"One of my first deliveries, as soon as I entered the home, this woman was precipitating her baby. Catching a football was not one of my forte's, but I caught this baby coming out of the birth canal."

Remarkably, the first 17 babies Steinberg delivered were all boys.

That season, he was named the Western Conference's Outstanding Scholar Athlete.

Steinberg earned the National Football Foundation's Distinguished Citizen Award in 1990.

Wild, Wild Finishes

Six decades before the crazy 2003 Fiesta Bowl conclusion, the Buckeyes won two games in the 1940s that were thought to be finished, the first as a tie and the second as a loss. Each included endings that were, well, let's say all that was missing was the Stanford marching band. They were just as unbelievable.

In the 1943 Illinois game, the score was tied 23–23 when Ohio State had one final chance to win the game from the Illini 23-yard line, but Bobby McQuade's pass into the end zone fell incomplete. The referee fired his gun, signaling the end of the game, as both teams filed into the locker rooms and most of the fans left Ohio Stadium.

However, one official had thrown a penalty flag during the final play, and it had gone largely unseen. As the officials huddled on the field, both teams were undressing in their respective locker rooms. Finally, the officials declared Illinois had been offside and agreed Ohio State would receive one more offensive play.

"We were in the dressing room, and I recall that most of us had taken our uniforms off when they made us come back on the field," Howard Teifke (1943, 1946–1948) said. "We couldn't believe it. It was amazing."

Ten minutes later, the two teams lined up, and little-known Johnny Stungis, a 17-year-old freshman, kicked a 33-yard field goal to win the game 29–26 for the Buckeyes. It was the only field goal of Stungis's career. It was also Paul Brown's final victory as Ohio State coach.

"Johnny Stungis," Teifke said. "I'll never forget that name. He was from Powhatan Point down on the Ohio River."

The 1947 game against Northwestern at Ohio Stadium had an even wilder, and longer, conclusion.

The Buckeyes, in Wes Fesler's first season as coach, were struggling to a 2–6–1 record that season, but the ending of the game against the Wildcats left them with one unbelievable memory. Trailing 6–0, Ohio State was stopped at the Northwestern 1-yard line with only 1:47 remaining in the game. The Buckeyes forced Northwestern to punt and then took possession at the Wildcats' 36-yard line with only 31 seconds remaining.

Two plays later, Northwestern intercepted Pandel Savic's pass and the clock expired as most of the fans left Ohio Stadium, believing the home team had sustained a shutout loss.

"I remember I had already pulled out my hip pads thinking the game was over," said Joe Whisler, Ohio State's top running back.

However, the officials declared that Northwestern had 12 men on the field during the play, thus giving Ohio State another play. This time, Fesler called for a running play, and Rodney Swinehart was tackled at Northwestern's 2-yard line, and again, the game appeared to be over. On the play, however, Northwestern had lined up offside, and the Buckeyes were given yet another play, in which Savic passed to Jimmy Clark in the back of the end zone for the touchdown to tie the game 6–6.

The ensuing extra-point attempt was blocked, and the game appeared to end in a tie. But once again, Northwestern was penalized for being offside. Finally, Emil Moldea made his second try at the extra point, and the Buckeyes walked off the field in disbelief as 7–6 winners.

"I was on the field for that play without the hip pads," Whisler added.

"I remember we got extra chances to win the game, but I didn't remember that many," Teifke said recently. "That was the game in which we kept getting so many guys hurt. We were scrambling at the end just to survive, and I don't know how we won it."

chapter 5

The Snow Bowl

The few brave souls who weathered the blizzard in Columbus for the November 25, 1950, Michigan game saw both teams combine to complete only three passes, punt 45 times, and fumble the ball 10 times between them. Ohio State's loss led to the resignation of Wes Fesler as coach and ushered in the Woody Hayes era.

As the snow stopped falling following the 1950 loss to Michigan, the "Graveyard of Coaches" would claim another victim. And a somewhat chubby man with a gap-toothed smile, fiery temper, and intense desire for hard work was on his way to Columbus.

The 1950 game against Michigan at Ohio Stadium is now infamous, because it was played in a blizzard, which turned what was supposed to be a football game into a mockery, a flurry of comical mistakes made by nearly frozen football players.

However, nobody was laughing afterward, because Ohio State lost the game 9–3.

The rivalry has never seen conditions as adverse before or since that November 25 game. That morning, it was five degrees and the wind gusted up to 40 miles per hour. Michigan spent the previous night in Toledo because it could not advance any further by bus. The schools' athletics directors (OSU's Dick Larkins and Michigan's Fritz Crisler) discussed canceling the game that morning. They decided not to, simply because more than 80,000 tickets were already sold, nobody had any idea how many fans would show up, and rescheduling it posed all kinds of problems.

Thor Ronemus, a junior guard for Ohio State at the time, recalled how the Buckeyes were getting dressed in the locker room and did not realize that it had started snowing harder outside: "It was blowing and getting worse and worse while we were inside. The team did not know about the serious discussion held by the powers that be as to whether the game should be called off," he said. "Our athletic director came into the dressing room to let the players have a say whether to play. Because we did not know about the blizzard and the temperature dropping and the wind blowing horizontally, we said, 'Sure, let's do it.'

"When we finally hit the field, I couldn't believe how bad it was. I had never seen a snowstorm like that—and still haven't."

The field's markings were invisible that day, and it wasn't much easier seeing the football, either. Part of the tarp that once covered the field was frozen to it.

The longest play from scrimmage was a 13-yard pass from Vic Janowicz to Tom Watson.

When Janowicz kicked a field goal to put the Buckeyes ahead 3–0, "it went up in a cloud of snow...it just disappeared," said longtime Ohio State sports information director Marv Homan.

"It was a nightmare," said Janowicz, who died in 1996. "My hands were numb. I had no feeling in them and I don't know how I hung onto the ball. It was terrible out there. You knew what you wanted to do, but you couldn't do it because of the weather."

The only touchdown of the day came when Michigan blocked a punt with 40 seconds left in the first half, falling on the football in the end zone. Ohio State coach Wes Fesler's decision to punt in the first place, instead of trying to run the clock out, unleashed a fury of criticism and was likely the impetus for his subsequent resignation.

"We faced too much time to close out the end of the period," Fesler said later. "Rather than take a chance of anything happening, I wanted to get the ball out of there."

"The blocked punt was the final disaster," said Ronemus.

The astounding statistics of the game: both teams combined to complete only three of 27 passes, to punt 45 times, and to lose 10 fumbles. Holding onto the football that day was as difficult as securing a greased rock.

The announced attendance was 50,503, but there probably weren't that many fans in the stadium, especially at the end. More than a half century later, however, millions claimed to have paid for the $3.50 tickets, braved the weather, and witnessed the game that day.

"There were times that fans would lose their footing and slide down the stadium steps toward us," Ronemus said. "As we looked up from the bench, it appeared as if people were coming down a water slide. It's a wonder we didn't have spectators killed that day."

Most Buckeyes maintained the conditions helped Michigan win the game.

"There is no doubt that on a normal day in November we would have whipped Michigan," Ronemus said. "We had a better team."

The loss, especially since it resulted from his ill-advised decision to punt before halftime, brought Fesler to a temporary state of depression. Almost as immediately as the snow stopped falling on the field, Fesler resigned under an avalanche of criticism from the legendary Snow Bowl.

Open the Door!

During the 1951 season, Woody Hayes's first at Ohio State, Thor Ronemus came down with the flu during the game at Pittsburgh.

*   *   *

Ernie Biggs kept me in the locker room after halftime with instructions for me to rest, and if I felt better, to shower, dress, and go visit with my family in the stadium. He had given me the key to the locker room. His only instructions were: "Be sure to be back to this dressing-room door with the key the minute the game is over!"

I had a nice visit with my family, but Pitt beat us and I was very sad and forgot Ernie's order. When I finally got back to the dressing room, the dressing-room door had been smashed. Ernie explained to me that Woody could not open it and bashed it down to enter. I said, "Ernie, please do not tell Woody it was me."

Every time I saw Ernie, until the day he died, I would ask, "Did you tell Woody yet?"

And every time, he would answer, "I would never do that to you, Thor."

And he never did. I would imagine Ohio State had to pay Pittsburgh for that door.

*   *   *

Robert "Rock" Joslin remembers it well. "The worst blowup I saw from Woody," he said, "[was when] he knocked the door off the hinges to get in."

Married Players

Through the 1950s, many more players were married during their playing careers than there are today. In those days, obviously, couples married at younger ages.

George Jacoby tells a story about when Woody Hayes called him into the office to discuss his poor grades following his freshman season.

"What's going on?" Hayes asked.

"I told him I kept going home to Toledo on the weekends to see my girlfriend," Jacoby explained.

"Is it serious?" the coach asked.

"I told him it was," Jacoby said.

"Then why don't you marry her and bring her down here with you?" Woody said.

"So we got married on August 11, 1951," Jacoby said, "and Woody was largely the reason."

Once married, Jacoby discovered that Hayes had a "Tuesday rule."

"[Assistant coach] Bill Arnsparger would knock on our door and remind us, 'No sex after Tuesday!' My wife and I didn't really understand that rule, and we always wondered who was telling that to all the single players," he said. "But Woody really liked Nina. She would come to practices and, if Woody was in a good mood, he would look at her, wink, and nod toward the bench. That meant it was okay for her to go sit down."

The Best of Everything

Even as far back as the early 1950s, Ohio State always had the best equipment—better than even those teams in the NFL.

"When I got to the Colts, I asked for some good equipment and they rejected me," Jim Parker said. "Woody had the best that money could buy. When you go to play football at Ohio State, they insist on the best equipment. Every player at Ohio State…their helmet is custom made for his head. You don't have to get somebody else's helmet.

"Woody always insisted on a Riddell helmet, and that's what I wanted in the pros. My teammates in Baltimore thought I was a prima donna, but I had never been hurt."

Aurealius Thomas, Case Study

Aurealius Thomas was a freshman lineman in the fall of 1954 when he became ill following a scrimmage at Ohio Stadium.

"It was about 105 degrees that day," Thomas said. "I worked about 45 minutes with the first team, and then they called for the second team. Well, I was a second-teamer, too, so I stayed on the field and worked with them for another 45 minutes. Then after our scrimmage, we did our running around the field. When it was all over, I went into the locker room to get an orange juice and the next thing I know, I am waking up in University Hospital."

Thomas suffered from heat exhaustion and a severe case of dehydration. He spent the next 28 days in the hospital and almost died.

"It was a serious situation, and it took that long for my body chemistry to adjust," he explained. "I had lost about 15 pounds. I couldn't see at first. Woody and all the other coaches would visit me, and they made it clear that I had my scholarship whether I ever played football again or not.

"When I look back on it, I realize I am blessed because others have passed due to heat exhaustion."

Because of Thomas's condition, a team of Ohio State doctors led by Bob Murphy studied dehydration and its causes and effects. They began weighing players before and after practices. They also convinced the coaches to allow players to drink as much water as needed during practices.

"Before then, we couldn't have water. Period," Thomas said. "They even changed the uniforms. They used to make the jerseys real thick so they could be worn for five years. They recognized that once the jersey got wet with sweat, it was like having a big wet blanket over your body and your skin could not breathe."

Thomas recovered fully, becoming an All-American in 1957.

The Graveyard of Coaches

Ohio State's football program earned that unwanted title throughout the 1930s and '40s simply because most of the Buckeyes' head coaches ended their tenure in the firing line, or they resigned under pressure.

To this day, Paul Brown is the last Buckeyes head coach who departed campus on his own terms. He joined the navy following the 1943 season but wanted to return eight years later.

In 1942 Brown had coached the Buckeyes to their first national championship.

Carroll Widdoes then arrived to lead the Buckeyes to a perfect 9–0 season in 1944, but the Big Ten wouldn't allow the school to accept a Rose Bowl invitation. A year later, after a 7–2 season, Widdoes demanded to return as an assistant coach—not as the head coach. For starters, he didn't like the pressure or the attention he got in the position.

"He was a kind and gentle man, but he simply didn't appreciate the pressure on himself and particularly on his family," said Jim Crane, who played end at OSU from 1945 to 1947.

In came Paul Bixler, another of Brown's former assistant coaches. Bixler lasted one season, his team finishing 4–3–2. He resigned, saying, "The pressure to win here is too much."

"By now, we were aware of the coaches' graveyard thing," Crane said.

Next it was Wes Fesler's turn. Fesler, a former Ohio State star in football, basketball, and baseball, seemed to be a perfect fit because he was well aware of the tradition and of the demand that would be placed upon his shoulders.

Fesler's teams went 2–6–1, 6–3, 7–1–2 (OSU's first Rose Bowl champions), and then 6–3 in 1950. The Snow Bowl loss was the final straw for Fesler, who also cited the job's intense pressure as his reason for resigning.

By then, the school's reputation as the "Graveyard of Coaches" was well entrenched.

The pressure to win at Ohio State was intense. The expectations were to win the Big Ten most seasons and to beat Michigan more often than not.

Sound familiar?

When Fesler resigned, a man named Woody Hayes was preparing Miami of Ohio for the Salad Bowl.

The Graveyard after Woody

Woody Hayes thrived as head coach of Ohio State from 1951 to 1978, but as we all know, he too was fired, but it was not for not winning enough games. Earle Bruce (1979–1987) and John Cooper (1988–2000) eventually suffered the same fate.

So when it is all said and done, every head coach since 1943 either has been fired or couldn't handle the pressure that becomes a fixture with coaching at Ohio State, except for Jim Tressel, the existing head coach, of course.

Another reason that Ohio State's last three coaches were fired: like it or not, the job is the pinnacle of college football. At other schools, head coaches come and go, leaving for better jobs where they have a chance to win national championships.

Is there a better job in coaching than being head coach of Ohio State? Is there an easier place to recruit great players or compete for national championships?

Where would Woody Hayes have gone to improve his career? Earle Bruce, a born-and-bred Buckeye? Even John Cooper?

In other words, as any Buckeye would tell you, there is no step *up*.

"They fired Woody," John Cooper said in 1995. "They have fired every coach to come through here. And maybe someday, they'll fire me."

Cooper was correct on that one, but his 2–10–1 record against Michigan and a 3–8 record in bowl games ultimately resulted in his pink slip.

Consider that the Buckeyes' program had 18 head coaches before Woody Hayes arrived in 1951, but that was common in the half century after the invention of the game of football. Coaches came and went from universities, because coaching wasn't a high-paying, stable business as it is today.

Nevertheless, largely because of Woody's 28-year tenure at Ohio State, the *Graveyard of Coaches* label has long been put to rest. Since 1951, the Buckeyes have employed only *four* head coaches.

Four coaches in more than 56 years—and counting.

chapter 6

The Woody Hayes Era

Ohio State football already had an aura and mystique about it before Woody Hayes arrived on campus, but the legendary coach will forever remain the heart and soul of the program.

How do you describe Ohio State's legendary football coach? **A**rdent. **B**enevolent. **C**ompassionate. **D**edicated. **E**ducated. **F**iery. **G**entle. **H**ot-headed. **I**ntense. **J**udgmental. **K**ind. **L**oyal. **M**otivated. **N**aval officer. **O**bsessive. **P**assionate. **Q**uotable. **R**eliable. **S**uccessful. **T**riumphant. **U**nwavering. **V**ictorious. **W**oody Hayes. **X**s and Os (not his strength). **Y**ea Ohio! (how he signed his name). **Z**ealous.

You can't summarize Wayne Woodrow Hayes with only one chapter, nor will I attempt to do so. This is a man about whom dozens of books have been written, a man who possessed as much depth as the Atlantic Ocean and as many sides as the Pentagon.

His official title was football coach, but he was essentially an educator with professorial status, a historian, a husband, a father, a leader, a social activist, a politician, and foremost, a teacher.

He was as complex as the space shuttle and yet as simple as a fullback dive play over right tackle. As his longtime assistant coach Esco Sarkkinen once put it, "You don't describe Woody Hayes in one word, one sentence, or one paragraph. You describe him with chapter after chapter."

We don't have that luxury here, but this chapter will illustrate a few of the many sides of Hayes.

Know this first: one cannot categorize Woody Hayes simply by the numbers that made him famous—205 wins, 13 Big Ten championships, and five national championships in 28 years at Ohio State.

For those who didn't know him, he was respected solely for that record.

For those who did know him well, he was loved and respected because of his character off the field. He was especially loved by his players once they graduated and were gone from Ohio State, because that is when many came to understand him better.

He was charming, and he was boorish. He was extremely profane in practice and a classic gentleman in mixed company. He was well educated and yet sometimes ignorant in so-called street smarts. As the years passed, many of his players have said they grew to realize their coach was the finest individual they ever knew, despite his flaws. And today, he is arguably Ohio's greatest and most beloved legend.

Here are a few of the things you may or may not know about Woody Hayes, the legend and the man:

- He was born on Valentine's Day, February 14, 1913.
- His father, Wayne, was the superintendent of schools in Newcomerstown, Ohio. Growing up there, "Woody," as he was called to distinguish him from his father, hung around

the local baseball fields and was befriended by a retired major league pitcher who managed on the semi-pro level at the time. From their first meeting, the legendary Cy Young loved the kid, giving him loose change to help keep the local diamond in shape.

- He was a member of the Sigma Chi fraternity at Denison, from which he graduated in June 1935. His roommate as a junior was Jim Otis, whose son later became one of Woody's star fullbacks at Ohio State.

- His first job was as a seventh-grade English teacher in Mingo Junction, Ohio, where he also was the high school's assistant football coach—all for $1,200 annually.

- He was almost fired from his first head-coaching position, at New Philadelphia High School, following the 1940 season. A superintendent cited "his behavioral problems," not his 1–9 record that season. Woody agreed to improve his behavior and control his temper, thus saving his job. He joined the U.S. Navy the following summer, before he coached another season.

- He lost his first-ever collegiate game as a head coach at Denison (18–13 to Otterbein) in 1946.

- Woody's brother Ike was an All-American guard at Iowa State. He died of a heart attack soon after Ohio State won the 1954 national championship in Woody's fourth season. "He was the toughest SOB you ever met," Woody once said, "but I could whip him."

- Woody lived in the same house at 1711 Cardiff Road in Upper Arlington from the time he accepted the Buckeyes job in 1951 until 1987 when he died.

   For much of that time, his telephone number was listed in the phone book. Often, following a loss, his wife, Anne, would talk to angry callers late at night. "I usually invited them over for coffee to talk it over," Anne often quipped. "But they never came. And sometimes, I just agreed with them and they would stop ranting."

- He earned $12,500 his first year at Ohio State, approximately the amount that Jim Tressel now earns in 48 hours, and he earned $42,000 in 1978, his final season. And money meant nothing to Woody. He frequently turned down raises and suggested the extra money be divided among his assistants. Most years, he drove an old, beat-up El Camino, which is a far cry from the huge car deals that coaches have today. By the way, the bed of the pickup truck was carpeted with AstroTurf for much of the 1970s. "I am not the Cadillac type," he once said.

- As far as hobbies, Woody didn't have many. He didn't fish, hunt, or play golf or cards like many coaches of his era. He never cared for exotic vacations. He didn't go to movies, unless it was the film that the team viewed the night before the game.

He was, however, a voracious reader of nonfiction.

"No matter when he gets home, if he gets home," Anne once said, "he will read for a half hour before he goes to bed."

That "if" illustrated his work ethic. Many nights, he fell asleep on his bunk in his office at the old Biggs Facility after watching film. He would spend the night there. By the way, the facility, which underwent a multimillion dollar renovation recently, is named the Woody Hayes Athletic Center.

The old man would be proud of it, though slightly embarrassed.

The Hiring

To say that Woody Hayes was a long shot to get the Ohio State job in 1951 is an understatement. When the search committee first sought to find a replacement for Wes Fesler, such high-profile names as Missouri's Don Faurot and Paul Brown, who already won a national title at Ohio State in 1942, were high on the list.

At 38 years old, Hayes was considered by most to be an inexperienced, small-college coach.

But Brown didn't exactly leave Ohio State the first time on good terms, and many people associated with the school didn't care for what they perceived as his large ego. Faurot wavered on taking the job, finally deciding to stay at Missouri.

That left Hayes, who wowed the committee during an impressive three-hour interview. He was educated, articulate, persuasive, and thorough. He was a teacher first, he told the committee, and a coach second. And he had won many games at Denison and then at Miami. It was a risk, of course, but a risk worth taking, athletics director Dick Larkins believed.

"Before I went to see them, I didn't think I had a chance at the job," Hayes once said. "When I left, I *knew* I had the job."

Earle Bruce will never forget their first meeting. He was trying to overcome a knee injury to make the 1951 team, Woody's first.

"A few weeks after he was hired, he called us all together and we put tennis shoes on to run his offensive plays in the gym," Bruce recalled. "Now, we were used to Wes Fesler, who wouldn't say shit if he had a mouthful. And I think that was the exact first word out of Woody's mouth when we all met him."

The First of a Legendary Era

Ranked third in the country, the Buckeyes beat Southern Methodist 7–0 on September 29, 1951, at Ohio Stadium—the first of 276 games Woody would coach at Ohio State.

"I think I was the only starting sophomore on that team," said Robert "Rock" Joslin. "I am a great trivia answer: I scored the first touchdown at Ohio State under Woody Hayes. I ran this little hook pattern, and Tony Curcillo threw it low, just off the grass. I got my hands down and picked it right from the grass and rolled over for the touchdown."

The Early Years

The first three seasons at Ohio State were not pleasant for Hayes.

He had overworked his players, who were not used to such extreme conditioning, especially during his initial season in 1951. At times, they somewhat rebelled on their way to a miserable 4–3–2 season, which concluded with a 7–0 loss at Michigan.

They also resented Hayes's offense, then the T formation. In 1950 Vic Janowicz had passed for 561 yards and 12 touchdowns and rushed for 314 yards and four more touchdowns to win the Heisman Trophy. In Hayes's first season, he completed only seven passes.

The popular joke around Columbus following that season: "Who's the only man ever to stop Vic Janowicz?" The answer: "Woody Hayes."

The Buckeyes then finished 6–3 for two consecutive seasons, and it appeared to some that Woody would be fired following the '53 season. At the time, he had a 16–9–2 record, including a 1–2 mark against Michigan.

Larkins (the namesake for OSU's recreation center), however, stuck his neck out for his third-year coach, and Woody survived to coach the 1954 season.

"The fans were tough as hell on him those first three seasons, but Woody got through it," said George Jacoby (1951–1953).

"I remember one game at the stadium, and I am not sure exactly when it was, but the crowd was chanting, 'Good-bye, Woody. Good-bye, Woody!'" Joslin recalled.

Woody used to tell the story that occurred the next summer, when he overheard neighbors having a barbeque. One of them remarked, "This is the year we get Woody!"

That season, the Buckeyes rolled to a perfect 10–0 record, including a 21–7 win over Michigan at Ohio Stadium and a 20–7 win over USC in the Rose Bowl. Woody Hayes had won his first— and Ohio State its second—national championship. Suddenly he had job security.

Now there was no stopping him.

"We played them one at a time," Woody said after the Michigan game. "We had an agreement that anyone who mentioned roses gets a punch in the nose, unless it's a lady over 80."

His teams would add consensus national titles in 1957 and 1968.

The 1961 team, Big Ten champions after a 50–20 crushing of Michigan, could have captured a national championship, but…

The '61 Rose Bowl Decision

If Woody ever had a right to exhibit his temper publicly, most fans would have understood when the school's faculty council voted not to allow the 8–0–1 Buckeyes to play in the Rose Bowl at the conclusion of the '61 season. The vote was 28–25.

Woody was informed of the decision as he arrived at a Cleveland booster-club meeting, at which he was the guest speaker. He promptly dropped his suitcase, exited the building, and took a long walk. For at least 90 minutes, he walked the streets of Cleveland. When he returned, he shocked everyone in attendance with his calm demeanor.

"I don't agree with those 28 'no' votes," he said that night. "But I respect their integrity, if not their intelligence."

Woody feared the decision would hurt recruiting more than anything else. His players, however, were angry and puzzled. Some still are.

"I still don't understand it," Paul Warfield (1961–1963) said recently. "I guess the faculty council didn't think bowl games and academics mixed too well, and they didn't let us go."

As a Recruiter

During Woody's 28 seasons at Ohio State, there were better tacticians in college football. Other head coaches were more progressive and obviously more innovative. Others were less stubborn and changed when certain plays or formations weren't successful. But there is little doubt that there was no better recruiter than Woody.

"Woody was an unrivaled master at recruiting," said Bill Conley, a former OSU player and recruiting coordinator. "From Woody, I learned to identify the key decision maker in the life of any recruit.

"Nobody recruited better than Woody. He was unmatched at the art of recruiting the parents as well as the player. Woody honestly believed that if you recruited the parents hard enough, the player would follow the wishes of Mom and Dad. More times than not, he was right."

That was Hayes's MO—to recruit the player's parents. He would sell them on education. He would sell them on developing their sons into men. He would sell them on Ohio State. He rarely mentioned football or the playing time a player would or would not receive.

"He talked to you about everything—everything but football," said linebacker Tom Cousineau (1975–1978). "Sometimes, he gave you the impression he wasn't interested in you for football, because he never talked about it. He left that to the assistants."

On the night before signing day, the Cousineau household hosted Michigan defensive coordinator Gary Moeller, Penn State coach Joe Paterno, and Woody—all at the same time.

"We all sat there and talked, but it was very uncomfortable," Cousineau said. "Coach Hayes was the first to leave. He went to the door, and I followed him. He turned around and told me, 'I'll be back at 7:00. You tell your mom that I like bacon and eggs, and pancakes would be nice.' Then he stuck out his hand and asked, 'Are you ready to be a Buckeye?'

"'Yes sir,' I said."

Hayes never coddled recruits, either, or told them what they wanted to hear just to sign them. He often challenged them.

As the Buckeyes prepared for the 1978 Gator Bowl in what would turn out to be Hayes's final game, linebacker Glen Cobb attended a practice in Ohio Stadium.

"It was a cold, wet December day, and not many recruits were there that day," he recalled. "Anyhow, I was standing along the sideline when Coach Hayes motioned for me to come over to him.

"When I reached Coach Hayes, he said, 'Son, do you see those linebackers over there?'

"I replied, 'Yeah.'

"'No, you will respond by saying, "Yes sir."'

"I corrected myself: 'Yes, sir.'

" 'Son,' he said, 'I want you to watch those linebackers today. You watch them. If after the end of practice you think you can play alongside them, then I'll give you a scholarship. If you don't, then get back on I-71 South and go back down to the farm and stay there!'

"I trotted off, and my thoughts turned to farm life," Cobb recalled. "It's a pretty good life really. I never got to play for him, but I did become a Buckeye."

Today, Cobb ranks as Ohio State's ninth all-time leading tackler, finishing his career with 336.

Somehow, some way, Woody had a sixth—and a seventh—sense when recruiting a player he really wanted. It was as if he had a network of private investigators working for him, telling him when and where a recruit may be at any specific time.

Here's an example from All-American tackle Kurt Schumacher (1972–1974):

*   *   *

A friend of mine (a girl I dated in high school) was attending OSU. She had some minor surgery back in Lorain, and her mother was going to drive her back to OSU on a weeknight. Jan asked if I could ride down with them so her mother wouldn't have to make the return drive alone. To the best of my knowledge, no one other than Jan, her mom, and my family knew that I was making this trip. As the three of us entered her dormitory lobby, you can imagine my surprise when we were greeted by Coach Hayes. He asked me if I had made all of my school visits, and I said that I had. He then went straight for the close: he asked if I was ready to commit to Ohio State.

In an effort to buy some time, I said I would need to speak to my sister (my parents died when I was 14, and my oldest sister took me in). Coach Hayes walked over to the pay phone in the lobby and got my sister on the phone. After a brief conversation, I came out of the phone booth and told Woody I was committing to Ohio State.

He then invited Jan, her mom, and me to dinner at the Faculty Club, and upon our arrival, there was a photographer from one of *the local papers waiting to capture a photo of Woody shaking hands with me to seal the deal. I never asked him how he knew that I would be in the lobby of a girl's dorm on that night, and I'll probably never know.*

*   *   *

Hayes's recruiting prowess is backed up by one statistic: he produced 56 first-team All-Americans in his 28 seasons.

His Uncanny Memory

Anyone who knew Woody well will tell you his memory was one of his personal strengths. He could remember dates, names, stories, the tiniest details, and specific conversations from decades earlier.

This is also a story from Schumacher about when Woody first visited him during the recruiting process: "After meeting Coach Hayes at the Cleveland alumni dinner, he can out to my home in Lorain. As the visit was coming to an end, I mentioned to Coach that my high school football coach, Doug Thompson, lived next door and I was sure that he would love to say hello. I could see lights were still on at his house, so I walked next door to let Doug know that Woody was at my home. Doug came over to say hello. As it turned out, Doug was part of the last class Coach Hayes recruited prior to leaving Miami to take the head-coaching position at Ohio State [1951]. Doug had mentioned that his parents were visiting from Toledo and that they also would like to say hello. Coach Hayes had recruited Doug 20 years earlier, and during that visit with Doug's parents, he recalled specifics of his conversations with them!"

When Woody asked a recruit about his goals after football, he would always remember them as their careers ended four or five years later, even if the players themselves did not remember.

"During dinner when he was recruiting me, I mentioned I wanted to major in business and maybe attend law school later," Brian Baschnagel (1972–1975) recalled. "After the draft [Baschnagel was selected in the third round by the Chicago Bears] but before graduation in June, Woody called me into the office."

"Brian, what are you going to do?" he asked.

"What do you mean, Coach?" Baschnagel asked.

Hayes then repeated himself, but louder. "What are you going to do?"

Woody Hayes takes a knee during practice on September 12, 1951, his first season as Ohio State's football coach.

"I don't know if you heard, but I got drafted by the..." Before he could get the words out, Hayes picked up a book and slammed it to the floor, screaming, "There goes your law degree!"

"After all those years," Baschnagel said, "he remembered that conversation we had at dinner during recruiting."

Marcus Marek (1979–1982), along with Cobb, was in the final class that was recruited by Woody but never got to play for him. That didn't mean the coach forgot those players.

"During my sophomore year, I remember walking across campus, and Woody Hayes and I were on the same path," Marek recalled. "I was thinking, 'He won't remember who I am.' Not only did he remember, but he remembered my parents' names and one of my friends from high school.

"'Didn't you have a friend who was going to Allegheny College?'" he asked.

"He never forgot people."

New Year's Eve will always be special for Rocco Rich (1971–1973) and his family. On that day, a day before the 1974 Rose Bowl against USC, Rich became a father.

"My wife had just delivered a little girl that day back in Ohio, and someone leaked it to Woody during practice," Rich said. "So he calls us all together and says, 'In honor of our victory tomorrow, I am hoping Rocco will name his little girl Rose Victoria.'

"I said, 'Okay, Coach, but I am not sure my wife will go for it.'"

Two years following the Buckeyes' 42–21 rout of USC, Rich was walking through the Big Bear grocery store behind St. John Arena when he bumped into Woody. They had been talking for about 15 minutes when the coach suddenly said, "By the way, did you name your little girl Rose Victoria?"

"I had to tell him we named her Dina Nicole," Rich said. "I was just amazed he remembered the story. We stood there and had a nice visit in the aisle of the grocery store. That showed what compassion he had for us and how he remembered everything about us."

Dina Nicole was the first of the Rich's four children and four grandchildren.

As a Father Figure

"That's exactly what he was to me and to a lot of other players over the years," said linebacker/fullback Bruce Elia (1972–1974). "When you leave home and you are 18 years old, you are really on your own for the first time. You could be up all night. You could be partying. You could become a failure. You could become anything, really.

"You are at an age where you are not a kid, but you are certainly not a man. You are sort of caught in the crossroads. Woody was the bridge for us. He kept you going from when your parents handed you off. He had promised my parents that he would look after me and that I wouldn't get to do just what I wanted."

"In the movie *Remember the Titans,* the coach asks the players, 'Who's your daddy?'" said Michael D'Andrea (1979–1981). "At Ohio State, Coach Hayes could have asked the same question. Woody became like a father to me."

As an Educator

His father was an educated man and drove Woody to become an educated man. And he wanted his players to be educated men. He cared as much, if not more, that they earned a degree as he did that they win games.

When players missed classes, he treated them as if they had fumbled. When they failed to get a degree, it was as if they quit on their teammates.

"We're not going to give these kids on the football team anything illegal, you can bet on that," he said once the NCAA probationary period passed in 1956. "But we are going to give them an opportunity to get an education. And I am going to see they get that education. We certainly owe them that."

"He never let me forget that I was at Ohio State for an education first and to play football second," Jim Parker, the All-American tackle, once said.

Woody even taught a university-accredited course, Fundamentals of Coaching Football, which high school coaches did anything they could to enroll in.

"It was a very hard course to get into," said Leo Hayden, part of the 1968 Super Sophomores. "But I was in it one year, and it always started at 8:00 AM. Well, one day, I had been up pulling an all-nighter, and I decided to sleep in and skip it. I figured, 'Well, Woody doesn't even know if I am there on some days.' But on this particular day, he was discussing the '14-15 play,' which is a tailback run that gave you a lot of options on how to read blocks and where to cut.

"He was saying something about the blocking of it and how the tailback read the guard's block, and then he added, 'Isn't that right Leo? Leo? Leo? That son of a bitch. He isn't here!' "

Woody called running backs coach Tiger Ellison, who promptly scurried over to Hayden's dorm room and began knocking on the door.

"There was this knocking, and I didn't say anything," Hayden recalled. "Then I could hear Tiger leave, and I figured he was going to get the resident assistant and come back and open the door. There was nowhere for me to go. In those days, I had a 32-inch waist, and there was about a 28-inch gap under the bed. Plus, there was a bar under the bed that made it difficult to get under there, but I sucked it up and got under there and held my breath. I thought, 'How embarrassing if I get caught under here.'

"Sure enough, two minutes later, I heard the key in the lock, and Tiger Ellison came into the room, opened the closet doors, and said, 'Son of a gun, he isn't here,' and he walked out. I waited five minutes and ran across campus and came busting into Woody's class before Tiger could make it back there. 'Coach, I am so sorry. I overslept. I won't let it happen again,' I told Woody.

'Don't you ever miss my class again!' he shouted.

"Let me tell you, Woody Hayes was a stickler about education. He would send coaches over to get you out of bed if you missed a single class."

One day, a professor called Woody to inform him that guard Ken Fritz (1976–1979) missed his class.

"The next day, Woody woke me up and went to class with me—all day," Fritz said. "Can you imagine the kids' reactions to see Woody Hayes walking in and sitting down in their classroom? I told him I would never miss another class."

There are dozens of stories from former OSU players, even those in the NFL, whom Woody would call and inquire about their progress toward a degree. He didn't once ask how life was in the NFL or how their individual careers were progressing.

"What are you doing toward your degree?" he would ask.

Once, he called up the Browns' Dick Schafrath and said, "You still need a course to finish that degree? Then you had better get back here and finish up!"

With that, he hung up.

"He was the motivating force for me to go to law school," said linebacker Stan White (1969–1971), who received his law degree in 1978.

And it wasn't just the sheepskin that Woody cared about. He hated wasting any idle moments with his players. If there was downtime, he gave them a course in his famous "word play," aimed at expanding their vocabularies.

He would order his players to learn one new word each day and memorize its spelling and its meaning.

"One time I used the word 'onlyest,'" said Paul Warfield (1961–1963). "He said, 'What? That word doesn't exist. There is no such word.' He was right. He knew the language."

After all, Woody majored in history and English at Denison University and was a stickler for teaching his players both subjects. He also was a professor in the truest sense of the word. Often, he tutored his players at study table, if a regular tutor was not available.

"He always told us that if we used the resources available to us, like the tutors, for example, there is no reason we shouldn't get our degree," said Leon Ellison, who graduated with a degree in communications. "After you earned a certain grade point average, you didn't have to go to study table, but I continued to go all four years because it helped me so much.

"And on many nights when I was there, he would be tutoring kids in English or history."

One time, on the team's bus trip to Michigan, Woody was reading the school's newspaper, *The Lantern,* when he suddenly ordered the bus driver to pull to the side of the road and stop. He stood up and lectured the Buckeyes on the fall of the Roman Empire. As it turned out, a writer in *The Lantern* had picked Michigan to win the game.

"Once he finished his lecture on how the Roman Empire was torn apart from within," Conley said, "Woody opened up the door of the bus, crumpled up the newspaper, and threw it outside."

Since one of the coach's favorite subjects was history, especially U.S. or military history, many of the Buckeyes' plays were named after famous battles, battleships, or planes.

Guard John Kelley tells a story from the 1966 game at Illinois to illustrate this point.

"Of course, it is well known that Woody was a real history buff. He would often drift off topic in our team meetings about how the play he was discussing reminded him of some battle or military maneuver," Kelley said. "We had plays named after airplanes and generals—Patton 1 and Patton 2, B52 or B56—and similar audibles that the quarterback would call. He sometimes drifted off into discussions about Sherman's march to the sea and how it reminded him of the off-tackle play that we so often ran. These transgressions could last a half hour or more as he truly seemed to enjoy enlightening us about history or military battles.

"Well, as we got into our sweats this day in Champaign, he called for a team meeting before we went out. So as we gathered in the locker room, he stood before us and began talking about Illinois. He began telling us the history of Abraham Lincoln. This went on for maybe 20 minutes, and he became so emotional about what he was telling us that he began to cry. Not sobbing, but tears were rolling down his cheeks. He loved Lincoln and could hardly get through that story."

Dr. Erwin Thal was a team manager from 1954 to 1957 and one of Woody's favorites. One time, Thal, who lived in Dallas, picked Woody up at the city's airport and took him to the downtown Fairmont Hotel.

"He was there for a roast or something," Thal recalled. "I had my 15-year-old son, Jeff, with me at the time. Woody picked up his room key, and the room number was 1911. He turned to Jeff and asked, 'Okay, what happened in 1911?'"

Since Jeff Thal couldn't come up with an answer, Woody invited both Thals up to his room, where they spent the next 90 minutes listening to the coach give a lecture on the history that occurred that year.

His Generosity

Woody never had much money after turning down all those raises, but he would give you the shirt off his back if he liked you, or knew you or trusted you, or if you were recommended to him.

If you were a former player, well, he would do virtually anything to help make your life easier. His loyalty was unquestioned, even by his enemies.

When Vic Janowicz was badly injured in a car accident and in a Chicago hospital, Woody put him on the team airplane after OSU played at Northwestern. He brought him back to University Hospital, where he stayed a month and made a full recovery.

It was Woody's generosity that got him in trouble with the NCAA in 1956. When a *Sports Illustrated* writer had visited Hayes to write a story on him following the 1954 championship season, the coach had mentioned how most of his players did not have money for their basic needs. And playing football at Ohio State prevented them from holding down jobs, so he would sometimes give them a few dollars to get them by.

As a result of his admission, the NCAA placed the Buckeyes' program on a one-year probation.

Woody and the Media

Generally, Hayes despised most sportswriters, especially those who worked for national publications. First of all, he didn't trust them, other than a chosen few who covered Ohio State on a regular basis, like his good friend Paul Hornung, who worked for *The Columbus Dispatch*.

If Woody was anything, he was honest. And sometimes, when reported, his honesty hurt him in the public's perception. Much of his disdain stemmed from the *Sports Illustrated* article that led to OSU's one-year probation. But overall, his relationship with the media correlated with the Buckeyes' success on the field. If they were winning, it was cordial. If they were not, it was strained, to say the least.

On Being Socially Aware

An outsider's perception of Woody Hayes could be of a narrow-minded Neanderthal. Nothing, and I mean nothing, could be further from the truth. He was more socially aware than the average man.

He was a progressive thinker on many subjects—subjects, that is, not related to his play calling, of course. In fact, he was among the first major-college coaches in his time to hire African American assistant coaches and to play black players in large numbers in the 1950s. And often he lectured his colleagues around the country on why it was the right thing to do.

During the energy crunch of the late 1960s and early '70s, he sold his car and walked anywhere he needed to go. And he told his players to do the same.

Leo Hayden said that one day, "Woody told us, 'Now don't drive over here anymore. We all have to do our part to save gasoline. Catch the bus over here or walk over here or run over here, but don't use your cars.'

"So one day I am driving to the facility early to get treatment, and there is Coach, walking down the street. I blew the horn, and he hopped in, and I was going to give him a ride. He asked, 'Leo, why are you driving to practice?'

"I told him I had to get there early for treatment."

"I don't give a damn," Woody said. "You know what I told you. Now let me out of this car, and I will walk the rest of the way."

"And he got out and walked," Hayden said. "It wasn't a gimmick for him. He believed in things like that, and he wanted us to believe in it, too.

"Now when I think that a college coach can make $32 million over eight years, boy, Woody wouldn't understand that."

As most people know, Woody also was very politically active, often stumping for Republican candidates at every level. And when there were anti-war demonstrations on campus during Vietnam, he was front and center on the other side of the line of scrimmage, so to speak.

Jim Conroy, a center, received a call from Woody one day in May 1970 that preceded a demonstration on the Oval, the heart of OSU's campus.

"It was during the period of the Kent State shootings, and there were upheavals on every campus," Conroy said. "It was the week after spring ball, and Woody, knowing I was one of the better students on the team, asked me, 'What are these people's philosophies? What do they believe in?'

"I said, 'Coach, I have no idea. I don't know.'"

So Woody came up with a covert operation by ordering Conroy to "infiltrate their ranks" and find out what books supported their beliefs.

"I go over there with my short hair and told them, 'Man, you have some good points here. I have to do some reading on this. What would you recommend?'"

Conroy promptly went to one of the university bookstores where Woody had given him his account number and bought three books. One was *Soul on Ice* by Eldridge Cleaver, and another was by Jerry Rubin, founder of the Youth International Party.

"I reported back to the old man with those books," Conroy said. "He was afraid they were going to shut down the university, which was their goal at the time, and he wanted to go to battle with them over it. But first, he wanted to learn what they stood for."

Within a few days, during a demonstration on the Oval, Woody grabbed the microphone and gave a passionate speech stating why the university should remain open. Conroy, Chuck Hutchison,

Dave Cheney, and many other linemen stood near the stage, acting as bodyguards just in case.

"Some kids were booing him, and some were cheering him, and we wanted to make sure nobody roughed him up," Conroy said.

At the base of the flagpole, which flew the U.S. flag, lineman Bob Trapuzzano sat next to his giant German shepherd.

"Bob was there to make sure nobody was burning that flag," Conroy said.

"While Woody was speaking, he was stating his opinion of why the university should remain open and he was using some football analogies, but you could imagine that those weren't flying

Woody Hayes is carried off on his team's shoulders after their victory over the number one–ranked University of Wisconsin in Columbus on October 11, 1952. Pictured are Tom Hague (No. 88), Dick Nosky (No. 54), and Bob Joslin (No. 85); the coach's hand is on the helmet of John Hlay, the Buckeyes fullback.

too well with that crowd. It just shows how much he believed in the university."

"Stand to His Right If You Want in the Game"

That was a credo many backup players on offense soon realized.

If things weren't going well on the field, Woody was reactionary at times and would grab the player closest to him if he wanted new blood in the game.

As a freshman, tailback Calvin Murray was told to do just that if he wanted to get a carry or two. Sure enough, when Ron Springs was injured during a 35–7 win at Southern Methodist in 1977, Woody turned to his right and grabbed Murray.

"You're going in," he barked.

"I said, 'Huh?'" Murray recalled. "The only thing he said to me was 'Don't fumble.'"

Murray rushed for 94 yards in relief of Springs and did not fumble once.

Yes, His Temper Is Legendary

Going back to his youth, Woody admittedly had a boiling point. And he passed it often, say about 10 times per day. For starters, losing the football on a fumble set him off. Losing a game usually did, too. So did someone disagreeing with him.

Examples of his temper definitely are in the thousands.

Just before leaving Miami of Ohio for Ohio State, Woody once smashed one of the school's trophies onto the floor in front of the school's athletics director, a booster-club president, and the Oxford, Ohio, mayor. The next day he came back into the athletics director's office and offered to pay for the trophy. Typical Woody.

Bo Schembechler, a former assistant and later Woody's chief rival, once said of him, "He was the most irascible man that ever lived and the worst guy in the world to work for. But I wouldn't change that experience for anything in the world."

One time, he heaved a film projector at assistant Bill Mallory.

"At times, he was like a volcano waiting to explode," said Sarkkinen, a Hayes assistant for 27 years at Ohio State.

It is also true that there were few players who passed through Ohio State who didn't receive a punch to the stomach from the head coach. It was his typical reaction to a play gone bad during practice. When they saw it coming, they just clenched their abdominal muscles and took it.

But they never laughed it off.

"That made him madder," linebacker Tom Cousineau said.

During one game at Illinois in 1977, senior team manager Lenny Davis was manning the offensive headset while standing behind Hayes on the sideline.

"We were in 'robust,' our goal-line offense, and it was either third-and-inches or fourth-and-inches when one of the coaches on the headset yelled, 'First down!'" Davis recalled. "So I yelled out 'First down!' Woody turned around and just punched me right in the stomach and screamed, 'Don't you ever yell "first down" unless you know it's first down.'

"I looked over at the players, and they are in hysterics. But we got the first down and won the game [35–0], and I got a punch to the gut from Woody Hayes."

Nothing set Woody off as did repeated mistakes during practice.

"In my sophomore year, I was a third-team guard," said Tim Wersel (1969–1972). "I backed up Phil Strickland. Phil was injured during one morning practice, and I was thrust onto the first team for that afternoon practice. I was as nervous as a whore in church. When we got to the scrimmage, Woody called 'Robust 26 on two' and I went offside. That was not good. I got up expecting the worst, but there was Woody rubbing his hands, tugging on his cap, only to shout 'Huddle up, next play.'"

Woody called the same play, and once again, Wersel jumped offside.

"Before I could move, he had me by the shoulder pads and started to hit me in the chest as hard as he could, screaming, 'You dumbass, you stupid sons a bitch,' and on and on. He grabbed my facemask and cranked it so hard that I was now looking at my teammates through the right earhole in my helmet. That is extremely embarrassing, not to mention painful. Football helmets fit snugly on your head for a reason. My teammates were at his back laughing quietly.

"His parting words were: 'Earle [Bruce], get him out of there, and don't ever put him back in.' All I can say is that Woody was truly a man of his word."

If you were an assistant coach under Woody, it is a sure bet that you were fired by him. Maybe twice or even three or four times. Then he would "rehire" you either within minutes, an hour, or if he was really mad, not until the next day.

"One time he fired me," said assistant Ed Ferkany (1972–1973). "We had a disagreement over a blocking scheme, and we are watching the film after practice one night and he shut off the projector and started screaming at me. He pushed me, and I pushed him. He said, 'Get out of here. You're fired!'

"I lived about two miles away, and I got to the front door, and my wife told me, 'Go on back. Woody just called and said you are not fired anymore.'"

But He Did Make Them Laugh

Many of the stories involving Woody are hilarious to his players all these years later, even if they weren't too funny when they occurred.

"It was prior to a homecoming game," defensive back Vince Skillings remembers. "Coach Hayes called for the second-team defense to go against the first-team offense. Well, all of the defensive starters went to the visitors' sideline and sat down on these folding chairs. Man, why did we do that?

"I didn't even notice Coach Hayes leave the middle of the field. I just saw players falling over chairs and beating feet toward the open end of the stadium. There was Coach Hayes running down the sideline, kicking over chairs, screaming, 'Get up! Get up! This ain't no goddamn country club!' Then he saw Al Washington still seated, and he picked up a chair and began chasing Al with it. Al's eyes nearly popped out of his head as he jumped up and took off running. Coach Hayes then started throwing all of the chairs into the stands, still screaming, 'This is not a country club!' We were falling all over ourselves with laughter. Later, I often wondered how he didn't suffer a heart attack."

Woody loved to tell his players stories, especially war stories. Sometimes, he was profane. Other times, he was profane *and* funny.

"He used to talk about the big battles in history and the wars," Jim Stillwagon said. "One time he was telling me about the guy from Ohio State who invented WEFT, which was a way to identify enemy aircraft. It stood for 'wings, engine, fuselage, and tail.' Woody called it 'Wrong Every F*cking Time.'"

He said, "By the time you figured it out with that system, the son of a bitch had dropped a bomb on you."

"I thought that was real funny," Stillwagon said. "So one day I was in the shower and I was telling the guys about Woodstock's theory on WEFT, and I noticed that he was in a bathroom stall listening. I could hear him chuckling about it. I could hear his cleats clattering on the floor because he was laughing so hard."

Sometimes, he said funny things during pregame speeches or during sideline meetings, even though he didn't mean for them to be funny. Michigan State had beaten Ohio State 32–7 in 1965, a day on which Spartan fans had tossed rolls of toilet paper onto the field to celebrate each touchdown.

When the Buckeyes made their return trip to Spartan Stadium two years later, Hayes gathered his team before the game and announced, "Do you know what today is? It's Operation Constipation! They're not going to be throwing that damn toilet paper at us this time! We're going to show them where to shove it!"

The Buckeyes won 21–7, the beginning of a 22-game winning streak that stretched to the end of the 1969 season.

One time, Woody stuck his head into the practice huddle and accidentally expelled some flatulence.

"We were trying to pay attention to the play call, but everybody was holding their breath," Murray said. "The minute he turned his back, we would get a breath and then snicker. Coach made us laugh a number of ways."

One time, the Buckeyes were having a terrible practice, making one mental mistake after another, when Woody stopped it. "I know what the problem is—you're not getting enough blood into your heads," he told the team. "Everybody, stand on your head!"

"So here we are, doing handstands," said end Dick Wakefield (1969–1971). "We were stopping traffic on Olentangy River Road. People were stopping their cars to watch this. And God forbid if you laughed. It you did, you did it quietly."

Many of the players on the '77 team will never forget the Pat O'Brien story.

During the week leading up to the Sugar Bowl, dozens of players hit the famous Bourbon Street nightspot and were indulging in the legendary Hurricanes—a fruit-punch concoction that includes several shots of liquor.

Woody walked into the courtyard where several players had drinks in front of them, but he figured they were just fruit punch because Hurricanes look no different than that. He sat down where several Buckeyes were seated.

"He said, 'Oh, those look pretty good,'" Leon Ellison recalled.

"Then he reached over and took a sip of one, and he figured out that juice was just for coloring," Cousineau said. "He got up, he threw that Hurricane against the wall, and the race was on."

Players scrambled to leave the bar without being seen by the coach. Several were crawling under tables, headed for the exit. Some were leaping over chairs and tables as if they were fallen linebackers. Starting the next night, there was an early curfew.

In a meeting before that game, Woody was ranting in front of the team, trying to motivate them to face Paul "Bear" Bryant's team. It was the only meeting ever between the two legendary coaches, in which Alabama won 35–6. It was Ohio State's worst bowl loss ever.

"He was saying, 'Bear this and Bear that,'" guard Ernie Andria said. "As he talked, his dentures kept sliding down. He kept shoving those teeth up into his mouth, and they kept falling down. Finally, he yelled, 'Dammit,' and he pulled them out of his mouth and held them in his hand as he continued his speech. We could barely understand him after that."

Woody had a quick wit, too, and often was not given enough credit for that, but his players always realized it. For example, and there are a million of these type of stories, guard Wayne Betz (1960–1962) pulled the wrong way during practice, crashed into the other guard, and caused a fumble.

"We got back into the huddle, and Woody asked, 'Betz, what kind of engineer are you studying to be?'"

"Chemical engineer, sir," Betz answered.

"I'll never drink another drop of water again!" Woody snapped, without missing a beat.

"He wasn't known for his humor," Betz said, "but Woody could be as funny as anyone."

He Was Always There

As far as what he accomplished each day, it was as if Woody somehow had 30 hours in his days, while everyone else had 24.

He was everywhere. If a former player was graduating, Woody was there. A birth? Woody was holding the baby in the maternity ward. ("One of the best days of my life was October 18, 1981, when my son Jimmy was born," Jim Otis said. "I held him first and Woody held him second, even before his mother.") A wedding? Woody would have walked the former player's bride down the aisle if asked.

He often attended any award ceremony for a former player, whether it was a Pro Football Hall of Fame induction or a company banquet that celebrated the smallest achievement.

"When I got inducted into the Pro Football Hall of Fame in 1983, I looked out into the audience when I was on stage, and you know who I saw?" Warfield asked. "Woody Hayes. That really touched me. He never told me he was coming. What a great man."

And there were times he was there when his players did not want to see him. Center Tom DeLeone (1969–1971) said Woody would frequently stop by the dorms, carrying a pizza or two.

"He would always bring pizza with him," he said. "It was almost like his disguise."

One day, DeLeone was studying in his room with two coeds, who had brought a few beers with them.

"I heard somebody shout, 'Woody's on the floor!'" he said.

"I stuck these beers under the bed and threw a blanket down there to make sure he wouldn't see them. Sure enough, he opened my door and he had a big box of pizza. He just said, 'Ladies, we have a big game this week, and you should probably leave now.' In my life, I never saw two girls move faster than that. He didn't offer me any pizza, either. He just turned the lights out and said something like, 'Go to bed.' Then he closed the door. It was about 8:30! But I went to bed."

Anne Hayes: A Saint and the Real Boss

Many friends and colleagues say that perhaps Woody's best feature was his wife, Anne.

"What a wonderful lady Anne Hayes was," Rex Kern said. "She was just as good a person as he was—maybe even better, because she had to put up with him."

Anne Hayes was, for lack of a better term, the First Lady of Ohio State football for almost 30 years. She was, by all accounts, a great recruiter, tutor, mother, and cook, and she kept Woody straight.

She had a heart as big as the entire campus.

"Let me tell you about Anne Hayes," Ferkany said. "I got out of coaching in '74 and took a job with Worthington Industries. I was driving back from Canton one day that year when I heard on the radio that Woody had had a heart attack. My wife just happened to be in the hospital at the time with back problems. We had five kids, and the oldest was 13. I would tell her to keep the kids home and safe until I would get there after work and fix them dinner.

"Well, there is a knock on the door that very night, and it is Anne Hayes. She had fixed this big pot of stew for us because she knew my wife was in the hospital. She had her own worries at the time because of Woody's heart attack, but that's the type of lady she was."

Anne often had former players and their families stay the night at the Hayes's house, before or after home games. Woody, after all, frequently stayed overnight at the North Facility watching game film.

"After I graduated, we continued to come back to home games," George Jacoby said. "One time, Nina was pregnant with our first son, and we stopped to see Annie after the game. We were getting ready to go home, and she said, 'George, Nina can't ride all the way up to Toledo like this. You just take one of Woody's double beds in the front bedroom. Don't worry about it. Woody watches film all night, and he won't be home until about 6:00 in the morning.'

"Woody had this big bedroom in the front of the house with two double beds in it. Well, Nina and I were sleeping in one of them, and sure enough, at about 6:00, the door opened and here came Woody. He went into the bathroom and then sat down on the edge of the bed. It was still dark. My wife woke me up and said, 'George, Woody's here. He's on the end of the bed!'"

"Coach?" Jacoby asked.

"Jacoby, what the hell are you doing in here?" Hayes responded.

"That was after I was gone, but he still recognized my voice," Jacoby said. "When Annie came up to Toledo, she would always tell people, 'My husband got into bed with this man's pregnant wife!' She always thought that was funny."

His Compassion

For every blowup, or "megaton" as insiders called them, for every temper tantrum, and for every time he berated an official, there are dozens of stories that reveal the softer side of Woody Hayes.

Undoubtedly, there are dozens of documented megatons but thousands of undocumented instances in which he showed his heart was as big as Ohio Stadium. We may never know all of them, because he wanted it that way.

Woody was just the opposite of today's celebrities who seek publicity for their good deeds. He did them every day of his life and went to great pains so that they wouldn't be revealed.

"In 1981, when my dad was on his deathbed, Woody found out and drove straight to Cleveland to be with him for all hours of the night," Ohio State coach Jim Tressel said. "It was a few years after he had been released at Ohio State, but Woody was still being Woody. He cared about people."

One of his regular routines was to visit Children's, University, and Riverside Hospitals unannounced and walk the halls, stopping in room after room to cheer up a patient. He usually carried either boxes of candy or flowers. Often, he would ask the head nurses, "Which patients haven't had a visitor recently?"

He always visited an injured player immediately, and then he would visit complete strangers' rooms. The staffs of all three hospitals knew him well. In fact, the running joke was that Woody spent more time in the hospitals than most doctors.

"Woody used to just walk the halls at all of the hospitals and drop in to cheer people up—people he didn't even know," Rex Kern said

Often, he would grab a popular player like Kern or Archie Griffin to accompany him.

"He would call me over after training table and say, 'Rex, you got any tests you are studying for?' If I said, 'No,' he would say, 'Let's go.' You knew where you were going—you were going to the hospital with him."

Diane DeMuesy was a nurse at University Hospital in the early 1970s. In one of the hospital rooms to which she was assigned was a young man dying of cancer. In the other bed in the young man's room was a Buckeye recovering from an injury. The young man with cancer was thrilled to be sharing a room with an OSU football player.

When Woody visited the injured player, he began chatting with the cancer patient. When the player was released, Woody continued to visit the cancer patient.

"Woody was so busy," DeMuesy said. "He could have made so many excuses not to come back. After all, the young man wasn't

Woody Hayes chats with some of his players at the start of the 1956 season, when it came out in a magazine article that the coach would occasionally give his players a few dollars to help them buy everyday necessities. From left are Hubert Bobo, cocaptain Bill Michael, Coach Hayes, Frank Ellwood, and guard Jim Parker.

part of Woody's life. But I would walk by the room, and there would be Woody, talking quietly to the young man. Why did Woody do it? Because that's the kind of person he was."

When the cancer patient died, an autographed football from the team and a Buckeyes poster were at his bedside. They were both gifts from Woody.

"That young man's last days were comfortable and happy," DeMuesy said. "The reason was Woody Hayes."

"There are literally hundreds of stories like that one," Kern said. "One time he was in the shopping center in Upper Arlington, and this man came up to him and told him how much he and his wife loved the Buckeyes and how he just wanted to shake his hand."

"Well, where is your wife?" Woody asked the man.

The man told Woody that she had cancer and was at Riverside Hospital. That evening, when the man went to visit his wife, Woody was already sitting by her bedside.

When the team returned following the 1974 Rose Bowl victory over USC, someone handed Woody a huge bouquet of roses at the Columbus airport.

"Woody decided to make a special trip to Riverside Hospital, and he asked the registration desk for names of patients who did not have any visitors that day," Bruce Ruhl said. "Then he passed out all of those roses to all those patients in the various wards."

"When I was in the hospital recovering from my injury in 1976," Ernie Andria recalled, "Woody stopped by one day with a box of chocolates for me, but he had just found out about a sick boy on the sixth floor. Bill Jaco was also visiting me that day, so Woody handed Bill $5 and told him, 'Go get Ernie what he wants—I am going to give the boy up on the sixth floor this box of candy.'"

Joel Laser was an All-American lineman at Akron St. Vincent–St. Mary. As he was being recruited in the winter of 1975, his mother Vera was dying of liver cancer. Hayes visited the household and spent two hours talking about everything—as usual—everything but football. When he left, Vera told her son, "Go to Ohio State. I know you will be well taken care of by that man."

"She went back into the hospital soon after I went to Ohio State, and Woody came to visit her," Laser said. "When she died, July 6 of that year, he went to the funeral. Then in August, my father had a nervous breakdown and was admitted to Akron General."

When Hayes heard about Laser's father during practice, he flipped the player, then a scout-team freshman, the keys to his El Camino with the AstroTurf in the bed and said, "Go visit him! Now!"

On the Monday before the '75 Michigan game, later that season, the Buckeyes were ranked number one with a 10–0 record.

"Woody's preparing for one of the biggest games of his life, and he calls me into his office and asks, 'How's your father?'" Laser recalled.

"He's back in the hospital, Coach," Laser told him.

The coach summoned team doctor Bob Murphy into his office. "Is there anything we can do for him?" Hayes asked Murphy.

Within two months, Laser's father was transferred to Harding Hospital in Columbus, then a mental-health facility.

"He recovered, later remarried, and lived a happy life until he died in 1995," Laser said.

"Understand this, that I was nothing but a scout-team guy for four years. I never played, which is still a sense of embarrassment for me. But I got a bachelor's and a master's degree from Ohio State within six years, all paid for because I had a scholarship and then worked in the athletic department. My mother was right—Woody Hayes was exactly what she said he was. He took care of me."

And then there were the little thoughtful things that Hayes did on a daily basis.

"My dad was watching practice in the spring on a fairly cold day," linebacker Dwight "Ike" Kelley (1963–1965) said, "and Woody noticed him and sent one of the managers in to get him a coat. He did little things like that all the time.

"In my four years there, I remember that Woody missed practice once. On that day, he had gotten word that a young student had just broken his neck playing intramural football. Woody left practice to go to University Hospital. He took an autographed football and stayed there with that boy until his parents showed up. Woody didn't want him to be alone."

Barney Renard, a backup tackle during most of his career (1973–1976), had been married and was close to graduating with a degree in pharmacy when his eligibility expired. His wife, Kim, then became pregnant.

"So the week before the next season, we were expecting our first child, and Kim was working at Children's Hospital," he said. "Woody asked me about my situation, and I told him, 'I will be fine as long as she could keep working and there are no problems with her pregnancy. If she can't keep working, I will be in trouble.'

"So Woody paid my tuition that year and also gave me a job that season (1977) of cutting up the film and breaking it down on

Sundays. Dick Mack and I would come in at 6:00 AM and put every detail of the film into a computer bank and look for tendencies. We would work until 8:00 at night. At the end of the season, Woody told me, 'If something happens and you need help, get back in here, and I will find something for you. I want you to graduate in June!' "

Woody always gave Renard money on those Sundays to pick up dinner and bring it back to the office. One night, he handed him money and told him to "go buy some chocolates."

"I got four boxes of that Russell Stover candy, and, as I pulled up to the facility, Woody was standing outside," Renard recalled.

"Let's go over to Riverside Hospital," Woody ordered, hopping into the car.

"Vince Skillings had blown out his knee the previous day, so we visited him, and Woody gave him a box of candy. I thought, 'What am I going to do with these other three boxes?' Then we stopped at another room, and another room, and another room. Woody gave out the remaining three boxes and visited with patients he didn't even know.

"Then he looked at me and said, 'Looks like supper will be McDonald's tonight because we have to get back to work.' "

Growing up in New Jersey and now living there, Bruce Elia often encounters the usual critics when Woody's name is mentioned. Most non-Ohioans have one limited memory of Hayes, stemming from his final game.

" 'Oh, you played for that crazy guy, Woody Hayes,' they will say," he explained. "I just say, 'Let me tell you, he wasn't crazy. He was only a good coach, but he was a great man.'

"I tell them about the time I was on the bus and it was very cold, but I just had a T-shirt on. Woody took off his coat and wrapped it around me. He looked at me and whispered into my ear, 'A fighter has to stay warm, right?'

"That man cared about people more than anybody I ever knew."

The late Bo Schembechler, who worked closely with Woody for six seasons as an OSU assistant, knew that better than anybody. It was Bo who delivered the most crushing loss of Woody's career—

the 24–12 shocker in Ann Arbor in Bo's first season. The loss surely cost Hayes a national championship.

"When I had my heart attack at the Rose Bowl, and then when I returned home, the first one to come see me there was Woody," he recalled shortly before his death.

"Then, when they honored me down there in Dayton, he drove down there to introduce me, and he spoke for 30 minutes. He wowed them, and I knew then that he wasn't feeling well. He drove home. And then he died.

"So if you ask me, 'Did I know Woody Hayes?' Yes, I knew him as well as anybody ever knew him. He was a great man."

On Responsibility

Bruce Elia still remembers all of Woody's little sayings and stories that would illustrate responsibility and accountability.

"He would take pens and pencils from his office home to do work—when he did go home, that is," Elia said. "Then he would always bring them back to the office.

"Somebody once asked, 'Why?'

"'Because they don't belong to me,' Woody shot back. 'They belong to the university.'

"As small as that story is," Elia said, "things like that taught us responsibility and about being honest. This was another one of his favorites: there was a little kid who worked on a farm and had to carry a calf every day. He did it day after day after day, picking up that calf and carrying it to where it needed to be. Then one day, that boy had done it for so long and had gotten so strong, that he didn't realize he was carrying a cow."

Tim Singer, a student manager from 1975 to 1978, will never forget this example from his senior season: "After the spring game, I was responsible for taking the film, once it was done and developed, up to the North Facility at night so the coaches could watch it and grade it. I flat-out forgot to do it. My parents were in town, and we went out to dinner. When I got back to my room, my roommate said, 'Coach [George] Chaump has called. Coach Hayes has called. Where is the film?'

"It was 11:00 at night, and Coach Hayes was still waiting for the film. I called the police, trying to get someone to open the lab door so I could get in and get the film. Nobody could let me in. So the next morning, I woke up and took the film over to the facility. Coach Hayes was sitting at one of those little classroom desks, right next to the film projector. He was sound asleep. I thought I was a dead man. I thought for sure he would blow up at me, but I had to wake him up, and I had to speak for myself.

"Coach, I just forgot," Singer told him. "I went to dinner with my parents, and I just forgot. I am so sorry. I am sure this is the last time you will see me."

He added, "I just knew I was going to be fired. He then gave me a heart-warming speech about responsibility, and he never raised his voice. Not once. I crept right back out of there, and I am alive to tell the story. But to think that he slept at that tiny, little desk all night waiting for that film…"

As a Motivator

Linebacker Thomas "Pepper" Johnson never played for Woody, arriving at Ohio State in 1982 and becoming an All-American by the time he was a senior. But he will never forget the two times the legendary coach sat next to him at the captain's table during team meals.

Earle Bruce had invited Woody to speak to his teams often, especially before the Michigan games.

"Woody and I were sitting there, and he was telling me how good these cinnamon rolls were. He always loved those rolls from the golf course," Johnson said. "He was telling me how to put a little butter on them and how to eat them. The next year, he sat next to me and we had the same conversation. Now, I looked out and saw 100 guys looking at me and Woody talking together. They were all wondering what we were talking about because it was an intense conversation. But they had no idea it was all about cinnamon rolls. That was one of those 'Call Mom and tell her what you did today' type of deals.

"The thing Woody told us was how to be a real football player. He told us he hated to see a guy miss an interception and then pound his fist on the ground or look at his hands like his hands let him down. Just because of what Woody said, I never did that after that, even in the NFL. I never looked at my hands if I dropped a pass. I tell my son that today."

"Motivation was his strength," Jim Stillwagon explained. "Was Woody a great Xs-and-Os coach? No. Was he a great leader? Yes. He could make an average player good. He could make a good player great. And he could make a great player a superstar."

Jim Parker always told a story about the time Woody wrapped his arms around him one day after practice.

"'Look up at that stadium,' he told me. 'Just look at it.'

"I looked up at the stadium, and he asked me, 'What are you thinking about? Just look up there and ask yourself if you are a better football player today than you were yesterday. Look up at the stadium and ask that of yourself.'

"I did. I looked up and asked, 'Am I a better football player today than I was yesterday?' He then told me, 'If it didn't say nothing back, then take your ass back out there and jog around the field four times.'

"Every day after that, I would look up there and think about what he said. I would ask myself if I was better today than I was yesterday. If not, I would go back and work on the weak things. That stayed with me all my life."

His Paranoia

There was plenty of evidence that Woody was paranoid of outsiders and opponents, or at least he acted that way. Often, he said he thought the Buckeyes' practices were being spied upon or that a visiting locker room might be bugged.

John Kelley described the pregame scene at Illinois in 1966: "He got us together again in the locker room before the kickoff and said in a very low and soft voice, 'Boys, I don't trust these Illinois sons-a-bitches, and they aren't above bugging this locker room, so I'm not going to talk very loud.'

"We could barely hear him as he went into his pregame speech. He said, 'I will write down our first play,' and he wrote '26' on the board (surprise…fullback off right tackle). The funny part, though, was that he really believed the locker room was bugged, and within five seconds he erased the play from the board and looked up at the vents and lights in the ceiling and said, 'I know this f*cking room is bugged.'

"We all sort of looked at each other and did not dare make any face or anything, because we were scared to death of him. He was still in his prime then and would just as soon punch you as look at you if he saw any silly faces or joking going on in a meeting. How many times we have laughed about that incident."

For the record, Ohio State lost 10–9 that day even though Gary Cairns made a then-school-record 55-yard field goal.

Practice, Practice, Practice

One of the secrets to his success on the field was the fact that he had his teams practice the things he believed in over and over and over again. It was the repetition—and I mean, repetition—of not only the fundamentals of the game but also of his basic plays that made his practices so effective.

"I am sitting in one of our meetings one time, and he looks at me and asks, 'Leo, I'll give you five bucks if you get this right: what did Paderewski say about practice?'" Leo Hayden recalled. "Paderewski was the famous pianist, and I had heard Woody say this many times before, so I answered: 'If I miss one practice, I know. If I miss two practices, the critics know. If I miss three practices, the whole world knows.'

"'Doggone right, Leo!' Woody shouted.

"That gives you an example of not only what he believed in," Hayden said recently, "but about how well-read he was. He knew the greatest people in every profession, and he used little stories and sayings like that to educate and motivate you. And all these years later, I can still remember them.

"Of course, I never had the courage to ask for my five bucks."

The stories of Woody's unquenchable thirst to practice are unheard of as they relate to today's game. For example, following the 7–0 win over Michigan in the final game of the 1960 season, he told an assistant to have Paul Warfield and Matt Snell meet him on the field. Both were freshmen and thus ineligible for the '60 season, but they had watched the Michigan game from the stands at Ohio Stadium.

An hour following the game, Hayes, unhappy with scoring only seven points that day, was thinking ahead to the 1961 season. He put the two future stars through an hour workout of practicing handoffs and passing, and it was all within NCAA rules that stated the final day of participation or practice coincides with the day of the final game of the season.

From what he learned in that one hour, he determined what part of the offense to plan for heading into spring practice four months later.

Quoting Woody

- "Eliminate the mistakes in football and you'll never lose a game."
- "No back in the history of football was ever worth two fumbles a game."
- "I try to get six or seven hours of sleep each night, and I try not to miss a meal. The rest of my time goes to football."
- "I love football. I think it's the most wonderful game in the world, and I despise to lose. I've hated to lose ever since I was a kid and threw away the mallets when I lost at croquet."

- "To me, there's nothing worse than being laughed at. I would rather be spit on than laughed at."
- "Every day as a football team, you are either getting better or you are getting worse. Every day as a person, you are either getting better or you are getting worse. Which do you want to be?"
- "The will to win is not as important as the will to prepare to win."

They Said It about Woody

Punter/kicker Tom Skladany (1973–1976) summed up his ever-changing feelings for Woody this way: "You were afraid of him as a freshman. You hated him as a sophomore. You liked him as a junior, and you loved him as a senior. He took you on an emotional roller-coaster."

Tressel, whose late father, Lee, was the longtime head coach at Baldwin-Wallace in Berea, Ohio: "My dad loved Woody Hayes. He did many things while coaching at Baldwin-Wallace that Woody did at Ohio State. If Woody watered down the AstroTurf, so did my dad. If Woody ran a certain play this way, so did my dad."

Who'll Stop the Rain?

One of Woody's favorite lines was, "If you have to fight in the North Atlantic, you train in the North Atlantic."

In other words, you need to practice in all kinds of weather because you may have to play a game in that same weather someday. Still, when the Buckeyes had a lot of work to do and it happened to be raining, he often asked for divine intervention.

"This is a true story, and I wouldn't have believed it unless I saw it with my own eyes," Lenny Davis said. "The buses pull up to the facility the week of the Michigan game in 1977, and it is pouring down rain. Nobody liked to practice in the rain, but we were going to practice whether it was raining or not.

"Woody walked out on that field wearing his scarlet wind-breaker, his glasses, and his black hat. He stood there and just raised his arms up to the sky, as if to ask God to stop the rain for a few hours. Immediately, it stopped raining! We just all stood there not believing what we just saw. That was amazing."

And other times, it did not work.

"Coach Hayes had this relationship with God, and he would always go out there if it was raining and wave his hands and try to make it stop," Calvin Murray said. "Well, this one time we were at the stadium and it was raining. He walked out there and did his traditional wave of his hands like he always did—and lightning struck the stadium at that very moment."

"Okay, take it inside boys!" Woody ordered, heading for the locker room.

"I will never, ever forget that," Murray said, laughing.

The Final "Megaton"

In the end, as many of his friends and colleagues had feared, it would be Woody's temper that ended his career.

Near the end of the 1978 Gator Bowl, with Ohio State trailing 17–15, OSU faced a third down at the Clemson 24-yard line. Knowing the Buckeyes were already in field-goal range, the offensive coaches decided to ride Art Schlichter's hot hand with one final shot at the end zone. At that point, Schlichter had completed 16 of 19 passes for 205 yards without an interception.

"[Assistant coach] Alex Gibbs gave me the play, and I shuttled it into the huddle," said guard Ernie Andria (1975, 1977–1979). "I told Art: '37 Streak and no interception! Art, throw it away if it's not there.' The play was designed as a streak pattern for Doug Donley down the right sideline."

"I was right there [on the sideline] when they called it," said Tom Cousineau, a team captain that season. "We were in field position where we could kick a field goal. The instructions were very clear to Art: 'If the play is not there, throw it away or sit

The ABC television cameras caught Coach Hayes's eruption on the sideline after Clemson's Charlie Bauman (No. 58) intercepted an Art Schlichter pass to seal the 1978 Gator Bowl in Jacksonville, Florida.

down in the middle of the field and we can still kick it.' I can still remember that conversation like it was yesterday."

As one of the most infamous plays in college football history unfolded, Schlichter dropped back but didn't see Donley, who was open, so he double-pumped before throwing a short pass underneath toward running back Ron Springs, who had released out of the backfield. A Clemson nose guard nobody had ever heard of then, Charlie Bauman, had been well-blocked to the left of the line earlier in the play but recovered to cut in front of Springs and intercept the pass.

Bauman's name is well-known all these years later, not so much for making the interception, but for running out of bounds along the Ohio State sideline. It was there and then that he took a right cross to the neck from Woody.

And with that, a legend's coaching career was finished.

Did Diabetes Contribute to It?

There is a theory among those who were closest to him that other circumstances led to Woody's reaction to the interception by Bauman. Woody was a diabetic. It was a condition he hid from many of his assistant coaches and players.

"I coached for him and did not know he was a diabetic until just a few years before he died," Ed Ferkany said. "We were in a hotel, and he pulled out a needle and gave himself some insulin. I asked why he never mentioned it, and he said he didn't ever do it in front of his coaches or his players because they may have seen it as a sign of weakness, and he didn't want his players to think he was soft or taking drugs."

Those closest to him agree that while he rarely paid attention to his health, he was especially negligent during that final week of December 1978. He wasn't eating balanced meals or taking his medication as prescribed, some say. Combined with the fact he hated stupid mistakes, the instructions to Schlichter were clear, and that he especially hated to lose, it all boiled over when Bauman stood before him, holding the football as a prize just a few feet from him in front of the Ohio State bench.

It was as if all the elements had formulated into the perfect storm.

"I really think that contributed to it," Archie Griffin said recently. "I think his diabetes…he just didn't take care of himself. Even Bo said something about that before he died. I never heard Dr. [Bob] Murphy [Ohio State's team physician] mention it, but others have."

"The real story [about the Gator Bowl] is that he didn't take care of his diabetes, and the fact is that he nodded off in the locker room before the game," Jim Otis said. "His blood sugar was all screwed up, but he never told anybody that. He didn't want to make excuses."

"We noticed," Andria said. "He was not making sense before that game. He was rambling and saying things we had never heard before."

Was He Fired, or Did He Resign?

To this day, you will read different accounts about the aftermath of that fateful night in Jacksonville, Florida.

When President Harold Enarson told athletics director Hugh Hindman to ask Woody to resign, he refused. Enarson then delivered the ultimatum that he would be fired if he did not resign.

"When we were in the dressing room after the game, everybody was saying good-bye to each other because we all knew it was the end," said Joel Laser, a senior on that team. "I watched as Hugh Hindman and [assistant athletics director] Jim Jones went with Woody into this separate dressing room for about 15 or 20 minutes.

"When they came out and left, they left the door open to this room, and that is when I saw the saddest sight I ever remember. I could see through that opening, and Woody was sitting in this chair, slumped over, just staring at the ground. I am sure that the reality of what he had done had just now hit him."

The next morning, Ohio State officials issued a statement that the coach had been fired. About the same time, Woody called friend and sportswriter Paul Hornung and told him he had resigned, thus leading to the lead story in the next day's *Columbus Dispatch* that the end officially was a resignation.

When the team's flight landed in Columbus, Hayes grabbed the intercom microphone and informed his players he "would no longer be their coach."

Whatever the terminology, Earle Bruce maintains to this day everything was done much too quickly by Ohio State officials.

"Enarson wanted to get rid of him, and he was just looking for a reason," Bruce said recently. "Ohio State had lost to Michigan three straight times, and those people were not happy with Woody. Hugo [Hindman] wasn't much help in stepping up for him, and he had coached for Woody. They were friends. He should have stood up for him.

"Woody loved Ohio State and devoted 28 years of his life to the school. They should have handled that a lot better. For crying out loud, they were paying him only $42,000 that final season. I will tell you this: if he had beaten Michigan those final three years, they wouldn't have fired him if he had *killed* that kid. But what they should have done is wait a little while and then bumped him upstairs as Football Coach Emeritus and kept him in the athletic department.

"But nothing needed to be done that night—or the next day."

He Often Apologized

Although he never did apologize after his career-ending punch, Woody did talk to Bauman years later about that night. And he often said, "I am sorry," in his own way over the years. No matter how small the blowup, if he ever realized later that he was wrong, he did something to make up for it.

One time, he blew up at Ohio State's groundskeeper for failing to cover the practice field before a downpour.

"He just went ballistic that day," Erwin Thal said. "Not only did Woody apologize, but he went out and bought the man a new suit coat and delivered it to him the next day."

Woody and Rex

Perhaps no player was ever closer to Woody Hayes than Rex Kern (1968–1970), the quarterback of his last national championship team. He was one of Woody's all-time favorites, if not his favorite, as the following story illustrates.

"That fall of my sophomore year, I was going to class from 8:00 AM until practice started, and I always had to take a sack lunch with me to eat on the run," Kern remembered. "One day of that Michigan week, I didn't have time to eat. We came into the meetings, and George Chaump, the quarterbacks coach, said, 'Rex, you don't look well. Are you okay?'

"I told him I had missed lunch. So we went out to practice, and I saw this manager carrying a McDonald's bag across the field. He walked up to George and gave it to him. George walked up to

Woody, and they talked before Woody called me over. He ordered, 'Rex, take this bag and go over there behind those tarps and eat this and then get back in there.'"

Then tackle Rufus Mayes told Kern, "Woody would let you eat McDonald's, but if it were anybody else, especially a lineman, he would have us eating grass if we were hungry."

There were times early in his career when Kern would change the play in the huddle before he ever got to the line of scrimmage. I mean, who would dare do that to a play that Woody Hayes had sent in? And he did it as a sophomore, as this story from the 31–24 win over Illinois illustrates.

"We scored the first two times down the field, and we are up 14–0," Kern recalled. "So we get down there to the 1- or the 2-yard line again, and Ray Gillian, our right halfback whom we called 'Cheese,' comes in with the play. It is 'Robust 26'—Otis again off right tackle. Otis got so many touchdowns, it was time for somebody else to score, so I said, 'Wait a minute. Cheese, do you want to score a touchdown? Do you want to score?'

"Finally, he said, 'Well, yeah.'"

"Okay," Kern said, "here's what we are going to do."

And he drew up a quick dive play for Gillian to take the handoff. He did, and he scored, making it 21–0.

"I knew I would be in trouble, so I ran off the field a long way from where Woody was standing on the 50-yard line," Kern added. "[Assistant] Rudy Hubbard met me and said, 'Rex, what play was that?'

"'Oh, I just made it up,' I told him.

"'Well,' Hubbard said, 'the old man wants to see you.'

"So, I slowly walked down there and stood beside Woody. He didn't say anything at first. A few moments went by, and he gradually turned his head and asked me, 'That wasn't the play we called, was it?' I didn't say anything. Then he said, 'You are awfully lucky it worked.'"

"We always teased Rex about Woody being his father," said offensive tackle Dave Cheney. "Rex was my roommate the first two years, and honest to God, Woody was up in the dorm room with him at least two or three times each week. He would be quizzing

A Buckeyes fan leaves a penny on Coach Hayes's tombstone for good luck prior to the 2006 Michigan game.

him on the offense and on all of the audible stuff: 'If it is third-and-four and they are in this defense, what are you going to do?' We realized he was just coaching him, but the truth is that Woody really liked Rex. There is no question he was his favorite."

Kern learned one very important lesson during his freshman season—if you go anywhere with the coach, do the driving. Woody invited him tag along to Avon Lake one winter night on a recruiting trip to see Dick Wakefield play a high school basketball game. The coach was behind the wheel.

"It is snowing like crazy, and the old man is talking about recruiting, off-tackle plays, and all kinds of things and not paying attention to the road," Kern said. "We can't see 10 feet in front of us, and he is going 60 or 65 miles per hour. Well, we start to hydroplane, and we do a complete 360 on this small country road.

We ended up in the same direction we were heading, and he just keeps driving. I didn't say a word. He didn't say a word."

Five minutes later, Woody looked at Rex and said, "You don't tell anybody that just happened, especially my wife, Anne!"

"We get to the game, and I am one step behind him," Kern continued. "Well, the people mobbed him as usual, and somebody said, 'Coach, I didn't think you would make it tonight.'

"I opened my mouth and said, 'I didn't think we would make it either!' All of a sudden, Woody grabbed my arm and squeezed. I took that as I had better be quiet on the issue. We got back to Columbus and I was telling [assistant coach] Tiger Ellison about it, and he said, 'Rex, one thing you've got to learn. If you go with Woody, you have to be the driver! Nobody lets Woody drive them!'"

Over the next four years and beyond, Woody and Rex came as close to having a father-son relationship that any coach and player could possibly have.

"The last time I was in Columbus prior to his death, we went to the Faculty Club for lunch," Kern recalled. "We always fought over who would pay. He would never let me pay. After we left, he said, 'Rex, you haven't driven down Woody Hayes Drive yet, have you? By God, we've got to go down there!'

"We did, and he loved it. I took him home, and I had made up my mind that I was going to tell him what he meant to me. Before we went in, I just said, 'Coach, I want you to know that I love you,' and I kissed him on the cheek. I think it shocked the old man. That was the last time I saw him alive."

March 12, 1987

Woody once joked that when he died, he wanted it to be on the 50-yard line at Ohio Stadium.

He didn't get his wish, of course. Ironically, for a man who was born on Valentine's Day and had given his heart to so many causes and to so many people, it was his heart that failed him in the end. He died in his sleep of a heart attack at his Upper Arlington home early in the morning.

A day earlier, Cousineau visited the coach at his office in the ROTC building on Neil Avenue.

"I had been carrying this large picture of him around in my trunk, and I wanted him to sign it," Cousineau said. "He was going somewhere on campus to make a speech, and he asked me to go with him. We came back, he signed this photo, and I finally got to express my feelings to him. I told him how much I cared about him, respected him, and how much he and Ohio State meant to me.

"The next day my wife called me and asked, 'What did you say to Woody Hayes yesterday?'

"I said, 'Why?'

"'Well, he died today,' she told me.

"I couldn't believe it. I was crushed. I believe I was the last player to ever see Woody Hayes alive."

Former players across the country were stunned and saddened that day. Many of them broke down and cried.

"I was in Fort Lauderdale with the Yankees, and my family called Barb, and then she told me," Hopalong Cassady said. "I won't forget the sadness of it—it was one of the saddest days of my life. He was a Buckeye's Buckeye. A real man. A great man. He lived and died the way he was, and he never changed in between."

A few days earlier, Archie Griffin had made plans with Woody to have lunch.

"I wanted him to meet my wife, Bonita," he said. "But we never got to do that. I was driving to work on March 12, 1987, when I heard that he had died. I just turned around, went back to my house, and sat down for a while. Then I went to the bathroom and cried.

"There isn't a day that goes by—and I mean not *one* day—that I don't think of Woody Hayes or my father. He was very, very good to me. He was a special person."

"There is no way to really explain what that man meant to me," Ike Kelley said, "but I know I cried like a baby on the day he died."

Former president Richard Nixon delivered the eulogy. The two first met in 1957, the year Woody won his second national championship and Nixon was vice president.

"I wanted to talk about football, and Woody wanted to talk about foreign policy. And you know Woody. We talked about foreign policy," he told the mourners that day. "For 30 years, I was privileged to know the real Woody Hayes, the man behind the media myth. Instead of a know-nothing Neanderthal, I found a Renaissance man with a consuming interest in history and a profound understanding of the forces that move the world. Instead of a cold, ruthless tyrant on the football field, I found a warm-hearted softie—very appropriately born on Valentine's Day—who always spoke of his affection for his boys and his family."

To this day, Kern admitted that the day of his coach's death will always be the saddest day of his life.

"Even now," he said, "it brings great sorrow to me."

Woody Would Have Loved This One

Once there was a man who went to heaven, where he was met by Saint Peter and taken to a gigantic football stadium to watch a game. Down on the sideline was a stocky man with silver hair, wearing a black baseball cap adorned with a scarlet Block O above the bill. He was running back and forth, jumping up and down, and gesturing to the officials and his players.

"Who is that madman?" the man asked Saint Peter.

"That's God," Saint Peter answered, "but He thinks He is Woody Hayes."

chapter 7

Earle Bruce:
Following the Legend

Earle Bruce, like his predecessor, was fiery and intense most of the time—but he also knew when to keep things on the lighter side.

Returning to the university he loved, Earle Bruce's head-coaching career at Ohio State began with a bang, as the Buckeyes came within minutes of winning a national championship in his first season. It ended eight years later with a rousing upset of Michigan.

Earle Bruce's road back to Ohio State—where he once had dreamed of being a player and where he was an assistant coach under Woody Hayes from 1966 to 1971—began in a hotel room in Miami on December 29, 1978, during a recruiting trip while he was head coach at Iowa State.

He had planned to drive from Miami to Jacksonville for the Buckeyes' Gator Bowl game that night.

"I told [OSU assistant] George Chaump I was coming up, but then I discovered it wasn't a three-hour drive as somebody had told me," Bruce recalled. "It was more like five hours, and I wouldn't have been there for the kickoff.

"So I stayed in Miami and watched it on television."

Midway through the fourth quarter, Bruce went downstairs to arrange for Orange Bowl tickets for a friend. When he returned to his room, the ABC TV crew calling the game was saying things he could not comprehend.

"I had no idea what they were talking about," he said. "The only one not talking was Ara Parseghian. The other guys were saying, 'He's lost it, he's got to go.' I was thinking, 'Who has lost it? Who has to go?'"

Bruce soon discovered what all the hubbub was about: Woody Hayes had punched a Clemson player.

"Oh my God!" Bruce said to himself. "Oh my God!"

The next day, Bruce flew from Miami to Chicago and caught a connecting flight to Ames, Iowa. He thought about the end of Woody's career...and contemplated a possible change of direction in his own.

Meanwhile, back in Columbus, Buckeyes fans and players were still in shock at what they had witnessed the night before. The media focused on Arkansas' Lou Holtz, also once an assistant on the Buckeyes' 1968 national championship team, as Hayes's possible replacement.

"The job comes open and there was a list of candidates: George Hill and George Chaump from Woody's staff, Lou Holtz and Don James at Washington," Bruce explained recently. "Now, when the media listed Lou Holtz as the favorite, I laughed my ass off, and I will tell you why: Lou Holtz was making $350,000 a year at Arkansas. Woody was making $42,000. Do you think he would go to Ohio State and take that kind of pay cut? So when Lou announced at the Hula Bowl that he didn't want to follow Woody Hayes, but he wanted to follow the guy that followed Woody Hayes, I knew that would be *me*. I would be that guy."

Sure enough, Bruce met with Ohio State officials in San Francisco during the coaches' national convention and asked if they would match the $36,000 he received from his Iowa State television show (bringing his total compensation to at least $78,000 annually). They agreed, and he was offered the job.

He walked into the lobby downstairs at the hotel, talked to the Ohio media a little, but kept the huge secret to himself...until he was named the Buckeyes' new coach two days later.

"I don't think the Ohio State people realized they were 20 years behind the times when it came to coaches' salaries," Bruce said. "Woody never asked for raises, and they never offered them to him.

"After I was hired, Woody called me and said, 'Congratulations. I am glad you got the job.' I don't think I ever was one of his favorites, because I never really played for him, but we always had a good relationship. I knew Woody wouldn't be a problem. He wouldn't overshadow me or do anything like that. In fact, that first year he stayed away entirely."

The Miracle at UCLA

The pollsters and media, however, were skeptical of Bruce's first team until it traveled to the Los Angeles Coliseum to take on 17th-ranked UCLA in the fourth game of the season. After all, with Hayes gone, the Buckeyes entered the season unranked for the first time since the 1967 season. Plus, they had squeaked by Minnesota by four points in the second game.

Even before kickoff, it would be a wonder if Ohio State could survive that game, let alone win it. Starting left tackle Tim Burke was on the sideline with a separated shoulder before two more offensive tackles were injured in *pregame warm-ups*.

"I can't play at that point due to the limited range of motion and pain in my shoulder," Burke recalled. "Then, in warm-ups, Bill Jaco, a fifth-year senior like me, and Joe Lukens, a freshman, get injured. Lukens pulled a muscle in his neck and can't keep his head up, which for an offensive tackle is a death sentence; Jaco turned his ankle badly.

"Earle was going crazy, telling line coach Bill Myles to 'put the whole damn offensive line on the bench, or we won't have anybody left to play the game.' Late in the second quarter, both Lukens and Jaco were struggling badly, and I knew that at least one of them, if not both, would not make it through the rest of the game. Coach Myles told me, 'Burke, you are going to have to go in for one of them.' At that point, I couldn't even take the pressure of someone bumping my shoulder, let alone think about playing.

"I went in for two or three series before halftime, but I was in ridiculous pain, and a young defensive tackle named Irv Eatman was kicking my ass. As we were running off the field at halftime, I was contemplating how I was going to play the second half in such pain. A trainer told me, 'After Earle is done with his halftime speech, come find me.'

"The team doctor told me I couldn't injure myself any more than I already had, so they said they would give me a shot to block the pain. They did, and in about 10 minutes, I felt no pain. I went to find Jaco and Lukens. I looked at both of them and realized Lukens couldn't be mended up to play, but Jaco possibly could. I pulled him aside and told him, 'Jaco, we are fifth-year seniors. This is it! We have to go in the second half!'

"Jaco looked at me with the same painful look I had on my face 15 minutes ago. 'Watch this, Jake,' I said, proceeding to beat the wall with my injured shoulder. Jaco was in shock. He knew I was in crazy pain 15 minutes earlier, and he was wondering how I would finish the game. He grabbed me and asked, 'How is this possible?'

"I told him—and he jumped up on one leg and hopped to the trainer and doctor. We came out onto the field, and I knew the UCLA coaching staff was just positive we were done for the day, since three of the four tackles we brought were injured. Those defensive tackles were planning on having a field day in the second half. When we took the field, Jaco and I peeled off from the team and made a run by the UCLA bench. Jaco was high-stepping, running backward, and I was doing windmills with both arms as we ran by them. I wish I had a camera, so I could have captured the look on UCLA's faces."

In the final minutes of the game, Art Schlichter drove the Buckeyes deep into UCLA territory, where he rolled out and passed to Paul Campbell for the winning touchdown. The 17–13 victory gave the Buckeyes a 4–0 record, which bumped them into the top 10.

After they rallied to beat Michigan 18–15 seven weeks later when Jim Laughlin blocked a punt and Todd Bell scooped it up to score the winning touchdown, Ohio State was 11–0, ranked number one, and headed to the Rose Bowl.

Bruce did a marvelous job soothing the wounds left from Woody's surreal departure. There was nothing like a win over Michigan and a Big Ten championship—the Buckeyes' first in four years—to expedite the healing process for a program that had resided under the darkest cloud in college football only one year earlier.

"We had a hell of a year," Bruce said. "We beat Michigan up there, and to that point, Ohio State had not scored a touchdown on them in four years, but nobody talks about that game now."

USC's Final Drive

The 1979 team would be mentioned often and would be celebrated as a national champion if the season had ended three minutes earlier.

The top-ranked Buckeyes took a 16–10 lead over USC into the final three minutes of the Rose Bowl, but the Trojans, behind Heisman Trophy–winning tailback Charles White, marched 83 yards to win the game.

If the defense had held on and stopped USC one final time, it would have given Ohio State its first national championship in 11 years and made Bruce an instant hero in Columbus.

"We played well, and we played a hell of a football team that day," Bruce said. "We just couldn't stop the isolation [running play with fullback leading White through the hole]. They ran that isolation at us over and over, and we couldn't stop it. If you can't stop the isolation, you deserve to lose—and we had had a good defense that year until that point."

The Trojans' final drive continues to haunt many Buckeyes defensive players and Bruce. Ohio State's defense was banged up by the time the Trojans took possession at their own 17-yard line. But by the end, USC's massive offensive line led by Anthony Munoz wore down OSU's smaller defensive front.

"I remember that I couldn't even see Charles White in the backfield behind those linemen because he was shorter than everybody else," said linebacker Marcus Marek (1979–1982). "All these years later, I may think, 'If I could have made one more play, or stopped the ball…' What I remember is how close we were."

Bruce, like several of the players from that team, believe the '79 team never received the credit it deserves.

"That's what bothers me today," said Cal Murray, a running back from 1977 to 1980. "That '79 team is a forgotten team. Nobody remembers that team. We had a great year and were Big Ten champions, and anniversaries come and go and nobody has any functions for us or mentions it. It just seems if you don't win a national championship, you are forgotten."

Heartbreaking Loss, Dark Shower

After the gut-wrenching loss, Ohio State was hit with another indignity—the locker room at the Rose Bowl had lost power.

"The doctors had those little flashlights [with] which they check players' eyes for concussions," said Chris Wherry, a team manager. "So everybody had to take showers with those little lights as the only light to see anything.

"Then I remember flying home, and we are headed back over the Rose Bowl. Coach Bruce told everybody, 'Guys look down at the stadium. We are coming back here some day, and we are going to win that thing.'"

Sadly, Bruce never chalked up a Rose Bowl victory, as the Buckeyes lost to USC again in the 1985 game by a score of 20–17 in his team's only other appearance.

A Player's Coach

Bruce was tough, demanding, and yet, still a players' coach. In short, just as they did for Hayes, his players loved him and always wanted to win for him.

"I remember during one practice in my sophomore year, he had seen all the other linemen and he was commenting how slow they were," recalled Bernie Brown.

"I can still beat you guys," Bruce said.

"Next thing you know, Earle is down in a three-point stance at the starting line and off he goes," Brown said. "He was about 20 yards downfield, running as fast as those short legs could carry him, when suddenly he pulled up, holding his hamstring. He barely made it across the finish line. Needless to say, we were all in tears laughing.

"The remainder of the day, he limped around from station to station, and we were all in the background smiling."

Bruce took many of Woody's philosophies and applied them. He often said, "You are either getting better or you are getting worse," as Woody did, and he even showered with players following practices, as Woody frequently did.

"I think Coach Bruce learned from Coach Hayes that it was important to spend time with the underclassmen who had their own dressing room," said quarterback Mike Tomczak (1981–1984).

"Well, one day, or should I say many days, players would talk with Coach in the shower just enough to distract him while a teammate would adjust the temperature of the shower. Most of the time, it would be on the colder side, just to frighten him some and to generate some laughter. The best time to surprise him was when he had soap in his hair or eyes and he couldn't find the handle to adjust the temperature back. Let me put it this way: he took many cold showers throughout his time at Ohio State."

A Man of Honesty and Integrity

Here's how linebacker Glen Cobb (1979–1982), a two-time captain, described Bruce: "I have to say that Coach Bruce was a man of integrity. Yes, he wanted to win with the best of them. However, he parted ways with coaches at some other institutions: he wanted to win the right way, without cheating. He spoke of integrity and its importance often. He spoke often about how a man is known by his friends, so be careful with whom you associate. He spoke about life after football and the need to grasp the bigger picture. I have the greatest respect for the man."

Brian Benio was a highly recruited linebacker from Atlanta in 1984. Living in the midst of SEC country, he admitted coaches in the South didn't always adhere to NCAA rules when it came to recruiting. There were offers of cars, women, and other enticements that were not exactly NCAA-approved.

"But when it came to Earle Bruce and Ohio State, all of their dealings with me were full of integrity and honesty," he said. "Earle and [assistant] Bill Conley impressed me with their enthusiasm for Ohio State. They cared about you as a person, and I could tell that. I had recently visited Georgia, and they were bragging about their 42 or 43 All-Americans. When I got to Ohio State, I realized there had been over 100.

"Chris Spielman was my host on my official visit, and he looked at me and asked one thing, 'All I want to know is are you serious about coming here?'

"Before I could get an answer out of my mouth, he added, 'Because if you are not, I am leaving now and I am not going to invest my time on you. We are serious about what we do here, and if you are serious, too, then come to Ohio State.'"

Later, as signing day neared, Benio had narrowed his decision to Ohio State and Miami, which had just won its first national championship a year earlier.

"When I was still undecided in the final week or so, Coach Conley was cool and calm, and he did not pressure me," Benio remembers. "Finally, I committed to Coach Bruce over the phone, and, as soon as I hung up, [Miami coach] Jimmy Johnson called. I told him I made a commitment to Ohio State, and he just went off on me: 'What the f*ck are you thinking? Do you know it snows in Columbus?' He continued to rant and rave and call me every name in the book. I handed the phone to my mom.

"That's why I became a Buckeye."

As a Motivator

One of Bruce's strengths was that of a motivator. After all, he had learned how to turn a player's switch from "off" to "on" from the master, Hayes.

During his first few weeks on the job in that winter of 1979, he called every player into his office one at a time.

Center Jim DeLeone, 5'10", 210 pounds, admitted recently that he "wasn't the best student, and I was a little wild." But what Bruce told him scared him straight and motivated him to clean up his act.

"It was me, Coach Bruce, and [assistant] Glen Mason," DeLeone recalled. "Coach Bruce looked at me and said, 'Son, you got a scholarship from Coach Hayes, so get your education.'"

"What do you mean?" DeLeone asked. "Will I get a chance to play?"

"Son, you are not the type of athlete we are looking for," Bruce told DeLeone. "You are not big enough, and you are a step slow."

"Then I got pissed," DeLeone said. "I knew I wasn't big. I mean, Art Schlichter was bigger than me, and he was the quarterback, but I was the strongest guy on the team. I told him, 'I will make you eat your words.' That spring, they tried to run me off."

DeLeone worked his way up from the bottom of the depth chart to second-string behind center Tom Waugh in 1979, became a much better student, and then started at center in 1980 and '81.

One day following his senior season, DeLeone told Bruce, "I told you I would do it."

"He didn't say anything back to me," DeLeone said. "He just smiled."

Most of the time, Bruce wasn't an easygoing, complimentary coach, either. He was fiery. He was intense. And he threw compliments around the practice field like manhole covers. If a player wasn't practicing well, he would stick the needle in.

"I remember one day I was having a difficult time at practice throwing the ball during a passing drill, and I heard Coach Bruce yell out 'Noel!' which happened to be one of his daughters' names," Mike Tomczak said. "Then he went into this story about how she could throw better, and make decisions better, and run the offense better than I could.

"I guess we all need a little encouragement, but the coach's daughter? Please. It got to the point where he replaced me on the practice field with another quarterback, and I didn't take a liking to his decision. So I challenged him for the first time and told him that he couldn't replace me, that I was a competitor and there was no one better to run this offense than me."

Tomczak said the two continued their conversation over breakfast the next morning at the Holiday Inn, where they would continue to meet for three years. It was the same ritual Hayes had practiced with his starting quarterbacks for most of his 28 years.

"We had many, and I mean many, breakfasts together throughout my career," Tomczak said. "He challenged me all the time, and I thanked him. However, he didn't have to insult me in front of my teammates. I guess he didn't have a choice due to the fact he didn't have any boys as children. I just wish he had had a son named Bart or Joe Willie."

No Dairy Products

Also like Hayes, Bruce believed in doing things a certain way—from the way the play-action fake was executed by a quarterback to what kind of shoes the Buckeyes wore to what kind of dessert the team should have at a pregame meal.

Earle Bruce is carried off the field on the shoulders of his players after Ohio State defeated Michigan 14–9 in Ann Arbor on November 21, 1981.

"It was before the Michigan game during my senior year [1983]," linebacker Clark Backus recalled. "We went out to the golf course for our dinner on Friday night, and it was cold, very cold. We were finishing our meal and then we had to go up to Ann Arbor that night.

"Those wonderful servers we had out there gave us ice cream. I could still hear Coach Bruce raising his voice: 'Don't you people know that having dairy products when it is cold out causes upper-respiratory problems? Doesn't anyone here realize that?'"

To this day, Backus said, he will not let his children have cereal and milk on cold mornings.

"Those were the little lessons you picked up around Coach Bruce," he said.

The Loudest Room on the Road

Nobody wanted to room with offensive lineman Ray Myers and fullback Vaughn Broadnax because the two had notorious snoring problems. It wasn't a problem for them, per se, but it was for anyone else who tried to sleep in the bed next to them.

"Apparently, there had been lots of complaints about my snoring the previous two years," Myers said.

Ditto for Broadnax, so the coaches came up with a solution— they put the two together for the 1982 season.

"This was not a problem because Vaughn and I were friends and got along very well," Myers said. "He snored so loud that I do not believe Coach Bruce ever opened our door for the bed check."

He didn't have to: the noise could be heard in the hallway of the team hotel.

The Sunshine Boys

Tackle William Roberts, linebacker Rowland Tatum, running back Cedric Anderson, and defensive back Doug Hill were out-of-state recruits in 1980. Roberts, Anderson, and Hill were from Florida, and Tatum was from California. Once they met and became friends and started hanging around each other, they were dubbed the "Sunshine Boys."

"Before every game, we got together and laid our plans and goals of what we were going to do," Tatum explained. "We had a lot in common and became close friends and still stay in touch to this day."

Tatum became known as the "Nicknamer," because he had a name for everybody.

"He called one guy who shall remain nameless, 'Misleading'— this player had huge biceps," Broadnax said. "But when he took his shirt off, it was quite apparent that sit-ups were not his priority."

Tatum and Hill made a pact during their sophomore year: no matter how tough it was, no matter the obstacles, they would each graduate from Ohio State.

"People had perceptions about us because we were football players," Tatum said, "but my mother had a Ph.D. and two of my brothers were schoolteachers. I wanted a degree, too. So did Doug. You know how some mornings you have trouble getting up? We would call each other and make sure the other one was getting up, going to class. We did that every day."

Hill and Tatum each received a bachelor's in education, one quarter apart.

"It is a testimony to what Ohio State brought to us," Tatum said. "I was from California, and when I was being recruited by UCLA, they put me up in the Beverly Hills Hilton and showed me around in a limo. When I visited Ohio State, I roomed with Tim Spencer and we went to the donut shop and he showed me the library. That was real. That was my style."

Pepper and Keith

Many teammates become lifelong friends, sometimes despite coming from various backgrounds.

But tailback Keith Byars and linebacker Thomas "Pepper" Johnson each found a brother when they met for the first time.

"During the OSU spring game prior to my freshman year [1982], the coaches told me I would be rooming with a guy named Thomas Johnson," Byars recalled. "When we met that day, we really didn't need an introduction. We just walked up and started talking to each other like we had known each other for all of our lives."

"He knew his roommate was named Thomas Johnson, but he thought that must be a white guy," Johnson said. "He walked up to me and said, 'Thomas?'

"I said, 'Yeah, just call me Pepper.'"

Byars added, "It was something like, 'What are you going to bring? You bring the TV. I'll bring the radio.' When coaches put roommates together, it is a crapshoot of whether it will work out, but in all these years, we've never had a cross word between us. It really was like meeting a brother I never knew I had.

"And that's how it went for Pepper Johnson and me. We bonded right away, and he's been my best friend since."

The pair became All-Americans together and ended up competing for years against each other in the same NFC East division of the NFL: Byars with the Philadelphia Eagles and Johnson with the New York Giants.

During one Eagles-Giants game, as Johnson chased Philadelphia quarterback Randall Cunningham, Byars blindsided his best friend with a vicious block that was replayed over and over in the ensuing days. To this day, it still is shown often on the NFL's greatest-hits show.

"Keith got me back," said Johnson.

Tomczak-to-Jemison Wins Fiesta

One of Bruce's biggest wins—of the non-Michigan variety, that is—came in the 1984 Fiesta Bowl.

The Buckeyes had dominated the game against Pittsburgh but had fallen behind 23–21 late in the game. As the clock ticked under a minute, they crossed midfield on Mike Tomczak's sharp passing. Then, from the Pitt 39-yard line, Tomczak saw Thad Jemison streaking wide open down the left sideline. His perfectly thrown pass put the Buckeyes ahead 28–23 with only 39 seconds remaining.

"The pass was supposed to go to Cedric [Anderson]," Jemison recalled recently. "But he was covered, and the cornerback went toward Keith [Byars]. There was nobody on me."

Jemison's next move was of the bonehead variety: he threw the ball into the crowd, earning a 15-yard penalty, which gave the Panthers hope after the kickoff. What Pittsburgh didn't have, however, was enough time to come back.

At the time, a guy by the name of Jim Tressel was the Buckeyes' receivers coach.

"Coach Tressel tells me every time he sees me, 'You almost got me fired!'" Jemison said, laughing. "Coach Tressel always talks about that. And Earle wasn't too happy with me, either. He really got on me."

Elevator Problems in Pasadena

One day following practice during the week of the 1985 Rose Bowl, Bruce gave his team final instructions for the night: "Don't be late for the Big Ten banquet tonight. Wear a suit and tie, and be on time. If you are not on time, don't bother to show up!"

The banquet was one of the annual highlights of the Rose Bowl trip, since several celebrities, actors, and actresses would be seated among the players.

On the way to their rooms following practice, several linemen bunched into the elevator at the team hotel, anxious to get to their rooms and get showered and dressed for the banquet.

"I think the elevator went up about four feet and just stopped," said linebacker Bill Harvey (1981–1984). "I weighed about 230, and I was the lightest guy in there. We might have had 4,000 pounds in that elevator. As we stood there shoulder to shoulder, stuck in that thing for about an hour, we were all worried about Earle. We knew we would be doing a lot of running the next day."

Finally, mechanics released the elevator as the players scrambled to their rooms. They arrived an hour late and spent the night avoiding their head coach.

"I know he wasn't too happy with us," Harvey said.

Beating Curfew and Texas A&M in Dallas

Linebacker Derek Isaman loves the memory of he and a few teammates racing back to the hotel to beat an 11:00 PM curfew before the 1987 Cotton Bowl against Texas A&M.

"A few of us probably had a few too many beers, and it got to be 10:30," he said. "We had Jeff Uhlenhake's dad's car, and we made a wrong turn and got lost trying to find our hotel. We exited the ramp at about 50 miles per hour, lost control of the car, and jumped the curb. We broke the front axle and had about 15 minutes until our curfew. The clock was ticking, but we persevered and continued driving on a wobbly wheel at 15 miles per hour and made it with just a few minutes to spare."

A few days later, the Buckeyes upset eighth-ranked Texas A&M 28–12 behind two interceptions returned for touchdowns—one by Chris Spielman and one by Michael Kee.

"The best overall game I had been a part of at Ohio State was the Cotton Bowl against Texas A&M," Spielman said. "They had three or four number one draft picks on that team, and everybody in Texas thought they were going to blow us out. I remember sitting in the press conference before the game and asking, 'What are we? I mean, hey, we're Ohio State.'"

Earle Arizona-Bound?

A few weeks following the Cotton Bowl victory, concluding the 1986 season with a 10–3 record after an 0–2 start, Bruce considered leaving the school he loved when officials from the University of Arizona called. They offered to pay him almost five times as much money as he was making at Ohio State to become the Wildcats' head coach.

He considered the offer for a few days and was about to accept it, feeling somewhat underappreciated at Ohio State.

Then he met with his staff, and a few convinced him that the '87 Buckeyes would have a shot at a national championship, what with Chris Spielman, receiver Cris Carter, and several other key seniors returning.

In the end, his loyalty to his alma mater won out over money, but 11 months after making the toughest decision of his life, he was out of a job.

1987 Turns into Nightmare

Bruce's final season, which once had so much promise, was doomed before summer camp had concluded. In August, Carter, who had led Ohio State with 69 receptions for 1,127 yards for what was a school record just a year earlier, was ruled ineligible by the NCAA after having accepted money from an agent.

"When [OSU athletics director] Rick Bay said, 'Cris Carter will never wear an Ohio State uniform again,' I had only one option, and that was to apply for the NFL draft," Carter said in 2003. "I didn't want to leave. I wanted to file that appeal, but Ohio State did not want to do that. I was upset at myself. Given what I knew about athletics, I didn't have to do what I did to get into that predicament.

"I admit that initially I was a little bitter, and, of course, my teammates were mad at me. The most vocal one of all was Chris Spielman. He is a no-nonsense kind of guy who does the right thing. He had a few choice words for me, and I understood that. I really did. I respected him so much."

The Buckeyes weren't consistent offensively that season, which included a 13–13 tie at LSU in the third game and a shocking 31–10 loss to Indiana in the fifth. Then came the three consecutive losses that sealed Bruce's fate.

Carter blamed himself.

"We didn't have the offensive leader that [quarterback] Tom Tupa needed," he said. "I faced the question that if that wouldn't have happened to me, we wouldn't have had a bad year and Earle wouldn't have been fired. I have to live with that."

Ironically, it was similar to the guilt that Schlichter felt nine years earlier when his intercepted pass in the Gator Bowl led to the infamous conclusion of Hayes's brilliant career.

His Legacy

Bruce's Buckeyes teams compiled a 81–26–1 record in his nine seasons, and if not for USC's game-winning drive in the 1980 Rose Bowl in his first season, it could be argued that Bruce's tenure and legacy at Ohio State would have been much different.

Reluctantly, he admits to agreeing with such a theory.

"I don't know," he said recently. "It probably would have been [different], but why beat dead horses? There is no sense in that. We didn't win the game in that Rose Bowl. I wish we had, but we didn't."

Bruce's teams never won a Rose Bowl, but he did have a 5–4 record against Michigan.

And like most of his predecessors during the Graveyard of Coaches days, Bruce, too, was fired.

The end came following those three consecutive close losses —by six points to Michigan State, two points to Wisconsin, and two points to Iowa. Two of those three were at Ohio Stadium, and president Edward Jennings decided to fire Bruce just hours after the November 14 loss to Iowa, in which the Hawkeyes completed a long desperation pass to win the game.

"We had the game won, but they hit Marv Cook on a pass," Spielman said. "In the end, I feel responsible for what happened to Coach Bruce. Losing to Iowa in our last home game was the toughest loss."

It was one week before the Michigan game.

"I don't think President Ed Jennings ever understood what that man did for the university," said Kirk Lowdermilk, an offensive lineman (1981–1984). "I really believe he deserved better."

Twenty years later, Bruce has trouble hiding his bitterness, but he distinguishes that from his feelings for his alma mater.

"I can honestly say that no one could have had the four years I had at that school," he said. "I love Ohio State. Do you hear me? *I love Ohio State.* I think of all the people and friends I made at Ohio State as a student, as an assistant coach, and as a head coach, let me tell you that I love Ohio State to this day.

"Now, that said, I don't like what the president did to me back then, and without him, I don't think it would have been done. So yeah, I dislike the president for what he did, but I don't let that overcome me today. That is not what I am all about."

The Final Game

Perhaps no Ohio State team was more motivated to beat Michigan than the 1987 squad, fired up to send Coach Bruce out with a ride on their collective shoulders.

To Bruce's credit, he and his assistants coached during the week as if nothing had changed.

"It was unprecedented for a coach to get fired before the Michigan game, and it was disturbing to me, to say the least," Spielman said. "But I was in awe of the way Coach Bruce handled himself throughout that last week. He put his feelings of rejection aside and got us ready to play."

As a tribute to their coach, Joe Staysniak had purchased headbands for the entire team, and the players wrote "Earle" across the front of each. They kept the secret until just before kickoff and then, in unison, wrapped them around their heads.

"We thought it was a great idea to honor a wonderful coach and a good man," linebacker Derek Isaman said.

Seeing those headbands was a sight that Bruce will never forget.

"We had the toss of the coin before the kickoff, and I look back there where the team is all lined up with their helmets off and something is on their heads," Bruce said. "I am thinking, 'What the hell are they doing? They know damn well I don't allow that stuff.' So I walk back to get closer and I see it says 'Earle.' Well, I can't say anything about that. I feel good about that all this time later, but we never talked about it much."

Following the 23–20 upset of the Wolverines, Bruce's fifth win over Michigan in nine attempts, the headband-wearing Buckeyes carried their fired coach, wearing a dark suit, a tie, and a fedora atop his head, across the field in celebration.

"I always thought to myself, 'You know, I never got one of those headbands. I wish I had one,'" Bruce said. "Well, before I went into the [College Football] Hall of Fame [in 2002], one of those former players gave one to me."

And today, along with the fedora, the headband rests in the College Football Hall of Fame as a tribute to the Hall of Fame coach who followed Woody Hayes.

chapter 8

The Cooper Years

John Cooper keeps a close watch on his team as they practice in the Louisiana Superdome in New Orleans on December 30, 1998, preparing to face Texas A&M in the Sugar Bowl two days later.

He recruited great players and won some big games, including victories over Notre Dame in 1995 and '96. At least two of his teams, in '96 and '98, were talented enough to compete for a national championship, but John Cooper will forever be known in Ohio by the numbers 2–10–1.

It was December 30, 1987, when I was walking through a Phoenix resort and bumped into Florida State athletics director Cecil "Hootie" Ingram. Hootie had played at Alabama for Bear Bryant. He knew football, and he knew coaching, as well as the talent pool of coaching candidates in major-college football.

Earle Bruce had been fired the previous month, and rumors spread that Ohio State was about to name the current Arizona State head coach as Bruce's successor.

"Tell me all you know about this John Cooper guy," I asked him.

"Let me tell you, you got the best coach out there, in my opinion," Hootie answered. "You got a real good one. You watch, someday this guy will win a national championship."

As we all know, John Cooper came close several times, but there would be no national championship victory cigar.

The John Cooper era at Ohio State—13 years in all—could be categorized as the good, the bad, and the ugly.

The good: it started with a 26–9 win over Syracuse, in which the Buckeyes did not commit a penalty or have a turnover for the first game in 27 years.

Cooper recruited dozens of talented athletes who helped win their share of games. Many of them went on to the NFL, where they had long and enriching careers.

The bad: despite that flawless first game, Cooper's first season (4–6–1) became Ohio State's first and only losing season of the previous 40 years.

No matter how talented, Cooper's teams could never reach college football's summit. Ohio State won three Big Ten cochampionships and played in one Rose Bowl (a 20–17 come-from-behind win over his former team, Arizona State, at the conclusion of the '96 season) during his tenure.

The most deflating loss was a 23–11 debacle to underdog Air Force in the 1990 Liberty Bowl, while the Buckeyes also sustained their most lopsided loss in school history under Cooper's watch, a 63–14 whipping at the hands of Penn State in 1994.

And the ugly: Michigan.

Ah yes, that M-word was already a dirty word for most Buckeyes fans, but when it is linked to Cooper, it represents so much heartache and frustration. Not only did Cooper have a 2–10–1 record against the Wolverines, it became apparent to most fans that he never fully recognized or understood the importance of the rivalry, let alone learned how to win "The Game."

To him, it was as if it was just another game on the schedule, one that happened to conclude each regular season. Once the heat was turned up for all of his failures in the series, he realized it was a game he needed to win. He just couldn't figure out a way, other than the aberrations in 1994 and 1998.

"The writers love to write how I can't beat Michigan," Cooper said in 1995, while his 11–0 team prepared for the Wolverines. "You get sick and tired of hearing people say you can't beat Michigan."

At that point, he was 1–5–1 against UM. That team, a nine-point favorite over Michigan, lost 31–23 in Ann Arbor.

"It's something I will live with the rest of my life," quarterback Bobby Hoying said moments after the '95 loss. "There's no Rose Bowl. There's no Big Ten championship, and I am a senior. I am not sure I will ever get over this."

Over the next six meetings, the Cooper-coached Buckeyes were a consistent 1–5 against Michigan.

What was confounding to most fans is that it was obvious Cooper's teams were usually more talented than Michigan, especially in 1993, '95, '96, '97, and '98. And Ohio State won only one of those games.

In 1993, Ohio State entered the game 9–0–1 and was beaten 28–0 in Ann Arbor, the day after Cooper received a contract extension. In '95 and '96, they entered the game with 11–0 and 10–0 records and hopes of a national championship, but Michigan, ranked 12th and 21st, respectively, upset Ohio State each time.

Once asked how Michigan week was different, Cooper answered, "You can't practice any longer or work any harder than you have every other week. You just don't get as many hours of sleep, and the phone rings a lot more."

Unlike Woody Hayes, Earle Bruce, and Jim Tressel, Cooper spent no more time preparing for Michigan than he did any other opponent. He did not save any plays or formations and rarely implemented anything new.

"I've never coached anywhere where you work on a team ahead of another team," he once said. "And I am not going to start now."

Losing to Michigan was one thing, but another was the fact that a few Buckeyes talked a good game before The Game. Maybe it was simple confidence, and maybe it was the pressure and frustration of not having beat the Wolverines enough. In 1995, for example, receiver Terry Glenn said on camera, "Michigan is *nobody*."

After the loss that cost the Buckeyes a shot at the national title, a game in which Glenn dropped three passes, Michigan coach Lloyd Carr admitted that Glenn's line was replayed over and over again for his players.

"It fired us up," Carr said.

Cooper, however, blamed the media more than he did his players.

"I warn these guys about it all the time," he once said, "but you know how reporters badger them until they say something."

The Comeback at Minnesota

October 28, 1989, will go down as a huge day in Ohio State football history. It is the date of the largest comeback not only in school history but in Big Ten history. (For more than 17 years, it also stood tied as the largest comeback in NCAA history, until Michigan State broke the record with a 35-point comeback over Northwestern in 2006.)

Just before halftime, Minnesota led the Buckeyes 31–0.

"Anything that could go wrong went wrong," quarterback Greg Frey said. "I never expect for us to get hammered like we did early in the game. It just snowballed in the wrong direction. I threw an interception and got sacked another time and fumbled. We had a special teams turnover. I just remember it happened so fast.

"When it was 31–0, I vividly remember kneeling on the sideline, and I made myself look up at the scoreboard. Sometimes you have to accept the fact that it is not our day, just get out of there and go home, but I made myself focus on getting back in the game."

On the last possession of the first half, the Buckeyes drove to Minnesota's 1-yard line. On fourth down, tailback Carlos Snow scored on a sweep. Frey then passed to Jeff Graham on a two-point conversion to make it 31–8 at the half.

"That kind of settled everybody down," Frey remembered. "It was very calm at halftime. Being down 23 points was a lot better than 31, and we knew we were going to get the ball first to start the second half. I said, 'Look guys, this is Minnesota...we can do this. It's not like we are playing Michigan.'"

The Buckeyes completed a long drive to begin the second half with a field goal. Frey then completed two touchdown passes to Snow and Graham, sandwiched around an option keeper for another touchdown.

For the winning touchdown, he passed 15 yards to Graham.

"We had two receivers split to the right, and when I came to the line of scrimmage and saw the coverage they were in, I had to hide my smile," Frey recalled. "I knew Jeff would be open and it would be a touchdown."

It was, and when Graham scored, accounting for the 41–37 win, Frey removed his helmet and raised his arms.

"The wire services ran a photo of me standing there, and it is always something I remember," he said. "I had never taken my helmet off before. I just stood there screaming with my arms up in the air."

A statistical oddity in that game: the Buckeyes had six turnovers and converted three two-point conversions. Frey finished 20 of 31 for 362 yards (third-best in OSU history) and three touchdowns.

"To this day, people come up to me and tell me where they were when they saw that game," he said. "It is amazing. It happens all the time."

Pitching at Yankee Stadium

One of the highlights of Cooper's career came on a baseball diamond.

The day after Ohio State beat Boston College 38–6 in the Kickoff Classic at the Meadowlands to begin the 1995 season, he was invited to throw out the first pitch of a New York Yankees game.

Yankees owner George Steinbrenner has always maintained a good relationship with Ohio State and Columbus, where the franchise's Triple A affiliate has resided for decades.

When he entered the dugout that day, Cooper was wearing one of the cheap Yankees hats that vendors sold inside the stadium. Then-manager Buck Showalter told Cooper, "You can't throw out the first pitch in that." He handed Cooper an authentic Yankees cap, and he promptly threw a strike to catcher Mike Stanley.

"From tiny Powell, Tennessee, to Yankee Stadium," Cooper crowed. "I've come a long way, huh?"

Despite his roots, Cooper considered himself a Buckeye at heart after a few years into the job. "You know, you might not believe this, but we had a buckeye tree on my property when I grew up," he said. "You think buckeyes only grow in Ohio? Come on. They're all over the place."

To illustrate his point, he pulled his lucky silver dollar and his lucky buckeye out of his pocket.

"I always carry them both," he said.

Beating the Fighting Irish

Aside from the 1997 Rose Bowl victory and his two lone wins over Michigan, John Cooper's greatest moments had to come in the 1995 and '96 meetings with Notre Dame.

Ohio State's history with Notre Dame is very limited, despite their proximity and standing as college football powers. The Buckeyes and the Fighting Irish had played in 1935 and '36, with Notre Dame winning each, 18–13 and 7–2, respectively. Notre Dame had held a 2–0 series lead and bragging rights over the Buckeyes for 60 years.

Ohio State had jumped to a 13–0 lead in the first-ever meeting with Notre Dame, billed as the "Game of the Century."

"Remember it like it was yesterday," Allen Murray, who was an Ohio Stadium usher, said in 1995. "It was my first season here.

Ohio State's Eddie George runs for a touchdown against Notre Dame on September 30, 1995, at Ohio Stadium.

Ohio State outplayed Notre Dame in that game. Had a 13–0 lead, but [Coach] Francis Schmidt took some of his good players out. Remember in those days, if you took them out, they couldn't return until the next quarter. It was a dumb move. We should have won that game. No doubt about it."

"That game was called 'Protestants versus the Catholics' around Columbus, and I happened to be one of the few Catholics playing for Ohio State," Charlie Ream said. "In the end, they threw a touchdown pass to beat us. That pass went from Bill Shakespeare to Wayne Millner and the saying went that 'a Protestant threw a pass to a Jewish boy to lead the Irish over the Buckeyes.'

"That was the only loss we had [in 1935], and that cost us the national championship. Let me tell you that we hated like hell to lose that game."

Legend has it that Notre Dame inquired about scheduling Ohio State throughout the '50s, '60s, and '70s, but Woody Hayes vetoed the idea. Those close to Woody speculated that he didn't want to add a second rivalry when he already was a part of the greatest in the sport—the rivalry with Michigan.

Woody died in 1987, the year that then–OSU athletics director Rick Bay agreed to play Notre Dame twice: in Columbus in 1995 and in South Bend the following year. Was it a coincidence that Ohio State finally agreed to play Notre Dame after Woody died? Only Bay knows for sure, and he's been long gone from Columbus.

"The fan inside me said, 'That's a great game, go for it,'" he told the *The Columbus Dispatch*.

Before the 1995 game, Cooper even wondered whom Ohio State's Catholic fans would root for.

"Somebody told me that's why Woody never scheduled them," he said. "I am not for it, either. If I was the Big Ten, I'd say, 'If you want to play us, come into the league.' Why play them?"

The hype for the 1995 meeting was huge, with end-zone seats at the Horseshoe selling for $300.

"Anybody and everybody who has ever done anything for me has called," Cooper said of the ticket demand.

The day, September 30, 1995, didn't start so well. Cooper fell face-first as he led his team onto the field.

"I thought I was going to get trampled," he said. "Our team was ready to play. They ran over me. I am not as fast as I used to be."

Ohio State crushed Notre Dame 45–26.

One of the happiest fans in the stands was a man named Fred Crow, who blocked an Irish kick with his left arm during the 1935 game. He had written into his will that if he should die before the

1995 game that his left arm be cremated and its ashes scattered in the south end zone of Ohio Stadium.

Crow lived to see the Buckeyes' victory that day but died five weeks later, hours before Ohio State was to meet Minnesota.

A year later, the Buckeyes went to South Bend and followed up with a 29–16 win over the Irish. It gave Cooper his only two wins over a Lou Holtz–coached team. Holtz's Arkansas teams had beaten Cooper's Tulsa teams seven times without a loss.

"We would bus down to Fayetteville, get our $150,000, get beat, give the kids a bucket of chicken, and bus home. Everybody in the athletic department was happy but me," he recalled.

Tressel's Buckeyes crushed the Irish 34–20 in the 2006 Fiesta Bowl. In that game, the Buckeyes rolled to 617 yards—the most ever given up by the Fighting Irish.

"If I have to hear the number 617 one more time," Notre Dame coach Charlie Weis said almost a year later, "I am going to puke."

With no future meetings scheduled, unless the two midwestern giants would meet again in a bowl, Ohio State has a 3–2 edge over Notre Dame.

Keep My Feet on the Ground

One of the greatest stories of the 1995 season was the emergence of wide receiver Terry Glenn.

Glenn, a former walk-on, entered his senior season with 15 career receptions. With world-class speed and sure hands, he delivered an All-American season, catching 64 passes for 1,411 yards and 17 touchdowns, which remains a school record. He was named Ohio State's first recipient of the Fred Biletnikoff Award.

Glenn's 253 receiving yards against Pittsburgh also remains a school record.

He had just one weakness: he wouldn't step onto an airplane, and thus, he had to drive to all of the away games. Depending on the destination, he would arrive late on a Friday night and not get nearly as much sleep as his teammates.

"Still," Glenn explained. "I am not flying. Can't do it. Don't ask me."

He wasn't the first Buckeye to encounter the fear of flying. Jim Parker once recalled the fact that Ohio State had to use two airplanes to fly to Madison, Wisconsin, because the airport's runway was not long enough to accommodate a larger airplane for the entire team.

"I didn't like to fly anyway," Parker said. "You almost had to hypnotize me to get me on an airplane. Even in pro football, I hated to fly. I always watched Woody. Whatever plane he got on, I got on. If he got on that one, I got on that one."

Which leads to a great story about one trip to Penn State in 1976. In the 1970s, the nearby airport at State College, Pennsylvania, had a shorter runway, too, so the Buckeyes used the two-airplane system: Red One and Red Two.

Red One included Woody Hayes, the assistant coaches, and the team's starters. Red Two included a few of the reserve players and other university personnel. When the pilot joked that he didn't know of the safety standards relating to the length of the airport runway, Woody replied, "Send in Red Two. If they make it, then we'll go in."

He may have been joking. Then again, he may not have been.

Clinching the Rose Bowl Berth

Even when the Buckeyes clinched a Big Ten cochampionship in 1996 by beating Indiana 27–17, with the Michigan game still remaining to be played, it didn't come easy.

Ohio State, ranked number two at the time, trailed the Hoosiers 17–13 in the fourth quarter when linebacker Andy Katzenmoyer forced a fumble, which defensive tackle Matt Finkes picked up and raced into the end zone for the go-ahead touchdown.

"Here's the neat story about that," Finkes said recently. "After I returned the fumble for a touchdown, I dropped the ball and the guys [teammates] tackled me in the end zone. We were celebrating in a pile, but there was still a lot of time left. This kid jumps over the fence and grabs the football and runs back into the stands. I went back and looked at it on the film, and you could see it.

"So after the game, we couldn't get off the field because all of the Ohio State fans were celebrating the clinching of the Rose Bowl. This kid comes up to me, pulls the football from underneath his shirt, and hands it to me as a gift. I have it today on my mantle, and it has the Indiana logo on it because it was their ball."

Later, when Finkes was playing a round of golf at Little Turtle Country Club outside of Columbus, a bag boy grabbed his golf clubs from his car and took them to the first tee for him.

"Remember me?" he asked. "I am the guy who gave you the ball at Indiana."

"I sent him a jersey and an autographed football," Finkes said. "I always thought that was a neat thing for him to do."

The Rose Bowl berth in hand, however, the Buckeyes were shocked by Michigan 13–9 at Ohio Stadium a week later. Even when he should have been celebrating his only trip to Pasadena, Cooper was commiserating yet another heartbreaking defeat to the Wolverines.

Germaine a Hero in Pasadena

Throughout the 1996 season, Cooper had alternated quarterbacks Stanley Jackson and Joe Germaine, who was clearly the better pocket passer.

By design, Jackson started and Germaine would come off the bench.

After Jake Plummer scrambled for a touchdown to give Arizona State a 17–14 lead over Ohio State in the Rose Bowl, the Ohio State coaches had a decision to make: Jackson or Germaine?

Only 1:40 remained in the game.

"Later, I heard the story," Germaine recalled. "Mike Jacobs was the acting offensive coordinator because Walt Harris had already accepted the Pittsburgh job, but he had stayed to coach us through the Rose Bowl. When they came to deciding who would go in on that final drive, there was dead silence. Coach Jacobs didn't say anything. Finally, Coach Harris said, 'We've got to go with Germaine.'

"They just pointed to me and said, 'Get out there.'"

Germaine, an Arizona native, drove the Buckeyes 65 yards in 12 plays. He finished the drive by throwing a five-yard pass to David Boston to win the game.

"We sent Dimitrious Stanley to the slot on the right and David out wide to the right," Germaine remembered. "The primary receiver was supposed to be Dimitrious, who would run a corner route. David would run inside on a hitch and then back toward the pylon. As I dropped back, I could tell they had Dimitrious defensed. They had him cut off. I looked down at Boston, and he was wide open."

As a footnote to the story, the Arizona State safety on the field chasing the play was Pat Tillman, who was killed in Afghanistan in 2004.

Once Jackson was gone, Germaine put together one of the finest seasons in Ohio State history for a quarterback. He completed 230 of 384 passes for 3,330 yards and 25 touchdowns in 1998. His completions, attempts, and yards still stand as Ohio State single-season records.

The PR Blunders

Losing to Michigan aside, Cooper did a few things to alienate fans. For starters, he made several commercials once he arrived in Columbus, one of which particularly made him a butt of jokes: it was a hot tub commercial in which the Ohio State head coach was shown taking a soak.

To some, it came off as if he was out to make a buck off the Buckeyes.

"There were things I would have done differently," he said. "I wouldn't have made as many commercials, but that's the way coaches around the country do it. Everything here that you do, you are compared to Coach Hayes. He didn't make commercials. He wrote books.

"The hot tub thing was stupid on my part. I was building a house, and some guy was putting a hot tub in it. He shot a commercial with me in it. Now this comes under 'you live and learn.'"

Another time, following the 1994 season, just days after his first win over Michigan, Cooper interviewed with LSU about the school's opening. He was angry that athletics director Andy Geiger had offered only a two-year contract extension following the 22–6 win over Michigan, which gave the Buckeyes a 9–3 record heading into the bowl game.

"Two years, can you believe that?" Cooper said the next year. "I can't keep my assistant coaches the way it is. My receivers coach had rented an apartment the past three years. He was afraid to buy a house because of the fear that they would fire my ass.

"The mood I was in...I would have taken the LSU job that day if [LSU athletics director] Joe Dean had offered it. But he never did."

Even some of Cooper's oft-used phrases, such as "I don't coach the players, I coach coaches," did not endear him to fans.

Recently, as Earle Bruce was asked about Jim Tressel and Florida coach Urban Meyer, two of his former assistants, he described them this way, and it could be disguised as a shot at Cooper.

"On the practice field, they are coaching, boy," Bruce said. "They're not over talking to alumni, or ex-players. They are in there with their players and their coaches....You know who the head coach is, because they are involved."

Which isn't exactly the way Cooper ran practices. Most of the times, he was twirling his whistle while watching from the sideline, carrying on conversations with media members, visitors, or former players.

At the same time, while many of Ohio State's fans never warmed to him, his assistant coaches loved working for him. For the most part, he was easygoing and he didn't require them to be in the office watching film at midnight. And he let them do their jobs without interference.

"I have so much respect for him," said current Illinois head coach Ron Zook, the Buckeyes' defensive backs coach from 1988 to 1990. "He is the greatest guy to work for."

However, there is no denying that Cooper didn't wrap his arms around Ohio State's tradition and its storied past. In fact, he resented it at times, and that cost him in the long run.

"One of the best things about this place is it's Ohio State University. But you know at the same time one of the worst things about it is it's The Ohio State University," he once said. "It's almost like Ohio State never lost before.

"I mean, name one coach they haven't fired. The thing that gets me about this place is that all the coaches I can name, all the athletics directors I know, have left here bitter. All of them. I don't want to leave here bitter."

Unfortunately, he did.

"I'll say one thing, and I may be boasting about this, but I am a good football coach," he once said. "My teams are always [fundamentally] sound. I don't cheat. They may fire me someday, but it won't be for cheating."

He was right about that, too. They did, and it wasn't.

In the end, Cooper won more games (111) at Ohio State than any coach besides Woody Hayes. He lost 43 games, 10 of which were to Michigan and another eight in bowls. His tenure at Ohio State, unlike that of Hayes, did make him a rich man, thanks to a $3 million buyout of his contract.

However, the figures that will be linked with him forever are *2–10–1.*

"You have to give John credit for one thing," Bruce said. "No coach in Ohio State history lost to Michigan as much and kept his job for as long."

Cooper still resides in Columbus, calls himself a Buckeyes fan, and has eased into retirement as a television analyst.

He is not revered by his players like Hayes or adored by fans like Tressel. He simply is John Harold Cooper, a Tennessee native who recruited great players but didn't fully embrace Ohio State's traditions or its past, and worst of all, couldn't win the big game.

Nor could he produce the championship season that so many Buckeyes fans wanted, needed, and had waited for all those long years.

Once he was gone, a buttoned-down, sweater vest–wearing young man who grew up in Berea and made his mark in Youngstown was about to arrive.

chapter 9

The Coach Called Tress

Jim Tressel and Buckeyes players and fans have had more to celebrate in his relatively brief tenure than during any period since the Hayes years.

Jim Tressel made a bold declaration to Ohio State fans the day he was hired. He later backed it up as his Buckeyes ended years of frustration by winning at Michigan. Then they did it again the following year. And they have continued doing it, winning five of Tressel's first six meetings with the Wolverines.

"I want to assure you that you'll be proud of our young people in the classroom, in the community, and most especially in 310 days in Ann Arbor, Michigan, on the football field."

It was January 18, 2001.

It also was obvious that the direction of the Ohio State football program was about to change.

James Patrick Tressel, hired as the university's 22nd football coach only hours earlier, stood on the basketball court at the Schottenstein Center, microphone in hand, and as much as informed frustrated Buckeyes fans better days were ahead.

With that simple statement, he told them that their football team's collective grade point average would be headed upward. He informed them their Buckeyes would start seeing the big picture in life, that they would embrace Ohio State's rich history, and that they would keep their noses clean off the field and get their hands dirty in the classroom.

And he told them their suffering at the hands of the Michigan Wolverines was about to be a thing of the past.

With that simple statement, Tressel received a standing ovation.

As promised, 310 days later, his first Ohio State team traveled to Ann Arbor, raced to a 23–0 lead, and held on to shock Michigan 26–20.

A year later, the Buckeyes beat the Wolverines again, 14–9, and then upset top-ranked Miami to complete the first 14–0 season in major-college football history, earning Ohio State its first national championship in 34 years.

Following his sixth season as head coach, Tressel's teams have beaten Michigan *five* times. Ohio State has a 62–14 record for a .816 winning percentage, the best of any coach of more than two seasons in school history.

"Expectations at Ohio State are always high," he said. "People like to talk about winning Big Ten championships and national championships and that type of thing. I guess my expectation coming in was to try to create a situation where you go to work and get better every day.

"Every day you evaluate what you did yesterday and how you can get better at what we did yesterday. We get good players. We have excellent coaches. People want to coach at Ohio State. Football players want to play at Ohio State."

"The two greatest days in our student-athletes' lives should be the day they walk across the stage to receive their diploma and the day they slip a championship ring on their finger."

With the thrilling 31–24 double-overtime win over the top-ranked Hurricanes in the 2003 Fiesta Bowl, Tressel's players were guaranteed one half of that statement would come true.

As for the other...

"There's only one reason to miss class, and that's because of a death in the family...your own."

For three decades, Woody Hayes stressed education and layed out the path for every player to receive a degree. Tressel has followed in those footsteps. He introduced his players to his Block O of Life—a model for success that defines goals in categories: football/family, spiritual/moral/ethical, personal/family, academics/career, strength/fitness, and caring/giving.

"With it, we have established a goal sheet that is given to each one of our players," he said. "We want the goals to be comprehensive. Players who say they want to do only enough to remain academically eligible to play in college and then go on to the NFL are selling themselves short.

"What we are trying to preach to our players is that this time in college is not a gap between high school and the NFL. This is life! This is what will fulfill you!"

Ohio State's collective team GPA and graduation rate has risen every year under Tressel. The days of a player not attending a single class and finishing with a 0.0, as happened under John Cooper, are history.

From 2001 to 2006, 97 Buckeyes were named Academic All–Big Ten, the most in the conference. In the fall of 2006, while Ohio State was rolling through the regular season with a perfect 12–0 record, 56 players had a GPA of 3.0 or above.

One of Tressel's first goals was to turn the Buckeyes program into a family. He wrote to former players, inviting them to drop by the Woody Hayes Athletic Center at any time for any reason. He instituted a routine of player presentations, designed for team-mates to learn more about each other.

As far as leadership, he did what Hayes also did: he made it clear that every Ohio State team belongs to the seniors. They are first and foremost in any activity, whether it is talking to the media or making crucial decisions that affect the entire team.

While the seniors lead, Tressel maintains, it is only natural that underclassmen will follow.

"The day he was hired," said defensive tackle Kenny Peterson (1999–2002), "he said, 'We want to be the class of college foot-ball. We want to be respected, and these people in this room will be a family. He constantly stressed it was all about "we" and "team." It wasn't about "me" or "I."'"

When recruiting, Tressel delivers the same message, which often has led to losing certain high school players that the Buckeyes had targeted. The fact is, his message is not always the message some recruits want to hear. There are five-star recruits who want to be told how great they are, who want to be begged to sign with Ohio State and promised playing time. Tressel refuses to do that.

"During the recruiting process, I felt he was really genuine," defensive tackle David Patterson (2003–2006) said. "I know that he knows every guy on the team's name and their hometown. I have a friend who played for another Division I school, and he said their head coach doesn't even know all their players' names.

"It's just good to see when you have a coach like Coach Tressel who really cares about all his players. No matter how busy he is, he takes time for any guy."

While he has developed a cocoon around the Buckeyes family, Tressel has protected it from spying eyes as well. Hayes didn't like the media much, either, but he used the forum at times, and his brutal honesty was always a hit with reporters. Tressel, on the other hand, limits the players' access to the media as much as he is allowed. He speaks to the media only when he has to, and doesn't want his players or assistant coaches to get too comfort-able in front of a microphone or notepad.

His unwillingness to open up and bare his soul, refusing to reveal his personal likes or dislikes or his views on anything other than football, has frustrated the media that covers Ohio State football on a regular basis. Furthermore, the team's practices generally have been closed to the media since he became coach, a contrast to the days when Cooper spoke with reporters on the sideline *during* most practices.

"I wouldn't give the media any zingers," Tressel once said. "I suppose there is a side to us that no one knows. We have a lot of fun with our players. To me that's part of the relationships with the players, and it can't be all work and no play. We try to play a little to make it fun for our guys. At the same time, we want to be caring and demanding of our players. Young people want to be in a situation where they are cared for."

At the same time, Ohio State fans and officials couldn't care less about such trivial matters, as long as their football coach wins enough games and beats Michigan enough times. Furthermore, his players get to see the side that the media wants to see—a coach who laughs and jokes and has a good time.

"There is a side of him that he protects from the media because I don't think he likes the media for the most part," said one player, who did not want to be identified. "He is a funny guy and he kids around with us all the time, but he probably wouldn't want me revealing that."

Doug Datish, the Buckeyes' All-Big Ten center in 2006, said, "Coach Tressel is Coach Tressel, 24 hours a day, seven days a week, 52 weeks a year."

And where he is these days is where he wants to be.

"I wake up every day and count my blessings that I am in a situation like this," said Tressel, who, in addition to owning school history's best winning percentage, has coached his teams to one national title and three Big Ten titles in his first six seasons at Ohio State.

"I am blessed to be where I am in a career standpoint. It is very hard for me to imagine being anywhere better than Ohio State. Coaching college football is like being in paradise. You have great kids. They are at a time in their lives where they are growing. It would be hard to imagine anything better than this."

His Lineage

Tressel was very close with his parents, Lee and Eloise, who died before his first game as Ohio State head coach, a 28–14 win over Akron on September 8, 2001.

"I had just lost my mother two weeks before, and we were playing Akron, where I had gotten my start coaching," he said.

Lee Tressel was one of the finest football coaches the Division III level has ever seen. He won 155 games in 23 seasons at Baldwin-Wallace, where Jim played quarterback from 1972 to 1974. He died of cancer in 1981.

"I got to watch my father work my entire lifetime—and to play for him as well," Tressel said. "My dad was one of the greatest coaches because he cared about every one of his players. He realized that the most important thing a player would ask was, 'Do you really care about me?'

"I have learned that players don't care how much you know, until they know how much you care. I learned that from my father."

Earle Bruce knew Lee Tressel and first noticed the similarities between father and son more than three decades ago.

"I tell him this once in a while—it's joking but it's not joking. The apple doesn't fall very far from the tree," Bruce said. "I knew his dad, and his dad was an outstanding man. He was successful in high school and college coaching like you wouldn't believe.

"I'd heard about him as a kid when I coached in Massillon and he coached in Massillon, so I'd heard about the Tressel boys. He went to Akron to start his career and then to Miami of Ohio and to Syracuse, where he was when I met him."

Tressel also learned his passion for Ohio State from his father. He developed it further when he served three seasons as a Buckeyes assistant coach from 1983 to 1985.

"It was my father's dream to play football for the Ohio State Buckeyes," he said. "He was recruited by the great Paul Brown to come to Ohio State. He played that spring of '43, throwing a touchdown pass to Les Horvath and running for two more touchdowns. After the spring, he enlisted in the U.S. Navy, giving up his dream of being a Buckeye so he could serve his country."

His First Stop in Columbus

While living in Syracuse, New York, coaching the quarterbacks for the Orangemen from 1981 to 1982, Lee Tressel's son received a call one day from Earle Bruce, who was in search of a new offensive assistant.

"I still remember meeting him at the Holiday Inn in Berea, at the corner of I-71 and Bagley Road," Tressel said. "He was very focused, and he knew what he was looking for. I had to hold my breath a week or so, but he called back and offered me the job. He said, 'Get here as soon as you can.'"

"When I interviewed him, like I said, he was like his dad," Bruce said. "I had the greatest respect for that man. I figured that's what the kid might be, and he was. He's a coach like his dad, a good coach."

In January 1983 Tressel arrived in Columbus as Ohio State's new quarterbacks and receivers coach.

"It was two years after my father had passed away, and I knew what Ohio State had meant to him," he said. "My father loved it so much, so I felt as if I was coming home."

For the next three years, Tressel became enamored with Ohio State's history and tradition. He read about the origins of such traditions as the Victory Bell, Buckeye Grove, gold pants, "Carmen Ohio," and "Across the Field."

"Those three years were fundamental to me in learning about the Ohio State tradition, and that is what makes Ohio State so special," he said. "That is why I believe it is important to expose those traditions to our players.

"For example, I had always heard about the Best Damn Band's skull session at St. John Arena before games, but I had never experienced it. I asked, 'If this is such a great tradition, how come many players and coaches don't know about it?' So we arranged to go over there and let the players see what it was all about. They loved it."

Before every game since he has become head coach, the Buckeyes attend the skull session and Tressel addresses the crowd.

He has done many other things to reach into Ohio State's past, such as honor the living members of the 1942 team, the school's first national championship team, with national championship rings. That stemmed from a meeting with Gene Fekete, one of the team's star players, at a golf outing in Columbus. As the two spoke, Fekete mentioned Tressel's huge championship ring from the 2002 season. Once he realized Paul Brown's team had never received such a gaudy token for their title, Tressel set out to correct history's injustice.

"He told me, 'I'm going to make sure every one of your members gets a ring, and all you have to do for me is get their sizes,'" Fekete explained.

Fekete did just that—and Tressel provided the rings.

While an assistant at OSU, Tressel was asked by Bruce one day, "Jim, what's your goal in coaching?'"

He said, "My goal in coaching is to be just like my dad, be a head coach at a small college and have a great program."

"So when the Youngstown State job came open," Bruce said, "I told him, 'That's your job. Go get it.' He was successful there, but I didn't realize that he'd been bitten by the Buckeye bug."

Four Division I-AA national championships, 135 victories, and 15 years later at Youngstown State, Tressel could have become a major-college coach any time he had wanted. He turned down several chances to interview for jobs, but the closest he came to leaving Youngstown was in January 1995, when the Miami Hurricanes wanted him to replace Dennis Erickson.

In the end, he decided to stay in Youngstown, and Miami turned to Butch Davis.

Becoming the Buckeyes' Boss

Within moments of the news that John Cooper had been fired, on January 2, 2001, Tressel made a monumental decision: if he ever was to leave Youngstown, this was the right time and the right job. He waited for the dust to settle in Columbus then called Archie Griffin.

"It wouldn't be accurate to say that I was in Youngstown, just waiting for the Ohio State job to come open," he explained six years later. "I didn't wake up every morning in Youngstown wanting to go there. There is something I learned from an athletics director many years ago. He told me, 'Keep your mind and your rear end in the same place, then you'll be fine.' Now he may not have said it exactly that way, but I heeded that advice.

"But when it was open, Ohio State didn't call me. I called Archie. I just sort of threw my hat in the ring. He listened and said he would get back to me."

"When he called me," Griffin recalled, "he basically said that he wanted me to know that he was interested in becoming the next Ohio State football coach. I told him he already was on our list [of candidates] and that he would be contacted.

"I knew all along he would be interested in the job. I just always felt that Jim was waiting for this job. Whether it is true or not, only he knows. I always felt that way. It wasn't a surprise to me when he called, and it wasn't a surprise to [athletics director] Andy [Geiger]. I knew him pretty well at the time. He had coached under Earle Bruce, and when I visited Youngstown, I would be with him on a few occasions…at banquets or I had played golf with him a little."

When Geiger and Griffin interviewed him, Tressel laid out an intricate presentation of what he would aim to accomplish as head football coach at Ohio State and how he would go about it—from the players' academics to community programs to recruiting. His main message was this: he wasn't just a football coach. He would be a teacher, a leader, and a father to his players, while transforming them from members of a football program into a family.

"I just talked about what I believe in, and this is how I would proceed, and thank goodness Andy Geiger and his committee decided to give me a chance," he said.

It was a similar presentation Miami athletics director Paul Dee saw six years earlier, calling it "the most impressive interview I have ever witnessed from a coach in any sport."

"He did an excellent job," Griffin said. "He was very impressive. It didn't surprise me at all. I knew he would be an excellent choice."

Geiger was blown away by Tressel, knowing he was the right man for the job.

"I had heard from other people who knew him what to expect from him," Geiger said recently. "He is a very impressive man."

The decision for Geiger and Ohio State president Brit Kirwan was easy: Tressel was their man.

They made it official on January 18, 2001.

That night, his "in 310 days" statement marked the beginning of a new era.

"When he said that," Griffin said. "I knew he understood what Ohio State was all about. It just confirmed to me that we hired the right guy."

Not that Kirwan, Geiger, or Griffin needed it, but confirmation of their choice came in the ultimate manner two years later, to the day, when more than 55,000 fans braved freezing weather at Ohio Stadium as the Buckeyes celebrated their first national championship in 34 years.

Preparing for Michigan Is Beating Michigan

Ohio State's rivalry with Michigan symbolized Tressel's favorite time of year as a kid. His father would be finished with Baldwin-Wallace's season, and the two would sit together and watch the Buckeyes play the Wolverines.

The period was from the 1960s, when Woody Hayes's team dominated the rivalry, to the years of the Ten-Year War between Hayes and Bo Schembechler.

"We didn't get to sit down with him much during the season, but it was our tradition to sit down with him and watch the Ohio State–Michigan game together as a family," he said. "My dad loved Woody Hayes, and he always rooted for the Buckeyes to beat Michigan."

Once he became Ohio State's head coach 23 years after Hayes's final game, Tressel certainly entered the rivalry in an advantageous position, following Cooper's 2–10–1 record in the series. As far as tough acts to follow, he did not face one. At

Michigan head coach Lloyd Carr and Jim Tressel meet on the field on November 18, 2006—a day that ended in Tressel's fifth win over "that team up north" in six tries.

that point, a Buckeyes win every other season would have thrilled fans.

But when he took a mediocre and unranked 6–4 team to Ann Arbor and jumped to a 23–0 halftime lead over the 11th-rankled Wolverines that first season, he looked like a sweater vest–wearing genius. Fortunately, the Buckeyes held on to win that game 26–20, or his proclamation would have come back to haunt him.

From that day in Ann Arbor, Buckeyes fans have fallen in love with Tressel, whose teams have saved their best performances on an annual basis for the Wolverines.

It is no accident.

So how has he done it? And why was he so confident he could do it in the first place?

For starters, when he took the Ohio State job, Tressel expected his players to realize the importance of the Michigan rivalry. He made them read books about it, as well as books about Ohio State's history. He also brought in several speakers to address it. He encouraged them to wrap their arms around the rivalry, to squeeze it, and to enjoy it.

These were players who, under Cooper, usually said they thought they could beat Michigan but then fell short in the fourth quarters of those games when the pressure peaked.

"He got us to believe we could win any game," said running back Maurice Hall (2001–2004), "especially the biggest games. Especially the Michigan game."

Secondly, Tressel prepares for Michigan all the time, much like Hayes did. A saying around the Woody Hayes Athletic Center goes, "What did you do today to beat Michigan?"

And it could be said in January, February, or any day in the off-season.

Whether it is his play calling or the schemes offensively and defensively, Tressel thinks about Michigan 365 days a year. On any day of the year, you could walk up to him and ask him, "How many days until you play Michigan?" and he would snap off the answer without looking at the calendar.

So could many of his players.

"When you have a rivalry like ours, you think about it often," Tressel said. "I think about trying to get good enough to prepare for that. It just so happens that every year it is your last game, so you're hoping to play your best football in that last game."

Thus, after spring practice and a summer spent often looking at Michigan tapes, he may have the Buckeyes working on certain formations or plays in August that will be perfect to spring on the Wolverines in November. And then he hordes them for that game, resisting any temptation to use them during even the closest games in September or October.

"That was the thing I remember when he got here," Hall said. "The players were asking, 'Why are we working on all this new and different stuff if we never run it in the games?' We had no idea why we were doing it."

They understood during that first Michigan game under Tressel, coming after the Buckeyes were soundly thumped by Illinois

34–22 at Ohio Stadium. He had saved an unbalanced-line formation, lining up one guard and two tackles to either side of the center, a surprise which Ohio State had worked on for months. It caught Michigan off guard from the start, as Jonathan Wells rushed for three first-half touchdowns and the Buckeyes built a large halftime lead.

In year two, in which Ohio State took a 12–0 record into the meeting in Columbus, the Buckeyes trailed 9–7 late in the game. It was exactly the type of game Cooper's teams would have lost. Ohio State was ranked higher—championship hopes in the balance—and heavily favored.

When the Buckeyes faced a second-and-goal at the Michigan 6-yard line, what did Tressel call? An option to the right, on which Hall scored easily.

What made the call so special?

"We had not run the option all season, but we had worked on it all the time," Hall said. "So when we called it in the huddle and then came to the line of scrimmage, I saw that all the Michigan linebackers were shifting to the inside, expecting one of our regular running plays they had seen on film from that entire season.

"All I had to do was catch the pitch and trot into the end zone. It was the greatest moment of my life. People to this day come up to me and mention that touchdown. That's an example of how he set it up."

Entering the 2004 game, the Buckeyes were struggling with four losses and were seven-point underdogs to Michigan at Ohio Stadium. Tressel unveiled a few new formations and plays, including a tight-end delay that caught the Wolverines by surprise. It didn't hurt that Troy Smith, inconsistent to that point because he had started only four games in his career, played the game of his life. He rushed for 145 yards and one touchdown and passed for 241 and two more scores as Ohio State upset Michigan 37–21.

For the 2005 meeting, Ohio State was coming off a game against Northwestern in which they had attempted 15 passes and rushed 54 times for 317 yards. Then against Michigan, Tressel had his offense spread the field with four and five receivers at times as

Smith operated the zone-read offense to perfection. He passed for 300 yards and ran for 37 more in a 25–21 come-from-behind win in Ann Arbor.

The following year, in the monumental number one versus number two showdown in Columbus, Tressel used a play in which he put speedy wide receiver Ted Ginn Jr. at tight end and called for a play-action bomb to him on second-and-inches. The Buckeyes had set it up by running powerful tailback Chris Wells on every second-and-short during the previous month. On this play, Smith faked to Wells and passed 39 yards to Ginn, which gave Ohio State a 21–7 lead in the second quarter.

Michigan did rally, but Ohio State held on to win the game by three points.

"It's always something like that," Hall said. "It has gotten to the point that none of the players ever question anything we are working on because we know it may be used in the biggest game of the season.

"Ohio State's players don't even think about it now. They know Coach Tressel is working on something. And we love him for it."

Tressel, however, downplays the theory that he has all the answers to the Michigan question, instead referring to a broken play Smith made in the 2004 game as an example of how his players play the largest part of the equation.

"Troy Smith spins and runs 46 yards?" he said. "Now, come on. I don't have any answers. If anyone pretends to think they have the answers, they've got a problem."

Another factor that has led to Ohio State's success against Michigan under Tressel, and it has been apparent in other close games as well, is a collective calmness that negates his players' chances to either panic or to believe the worst is about to happen.

Ohio State trailed Michigan 9–7 in the fourth quarter in 2002, 14–7 early in the 2004 game, 21–12 in the fourth quarter in 2005, and 7–0 after the first series of the 2006 game. The Buckeyes won every one of those games.

"Teams take on the personality of their coach. That's why you see us with our calm demeanor, our very businesslike demeanor,"

Patterson said. "Coach Tressel, before a game he can give you a speech to get you ready to go, but it's not going to be the 'Go win one for the Gipper' speech. It's going to be, 'Guys, we need to go out there and take care of business.'"

"And we never panic if we get behind or things don't go right," Smith said, "because we never see our head coach panic or get too excited. We know we have the weapons to come back and win any game."

Tress and Troy

Much like Woody Hayes and Rex Kern, who became closer as the years passed, almost to the point of having a father-son relationship, Tressel's relationship with Troy Smith evolved into one as close as one between a coach and player could possibly be.

From the beginning, it had as far to grow as any relationship, especially since Justin Zwick was recruited in the same class. Zwick, widely thought to be the superstar of the future, represented the school's most heralded quarterback recruit since Art Schlichter in 1978.

Smith, on the other hand, was signed as an "athlete," and media reports listed him as the final recruit in the 2002 class.

"Well, Troy wasn't the last guy that signed that year, I think that has been turned into folklore," Tressel explained. "I don't know when his fax came in and what time he signed, but we recruited Troy in the summer before his senior season and offered him a scholarship well in advance of the end of recruiting."

However, Zwick was given first crack at the job, once Craig Krenzel, who led Ohio State to the 2002 title, departed following the 2003 season.

It started well, as Zwick passed for 324 yards and three touchdowns to lead the Buckeyes on a two-minute drive that led to Mike Nugent's 55-yard field goal to beat Marshall 24–21. The next week, Ohio State went to Raleigh and beat North Carolina State 22–14 for a 3–0 start to the season.

Then came the nightmare: the Buckeyes lost at Northwestern, to Wisconsin, and then in a 33–7 blowout at Iowa, in which Zwick injured his shoulder.

That opened the door initially for Smith, who took over and had a 4–1 record as a starter down the stretch. It was his brilliant and surprising performance in the 37–21 upset of Michigan at Ohio Stadium that was his coming-out party.

That game, and the practices leading up to it, led Tressel to believe he had the star quarterback of his future.

"He showed us back in '04 that he could make some plays," the coach said. "But would he do it consistently?"

The next pothole for Smith emerged when it was revealed he had accepted $500 from a booster earlier that summer. Ohio State suspended him for the Alamo Bowl and for the 2005 season opener, games the Buckeyes won with Zwick at quarterback.

"Staying home, watching that game on TV, you can't even begin to understand how low I was," Smith explained of the Alamo win over Oklahoma State. "Everything I had worked for to that point...I felt like I had thrown it all away."

Tressel went to bat for his player, believing he was worth saving. While the Ohio State administration discussed how to punish Smith, and since it was an NCAA violation, not just a team rules violation, many factors were considered. Tressel had banked much collateral in his time at Ohio State, and he used it in defending Smith.

In the end, he has proven the gamble was worth the risk.

"I think all of us would have to admit that we grow through our sufferings," Tressel said of Smith. "He's taken the opportunity to grow from things he's suffered through."

"It messed with me mentally and emotionally," Smith said of the suspension, "because I was not with my team."

After both quarterbacks split time during the 25–22 loss to Texas in the second game of the 2005 season, Tressel made the final decision to go with Smith for good. Following a 17–10 loss at Penn State, he led the Buckeyes to seven consecutive victories and to a perfect 2006 regular season before the disastrous loss in the BCS championship game to Florida.

The results, a 19-game winning streak, and another Heisman Trophy for a Buckeye—the first for an Ohio State quarterback—provide overwhelming evidence that Tressel made the correct decision.

"You could kind of sense how things were going, and we thought that was the right thing to do," Tressel said of his decision following the loss to Texas. "I can't point to any empirical evidence. Sometimes you've got to say, 'It's time to go to the left.' You might be right or you might be wrong."

Smith always was a good runner for a quarterback, but he spent most of his Heisman Trophy–winning season in the pocket, rarely scrambling. During the 42–39 win over Michigan in 2006, Tressel trusted him enough to go to a four- and five-wide formation again. For the most part, he abandoned the running game and put the outcome in Smith's hands.

Smith's decisions on the field, resulting in an incredible career touchdown-to-interception ratio of 54–13, usually had been flawless, and it became obvious the coach *trusted* his quarterback as much as he ever trusted a quarterback.

"*Trust* is a strong word, and I've always thought I could trust Troy Smith with my life," Tressel said.

So he had no problem trusting him with the outcome of a football game.

Following his 29-of-41 day for 316 yards and four touchdowns—all records for a Buckeyes quarterback against Michigan—it became apparent that Smith had wrapped up the Heisman. Even Tressel, who rarely speaks on such matters, said so moments after the game.

"I would think that he clinched the Heisman," Tressel said. "I don't think there would be any question about that."

Throughout the 2006 season, Smith, once outspoken and boastful, even started talking like Tressel, in measured tones centered on content of "team first, me second." As the winning streak mounted, he deflected credit as if he wore a mirror on the outside of his uniform.

For example: "It's not that I am 3–0 against Michigan. It's not about me beating Michigan. It's the team that lined up and took the field every year I got to start against Michigan. They are also 3–0."

Two scenes illustrate how close the coach and quarterback became. When Smith was introduced before the Michigan game, he ran into the arms of Tressel at the middle of the field, and the two bear-hugged. When he thanked his coach while giving his Heisman acceptance speech three weeks later, Tressel had tears in his eyes for the first time publicly as the Buckeyes boss.

"The guy is out there [on the field] when it is 80 degrees, in a white shirt, tie up to his neck, and a sweater vest—and he's not even sweating," Smith said. "So if you can get into a situation where you can shake and rattle him, you've done *something*."

Smith, despite the heartbreaking loss to Florida in his final game, described his transformation during his five years at Ohio State this way: "It is more about my life than football," he said. "I got there as a boy and left there as a man. There are plenty of reasons, but the biggest reason? Coach Tressel."

chapter 10

Fiesta Time, Title Time

Jim Tressel celebrates on the podium after Ohio State beat Miami 31–24 in double overtime in the Fiesta Bowl on January 3, 2003.

It went down as one of the greatest games in college football history. Huge underdogs entering the 2003 Fiesta Bowl against top-ranked Miami, Tressel's second Ohio State team stunned the nation that night in Tempe, Arizona, to bring home the school's first national championship in more than three decades. The Buckeyes became the first team in history to win 14 games in one season.

Thirty-four years.

Thirty-four *long* years.

A college football power with the rich tradition and history of Ohio State should never have to wait 34 years between national championships.

But that was the period from the season the Super Sophomores, led by Rex Kern and Jack Tatum, gave Woody Hayes his final title in 1968 to the 2002 Buckeyes team that persevered, scratched, and clawed—winning six games by a touchdown or less—its way to a championship.

Jim Tressel's second team at Ohio State wasn't nearly as dominating as many talent-laden Buckeyes teams that didn't win national championships. But they saved their best effort for the final victory, a 31–24 double-overtime thriller over heavily favored and top-ranked Miami on January 3, 2003, in the Fiesta Bowl.

"We won the championship that night," All-American safety Mike Doss said. "But the whole thing started in the second half of the Outback Bowl the year before. We came back from 28–0 down [to South Carolina], still lost, and said we would never feel that way again."

And they didn't.

Not that anyone but the Buckeyes themselves expected them to shock Miami that night in the desert—least of all the top-ranked Hurricanes, riding a 34-game winning streak and aiming at their second consecutive title while entering the game as a 12-point favorite.

"The week before the Fiesta Bowl, you would have thought Miami was out there just for the joy of it," linebacker Cie Grant said. "It was a given that they would be crowned national champions again, but we didn't go out there to roll over. We practiced like we knew we had to dominate the game. We practiced all week at game speed. And we knew that Miami did not really know how good our defense was."

Punter Andy Groom, whose powerful leg kicked the Buckeyes out of danger throughout the season, said one of the best parts of the season was the week leading up to the game. During the previous two Outback Bowls, each resulting in losses to South

Carolina, the team was fragmented and sometimes distracted. But just like throughout the entire 2002 season, the Buckeyes were focused and in harmony while preparing for the school's first shot at a national championship in 23 seasons.

"They had a hospitality room where we could all come together and relax and play a number of different games," Groom said. "I can still see [defensive end] Darrion Scott sitting there with his shirt off, playing cards. Or [defensive tackle] Kenny Peterson talking junk all the way to the championship game of pool. Those are the times I will miss the most.

"I can honestly say that the one thing that this team possessed was that everyone cared for each other and loved one another. I would go to bat for anyone on that team."

At the team's final practice, former quarterback Mike Tomczak told them, "I have never been this excited and pumped up since I played at Ohio State. I want each one of you to go back to the hotel tonight and write this down: '2002 national champions.' Because if you don't write down your goals, they won't come true."

Most every Buckeye did just that. Some even wrote it and stuck the paper inside their helmets before the game.

Minutes before they exited the locker room, Tressel told his team: "Seize this opportunity! If you are a junior, sophomore, or freshman, don't think you'll ever get here again and have another chance. This is your chance! Seize it! It has been 34 years since Ohio State last won a national championship. Know that you are playing for all of Ohio State's fans, alumni, and former players. Now go do it!"

Peterson remembers the approach to that game very well.

"We were not being coached to come from behind that night," he said. "We were being coached to smack them in the mouth."

Tressel recently recalled the start of the game.

"Our first two plays, we have 12 guys on the field on one because [Chris] Gamble wanted to start both ways. On the second play, our running back lined up on the wrong side and we didn't have a guy to hand the ball to," he recalled. "We were nervous and hyped, but we settled down.

"That team fought from beginning to end. And in the end, they had what it took to be champions."

Sea of Scarlet

Amazingly, Sun Devil Stadium appeared to be just another day on the banks of the Olentangy—it was filled with Ohio State fans, who made up more than 90 percent of the 77,502 in attendance.

"When we went out for warm-ups that night, we knew it would be a home game," Kenny Peterson said. "We were thousands of miles from home, but we felt we were at home."

"As I think back to that magical night," Andy Groom recalled, "everything about the game was breathtaking. Seeing the sea of scarlet in the Fiesta Bowl was a sight for sore eyes."

The Plan

The game plan illustrated Tressel's excellent ability to X-and-O with the best of them. He employed quarterback Craig Krenzel, who had rushed for only 368 yards during the season, almost as a third running back.

While tailback Maurice Clarett gained only 47 yards rushing, Krenzel took the snap and powered off guard and tackle time and again, totaling 81 yards and two touchdowns on 19 carries.

"That's still one of the great trivia questions: 'Who was the leading rusher in that game?'" Tressel said four years later. "It was Craig Krenzel, our quarterback."

While preparing for the game, Tressel and his offensive assistants had noticed that Miami played so much man coverage on defense, its linebackers had trouble staying in position to defend a running game that featured the quarterback.

On the other side of the ball, Miami's offensive line had trouble blocking the Buckeyes' quicker defensive front. Ohio State sacked Miami quarterback Ken Dorsey four times and pressured him on several other passing attempts.

The other key: Miami committed five turnovers to the Buckeyes' two.

The final numbers that counted: the 2002 Buckeyes became the only team in major college history to finish a season 14–0.

The Interference Call

Ever since the game ended, Miami fans and players as well as much of the national media have cited the Hurricanes were robbed of the title by an official's call. Furthermore, national television pundits have also continued to refer to the call as either "terrible, unjust, awful,"—pick an adjective—when either the game or the Buckeyes' national title is mentioned all these years later.

Let's replay the situation: Miami had a 24–17 lead in the first overtime when the Buckeyes faced a fourth-and-goal from the Hurricanes' 5-yard line. As the offense huddled around Tressel on the sideline, Krenzel suggested a "fade-stop" route by receiver Chris Gamble. The play would be called in a five-wide formation in order to spread out Miami's defense and guarantee man coverage.

Gamble would be covered by freshman cornerback Glenn Sharpe.

As Gamble stepped into the end zone, Sharpe immediately made contact, and the two players became entangled. As Krenzel released the pass, the two then separated for an instant. As the ball arrived, Sharpe wrapped up Gamble again and the pass fell incomplete.

While Gamble protested, believing he was interfered with, Miami players and coaches stormed the field, believing the game was over. The line judge of the Big 12 officiating crew closest to the play signaled incomplete. Field judge Terry Porter grabbed for his flag, hesitated, and then finally flung it to the turf. He then made the hand gesture for defensive holding as fireworks prematurely exploded over Sun Devil Stadium.

"I was looking all over for the flag," Tressel said, "and then it sailed out there and I said, 'Hallelujah.' "

"I was sitting on the bench, head down, practically in tears," Ohio State cornerback Dustin Fox recalled. "Miami rushed the field. Then I saw the scoreboard read, 'Marker Down. Marker Down.' "

"I fell to my knees," running back Lydell Ross said. "Then I heard the [PA] announcer say, 'Flag on the field.' "

Miami's Glenn Sharpe interferes with OSU's Chris Gamble in the final seconds of the 2003 Fiesta Bowl, setting up the Buckeyes' double-overtime victory.

As the replay was showed to the nation on the ABC broadcast, analyst Dan Fouts, calling the game with play-by-play legend Keith Jackson, shouted, "That's a terrible call…that's a terrible call."

Fouts's fervent protests and the ABC replay helped form much of the nation's opinion. There is more to the story, however.

What the sideline replay showed was the play from the point which Krenzel released the ball. It never showed the initial contact between Gamble and Sharpe. Also, Miami secondary coach Mark Stoops, the brother of Oklahoma head coach Bob Stoops and Arizona head coach Mike Stoops, gave Sharpe these final instructions during the Ohio State timeout before the play: "Get up in his face! Get into his grill! They won't call you for anything on the final play of the game!"

He couldn't have been more wrong.

Porter explained his call this way: "I replayed it in my mind. I wanted to make double-sure it was the right call. I saw the guy holding the guy prior to the ball being put in the air. He was still holding him, pulling him down while the ball was in the air. I gave the signal for holding. Then I realized it should be pass interference because the ball was in the air."

Gamble agreed, "He was all up in my shoulder pads, in my helmet. Yeah, it was interference."

Actually, Porter's original thought of calling holding on the play would have been the proper call since Sharpe did hold Gamble as he released from the line of scrimmage. Furthermore, the penalty yardage—half the distance to the goal and an automatic first down—would have been the same as with pass interference.

Porter's biggest mistake was not his call—it was his delay in making the call in the first place. It gave the impression that he was not sure of his conviction of seeing the penalty.

Four years later, Porter said the call comes up during conversation constantly.

"I did the right thing," he said. "I got it right. What if I had not made that call? Then Ohio State would have been cheated."

Here's another part of the story that the critics don't acknowledge, or even remember for the most part. The Big 12 officiating crew missed a crucial call in the final minutes of the fourth quarter, which greatly benefited Miami.

On a third-and-long, Gamble ran a sideline pattern near the Ohio State bench. He first was grabbed and then held but broke free and caught Krenzel's pass before he rolled out of bounds. There was no holding call. And to top that, the officials ruled the pass was incomplete. Remember, the game was played before the NCAA implemented instant replay.

Thus, the Buckeyes had to punt, leading to Miami's tying field goal on the final play of regulation.

"They got some calls, and we got some calls," Gamble said. "I think things evened out."

Cie Can Carry a Tune

As the 2002 championship season was about to begin in August, Cie Grant was running late one night for one of the seniors' weekly presentations. It is a ritual that Tressel started soon after he was hired in order for players to get to know their teammates better.

"Late in the summer, I had missed one of the seniors' presentations in front of the team," he explained. "The seniors give reports on themselves to the entire team, and I had missed Mike Collins's report. Coach Tressel asked, 'How are we going to punish you? I know, you have to sing "Carmen Ohio" in front of the team.'

"I had sang in the church choir a little, so I sang 'Carmen Ohio' in front of the team that night—and I ended up singing it each Friday night in front of the team before our next game."

Cie Grant pressures Miami quarterback Ken Dorsey to help seal the Buckeyes' 2003 Fiesta Bowl win.

On the bus ride over to the national championship celebration in Ohio Stadium two weeks following the Fiesta Bowl, a few assistant coaches asked Cie to sing the alma mater one more time—this time during the ceremony.

"I said, 'My last time singing in front of anybody was the night before the Miami game,'" Grant said. "Then Craig Krenzel came up and asked me again. He wanted to get it on tape. I really didn't want to do it."

At the conclusion of the celebration, attended by more than 55,000 fans in freezing weather, athletics director Andy Geiger called Grant to the microphone.

"I told the other seniors, 'We've always had each other's backs, so you've got my back today. Don't let me down,'" Cie said. "It was cold and I hadn't warmed up my voice yet, but the rest is history. I am very glad I did it."

Grant had ended the championship game by pressuring Miami quarterback Ken Dorsey, forcing his errant pass on the game's final play. And then he brought the house down with his voice.

It was January 18, 2003, two years to the day Tressel was named Ohio State's 22nd head football coach.

And it was a perfect ending to a perfect season.

chapter 11

"The School Up North"

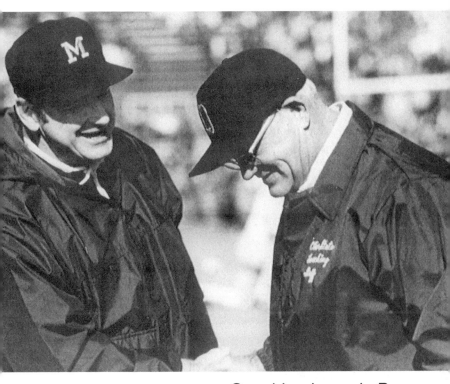

*Coaching legends Bo
Schembechler and
Woody Hayes share a
laugh prior to one of
their meetings during
the 10-Year War.*

A rivalry unlike any other, Ohio State–Michigan has it all. More than 100 years of head-to-head battles have produced some of the more memorable games in college football history.

The Ohio State University Monthly magazine called it "the biggest game of all Ohio State athletics to date," and the subsequent Buckeyes victory resulted in "the biggest celebration Columbus has ever seen."

Sound like the Buckeyes' 1975 victory over Michigan?

Or the 2002 win that sent them to the Fiesta Bowl to play for the national championship in Jim Tressel's second season?

Or the 2006 win over the Wolverines in the gigantic showdown of the nation's top two ranked and undefeated teams?

Try October 25, 1919, when the Chic Harley–led Buckeyes defeated Michigan 13–3 for the school's first-ever victory in a series that began in 1897. Understand that our predecessors didn't care much for the school up north, either, dating back as far as the turn of the century.

Throughout the 100-plus years of its existence, Ohio State–Michigan has been called the Greatest Rivalry in Sports.

Sports fans on the East Coast will contend that title belongs to the Yankees–Red Sox. That's baseball, for gosh sakes. Fans in the South may say it is Auburn-Alabama. That consumes only one state. How about Army-Navy? Great tradition, but the service academies have long ago dropped from the hierarchy of college football.

Ohio State–Michigan has captivated not only fans from both states, but football fans across the world simply because it possesses all the ingredients: tradition, excellence, longevity, and hatred (or at least a strong dislike). And more often than not, it matters to the college football picture as a whole.

Usually, it is played for the Big Ten championship. Sometimes, one team or the other is vying for a national championship.

To put it simply, after all the other kids are disposed of in violent fashion, it's as if the two bullies of the Big Ten neighborhood are meeting in the backyard to determine who will become king of the hill.

The rivalry created the gold pants club for the Buckeyes and earned Michigan players such as Tom Harmon, Desmond Howard, and Charles Woodson their Heisman Trophies. It gave Bo Schembechler his greatest career victory—a 24–12 upset of his mentor Woody Hayes in their first meeting in 1969—and his biggest disappointment, the 10–10 tie in 1973 after which the Big Ten voted to send Ohio State, not Michigan, to the Rose Bowl.

It brought us the legendary "Snow Bowl" of 1950 and made Buckeyes kicker Tom Klaban famous and Michigan kicker Mike Lantry, who missed game-winning field goals in 1973 and '74, infamous. It made Michigan tailback Tshimanga Biakabutuka rich and Eddie George heartbroken. It made heroes out of forgotten players and goats out of star players. In this rivalry, Ohio State produced its most-famous goal-line stand (1974), 99½-yard drives (1954 and 2004), and two-point conversion attempt (1968) in school history.

And it made John Cooper as popular in the state of Michigan as a good set of snow tires.

The standing date every year comes on a usually cold Saturday in late November. For the other 364 days of the year, the past game is discussed while the next one is anticipated.

"How did our great rivalry get started?" Hayes once asked rhetorically. "The real fight started back in 1836 when Andrew Jackson, that wily old cuss, took Toledo away from that state up north and gave it to us."

True story. Ohio-Michigan sparks first flew over Toledo!

And it carried over to the football field in 1897, when Michigan's premier university and Ohio's flagship university first competed in what was a relatively new sporting event.

The two teams met 15 times before Ohio State ever won a game—the first being that 13–3 win in Ann Arbor in 1919. In fact, Michigan so heavily dominated the series for the first half century that Ohio State won only 12 of the first 48 games through 1951.

Hayes and his emphasis on preparing for Michigan hating Michigan, and, especially, beating Michigan changed all that.

From 1951 through 2006, the Buckeyes held a 28–26–2 edge in the series, despite Cooper's failures.

Hayes hated to even say the M-word, although he slipped and did a few times, according to his players and assistants. To this day, some of his players, such as Rex Kern, won't say it.

"I got a speeding ticket once in that state up north," Kern said recently. "As I tried to talk my way out of it, and realizing I couldn't,

I told the officer, 'Now I understand why my football coach didn't care much for this state!'"

And about that old legend about Woody not wanting to buy gas in the state up north...that's true, too.

When he and assistant Ed Ferkany were returning to Ohio from a recruiting trip in 1972, they were just a few miles north of the border when Ferkany noticed the gas gauge was near empty.

"I had just been hired and didn't know Woody that well yet," said Ferkany, who now lives in Naples, Florida. "I had been there only three or four weeks. It was about 9:30 or 10:00 that night in February, and it was snowing. We had a rental car with no radio. When we left Detroit, I looked at the gas gauge, and it was just below the one-eighth mark. Then we get down to I-75 and the needle is on the top side of empty.

"I said, 'Coach, we had better pull over and get some gas.'

"'No, no, keep going,' he said.

"The gauge kept getting lower and lower, and finally I said, 'Coach, we have to get some gas!'"

Finally, Woody blew up and started into a tirade: "No, goddammit! We do not pull over and fill up! And I'll tell you exactly why we don't. I won't buy one goddamn drop of gas in this state. I will push this goddamn car to the Ohio line before I give this state a dime of my money! The tax on the gas we pay for will just wind up supporting that football team up here, and that is not going to happen!"

Ferkany, fearing he soon would be pushing a rental car across the state line on a cold winter night, continued driving. He reached Ohio and pulled into the first gas station he saw.

"We barely made it," he said. "There couldn't have been a few drops in that tank. Over the years, that story has grown and has been twisted so much. I even read once that we had to push the car across the state line. That never happened. But it is true that Woody did not want to ever buy gas in the state of Michigan. I was a witness to it."

It was no secret that Woody didn't care for the whole damn state of Michigan. He didn't like the universities, including Michigan State, and sometimes, he even made light of his distaste.

For example, senior center Jim Conroy, a Phi Beta Kappa, blew out his knee the week before the Michigan game in 1970.

"The old man came in to see me, and I was all packed in ice and pretty drugged up from whatever Dr. [Bob] Murphy gave me," Conroy remembered.

"I understand you want to go to law school?" Woody asked.

"Yes, sir," Conroy replied.

"I'll help you get into any law school you want," the coach said. "Just let me know."

As he walked away, Hayes said, "Yep, any one of them...except one."

"He looked back at me and smiled," Conroy said. "I knew which school he meant, without him saying it."

Conroy received his law degree in 1974 from Ohio State.

"How did Woody feel about Michigan?" Randy Gradishar asked. "Let me illustrate [his feelings] with one story. One time we were at the Quarterback Club and the team was being introduced. A freshman had on a blue tie. Woody took one look at that blue tie and walked over and whipped it off that freshman. The audience went wild.

"We learned quickly that tradition dictated we wear ties of scarlet and gray, but we didn't know much about fashion."

A team's success and legacy is decided in the rivalry. Ohio State's history is littered with teams that lost a game or two and would otherwise be declared one of the finest in school history. But if one of those losses came to Michigan, they became forgotten teams.

"We've had 11–1 and 10–1 football teams that lost to Michigan and they're not even mentioned in the second breath," Bruce said. "If you don't win the Ohio State–Michigan game, you have a big problem."

The Intensity

Other schools in other rivalries contend the intensity level is just as high, but Buckeyes and Wolverines would doubt that.

There were times in Ann Arbor that Hayes actually wanted his players to challenge Michigan to a pregame fight, right in the tunnel the teams shared leading out to the East sideline.

Before the '75 game, which Ohio State entered undefeated and ranked number one, he told his team, "If those sons a bitches want to fight, get ready because we'll fight 'em right outside these doors."

He then ordered all of his second-team players to the front so they would come out first. Woody was thinking ahead, not wanting any of his starters either injured or kicked out of the game for participating in a pregame mêelée.

"Let me tell you," Bruce said, "there is nothing—and I mean *nothing!*—as intense as Ohio State–Michigan."

Clark Backus, a linebacker (1981–1983), was a teacher at West Point in 1998 when he met Army's linebackers coach, who just happened to be a former Wolverine.

"I had become a faculty mentor to the Army linebackers," Backus said. "I was looking through the press guide one day, and I saw that the outside linebackers coach was from Michigan. He played in the '90s, and I thought I would say hello and introduce myself to him. One day I hear my name being called, and it is this coach. The first thing he asks me is, 'How many pairs of gold pants do you have?'

"I told him I had two," Backus said.

As the two talked, Backus had a burning question. Finally, he asked the assistant coach, "This isn't to demean the Army-Navy game in any way, but you are an ex-Michigan player now coaching in this rivalry, so which one is the best?"

The former Michigan player didn't say a word for a moment. He just shook his head and smiled, paused, and then said quietly, "This one just doesn't compare."

"I knew immediately what he meant," Backus said. "There is no comparison to Ohio State–Michigan."

The intensity started with the attitude from the Ohio State coaches immediately following the previous game. Under Hayes and Bruce, every Buckeye knew it was a week not to be taken lightly in any way, on any day.

"You learned very quickly playing under Coach Hayes that beating Michigan was top priority," said receiver Doug Donley (1977–1980). "Every practice during the season was intense, but practices during Michigan week were especially gut-wrenching. Any fumble, interception, or missed assignment caused an eruption of large magnitude. Players and coaches were on pins and needles all week. You didn't talk or laugh during the week. It was war."

The Myth of the Two-Point Conversion

There probably is no play in Ohio State football history that has turned from fact into fiction like the famous two-point-conversion attempt near the end of the 1968 Michigan game.

Like the running-out-of-gas story, this one has been told and retold so many times that many inaccurate versions exist. But here's what really happened:

With undefeated and number one–ranked Ohio State leading 44–14, the Big Ten championship and Rose Bowl berth were secured. Most of the starters were on the sideline as the Buckeyes drove deep into Michigan territory and the clock ticked to under two minutes remaining. Ohio State faced a fourth-and-goal at the Michigan 2-yard line. Bill Long was in at quarterback, and Paul Huff was at fullback.

"I tapped Woody on the shoulder, and I asked, 'Coach, do you want that touchdown?'" Jim Otis recalled.

"He just said, 'Go in and get it! And you call the play!'

"So I went in and I looked around. The best lineman in the huddle was Dave Cheney at left tackle. I looked at Dave and said, 'Now, Woody wants this touchdown, and he wants it over you!' I got the touchdown over Dave, and the old stadium was rocking like it never rocked before."

It was Otis's fourth touchdown of the day and 17th of the season.

At that point it was 50–14 with only 1:23 remaining, but there was a subsequent confusion in the huddle following the touchdown.

"Here's why there was confusion," said Long. "Our long-snapper had been hurt earlier in the game, and he wasn't in there.

So we lined up and I called, '27 Pass,' which was designed for the halfback. I remember seeing the play, but nobody was open. I threw it into coverage, and it was incomplete."

Cheney recalled it this way: "The truth is that Jim Roman was our kicker, but he had to go in at center, so we didn't have a kicker in the game."

"Dave is right," Long said. "That is why we didn't have a kicker in there. Roman went to fill in for the center."

Ohio State's official play-by-play sheet from that two-point-conversion play reads: "Long's pass intended for Pollitt incomplete, too long."

What nobody can figure out is why Bill Pollitt, a linebacker, would have been the intended receiver on the play.

"Well, I did play on special teams, but I don't remember being in on that play," Pollitt said. "I remember the game, the touchdown, but don't remember that two-point conversion."

"He had to be lined up at tight end," Long said. "But I don't remember it, or remember throwing it to him. I think I threw it away, and he must have been the closest one to it. I just know that everybody was covered."

This is the part that was never forgotten and has become a legendary quote from Hayes. When asked by a reporter after the game why he attempted to go for two points, Woody said, "Because they wouldn't let me go for three!"

"That's how bad he wanted to beat them," tight end Jan White said. "He was upset when we didn't get those points."

Which is true. He was upset. But the truth is, unlike the legend, Woody never preplanned to go for two in this case. It only happened because the right personnel was not on the field.

And the myth has developed and been believed by many, even those who were there that day; not only had the coach ordered it, but the two-point conversion was *successful*. Even many sportswriters and resources over the years have been mistaken when referring to the two-point attempt.

"I could have sworn that we made that two-point conversion and that Woody decided to go for two," said Bruce, an assistant coach who was in the press box in 1968. "I know I was upstairs, and I remember screaming into my headset, 'No! No! Don't go for two!'

"And that came back to haunt us the next year because Bo came in there as the new coach and used that for a whole year to fire them up."

Cheney added, "That thing has gotten so blown out of proportion over the years, the play and everything else about it, I sometimes even wonder if Woody ever said that line: 'Because they wouldn't let me go for three.'"

Michigan Did Those Things, Too

Michigan, already leading 55–6, kicked a late field goal to add insult to injury in the 1946 game at Ohio Stadium.

"I remember screaming at one of those Michigan players, 'What the hell is wrong with you?'" center/linebacker Howard Teifke said. "We didn't think they should be doing that just to beat us even worse."

The 10-Year War

Ohio State's failed two-point conversion and 36-point victory in 1968 set up the 10-Year War between Schembechler and Hayes. For starters, it helped get Michigan coach Bump Elliott fired.

But the seedlings for the Schembechler-Hayes battles were planted much earlier. Bo worked on Woody's staff for six seasons. They ate together, traveled together, watched film together, and mostly, fought together.

Bo was one of the few assistants to stand up to Woody mostly because he had the same temperament as his boss. He hated to lose either a game or an argument.

There was the time Bo threw a chair at Woody in 1961.

Eight years later, when his Wolverines upset Hayes's number one Buckeyes in Ann Arbor in Bo's first season as UM head coach, it served as the shot heard 'round the college football world. And war was declared by both sides.

At the end, thanks to three consecutive Michigan victories, from 1976 to 1978, Bo stood victorious with a 5–4–1 advantage over his mentor. He always said, however, that the war ended prematurely with Hayes's subsequent firing.

"I wish we could have gone on competing against each other forever," Bo once said.

Broken Hearts, Broken Camera

One huge advantage Bo had was that he knew Woody better than Woody knew himself.

He knew the Ohio State coach's tendencies in certain situations, and he knew how he coached. And that, more than anything, led to the toughest loss of Woody's career simply because the 1969 team was seemingly invincible, riding a 22-game winning streak when it headed to Ann Arbor.

Following the 24–12 loss, Woody always told his protégé, "You'll never win a bigger game than that," to which Bo would reply, "You're right!"

"It was just an ugly day and, without question, the worst loss I ever experienced," Rex Kern said. "When did I get over it? I haven't."

During the game, ABC broke in a new camera technique—a roving cameraman on the sideline. That didn't sit too well with Woody as the Wolverines pulled away in the second half.

"I was carrying the telephone for Woody and, deep into the second quarter as the game started to slip away from us, that cameraman was sneaking closer and closer to Woody," said Paul Caswell, a team manager that season. "He was supposed to stay outside of the bench lines, but he continued to get closer, probably because we were frustrated and losing.

"One time, Woody turned around and growled at us about it. He told us, 'If that guy gets any closer, you will be walking back to Columbus.' Well, we told the guy to stay away, and once as he was walking backward away from us, he fell ass-over-teakettle over the bench and the ABC camera got smashed. Later, ABC wanted Ohio State to pay for it, but there was nothing in the television contract back then that allowed him to get that close. That guy was really upset with us, but we didn't want to walk back from Ann Arbor."

Revenge Game

The Buckeyes spent the 1970 season staring at two numbers. They were stitched into the floor mats at the North Facility. They were painted on the walls of the locker room. They were written on meeting sheets and playbooks and menus. Just about everywhere.

"24–12."

The score of Michigan's monumental upset in Ann Arbor the year before. Hayes wanted no Buckeye to forget.

The week of the 1970 game, Woody pulled one of his often-used motivational ploys. He had noticed a few players on the sideline of practice shooting the breeze and not paying attention, and he started screaming at Bruce.

"Earle, they won't play for me! They won't play for me!" he screamed. "My God, it's Michigan week, and they won't play for me!"

"Now, I think that is the only time I heard him say the M-word," Kern recalled. "He always used the other term for them, but he said it that time. John Hicks was our right tackle, and he had never seen Woody like this. Tommy DeLeone, our center, screamed, 'Come on, Rex, get us ready! We'll play for him! We'll play for him!'

"It was so effective."

A record crowd of 87,331 filled Ohio Stadium for the game, which the Buckeyes won 20–9.

"It was probably one of the most raucous crowds to ever be at an Ohio State game," linebacker Stan White recalled. "We had seen that score, 24–12, for the next 12 months after the [1969] game. It was on the rugs at the facility. It was on everyone's mind. It was revenge time.

"I intercepted a pass late in the game and returned it to the 9-yard line. I played for 21 years, including 13 in pro football, and you know what? On that interception, it was the only time I ever heard the crowd late in the game. As I jumped to catch the ball, I was struck by the booming explosion of the crowd. The moment is seared in my memory, and it is as real today as it was all those years ago."

Motivational Speeches

Before the 1972 game, Woody invited Jim Stillwagon back to address the team. As Stillwagon tried to talk, the head coach continued to interrupt him with his own words...and a punch to the stomach for emphasis.

"Yes, sir, yes, sir, you're doing great Jim, but tell them how it really f*cking was," Hayes said, pumping his fist into Stillwagon's midsection. "Tell them it's like a war."

Then came another punch.

"You gotta beat those sons a bitches."

Another punch.

"Tell 'em, tell 'em, Jim."

Another punch.

It was difficult for the former All-American nose guard to speak a word since he was having the wind pummeled from his gut.

The Buckeyes loved the display and turned it into a 14–11 win behind two of the greatest goal-line stands in school history, when Michigan quarterback Dennis Franklin was stopped twice on fourth downs—at the OSU 2-yard line in the first half and inches from the goal line in the second half.

Fit to Be Tied

One of the true classics of the series was played in 1973, when the Buckeyes went to Ann Arbor ranked number one again. Their closest games that season were two 24-point victories. They entered the game averaging 40.1 points per game and allowing only 3.7. In fact, the defense had recorded four shutouts and let opponents score a touchdown in only three games.

In other words, this Buckeyes team was on its way to becoming not only the greatest in Ohio State history but also one of the greatest teams in college football history. The Wolverines were ranked number four and were 10–0.

The hype for the game was unparalleled in the history of the series.

"We had beaten Iowa pretty good the week before [55–13], and a lot of the starters didn't play in the second half, which was the norm that season," quarterback Cornelius Greene recalled. "That just made the wait seem longer. It was like time stood still that week. Saturday took forever to get here."

"George Hasenohrl had to lead interference for all of us to get from the bus to the locker room," Dan Cutillo said. "Michigan fans were throwing rocks through the locker room windows. Running onto the field, John Hicks reaches up and tears the 'M Club Supports Wolverines' football banner. Michigan fans were going nuts, and they were so close to our sideline. My eyes were big as saucers."

To this day, Hicks denies tearing down the banner, but whoever did it outraged Michigan fans and players.

"I was unjustly accused," Hicks said. "That got torn down when we were coming out, but I wasn't the one who did it. But nobody wants to claim it, so they just blame it on me."

On the opening kickoff, kicker Tom Skladany sustained a broken leg and dislocated ankle when trying to make the tackle.

"It was a gruesome injury," Skladany recalled. "I remember Doctor Bob [Murphy] told me not to look."

When Hayes asked the doctors about Skladany's condition, they said there was no way he could kick. "Well, at least tape him up so we can use him for punting," the coach snorted.

Ohio State jumped to a 10–0 halftime lead and had shut down Michigan's option offense. Late in the third quarter, Woody gambled on a fourth-and-two at UM's 42, and when Greene was stopped short, the momentum changed.

Michigan quarterback Dennis Franklin started gaining yards on the option and hitting big passes when he needed them. After a Mike Lantry field goal, Franklin ran the option 10 yards for the tying touchdown.

On UM's next possession, Franklin landed awkwardly on his right shoulder and broke his collarbone after throwing an incomplete pass.

Meanwhile, on the other side, Greene was playing with an injured thumb, which prevented Woody from calling any passing plays. For example, on third-and-six at Michigan's 38-yard line, which represented Ohio State's last good chance to win the game, he ran Archie Griffin off tackle. The Wolverines had nine men near the line of scrimmage and made the tackle after a three-yard gain.

"The thing is, we had practiced all of this option stuff to get wide on them and we even had an option pass from Corny to [wingback Brian] Baschnagel that would have worked for a touchdown, but Woody wouldn't call it," said Ed Ferkany, an OSU assistant from 1972 to 1973. "Bo knew we were going to run right between the tackles, and we did. There is no doubt in my mind that was one of the greatest teams of all time. All we had to do was score once more."

With little more than one minute remaining, Woody replaced Greene with Greg Hare, the better passer, but his first pass was intercepted. That led to Michigan's Lantry missing a 44-yard field goal with 24 seconds remaining. It was wide left.

"We had a near mutiny after that game," Ferkany said. "Woody was so stubborn sometimes."

Woody's conservative play calling in the Michigan games, and the fact that Schembechler realized his rival would be conservative, frustrated all of his assistant coaches.

It also circumvented all the extra work the Buckeyes put in to prepare for Michigan.

"We would practice many times twice a week for the Michigan game, up to six or seven weeks earlier," Baschnagel said. "That taught me how important it was."

The game ended 10–10, and Michigan fans celebrated, thinking their team was headed to Pasadena. The Big Ten had recently abolished its "no repeat" rule concerning the Rose Bowl, and OSU had been to Pasadena the year before. So the consensus feeling was that the Wolverines would be headed west.

"It was not a loss," Baschnagel said, "although it did feel that way after the game."

Michigan's band even played "California Dreamin'" as both teams left the field.

"We outplayed them in the second half," Schembechler crowed.

With everything being equal, everyone, even Woody, assumed the Wolverines would be playing in the Rose Bowl.

By the next morning, Woody's assistants were still furious with him for his conservative play calling. In fact, they had planned to boycott the coaches' meeting when the call came in: Ohio State, not Michigan, would represent the Big Ten in the Rose Bowl, according to a 6–4 vote of the conference's athletics directors. Many said that Franklin's injury affected their vote. The Big Ten had been losing to the Pac-10 with regularity, and the athletics directors wanted the best chance to win the Rose Bowl, so they chose the Buckeyes.

Schembechler was outraged.

"I am very bitter," he said. "It is tragic for Big Ten football. This is the darkest day of my athletic career."

To this day, Wolverines everywhere are bitter. Bo never forgave those involved in the decision and went to his grave bitter. He even spoke about it publicly just four days before he died.

"We got *screwed*," he said. "And I mean that as it sounds. It was a terrible decision. I always believed that—and I always will."

Ohio State went on to clobber USC 42–21 in the Rose Bowl to finish 10–0–1 and probably was the best team in the country that season, finishing number two in one poll and number three in the other.

But in the end, the tie and the ensuing controversy only intensified the rivalry.

Klaban's Leg Saves the Day

The Buckeyes beat the Wolverines in 1974 without scoring a touchdown, thanks to Tom Klaban's four field goals that resulted in a 12–10 win.

Listen to what Woody said before that game: "By comparison, the World Series and the Super Bowl don't compare to our rivalry."

It was the first time the Buckeyes were held without a touchdown in eight years.

Again, Lantry missed a field goal that would have won the game, a 33-yard attempt with only 18 seconds remaining.

"Up until the Michigan game, we had never had an outcome riding on the kicking game," Baschnagel said. "But Tom came through."

Klaban was Ohio State's first soccer-style kicker, and his success in that victory over Michigan helped convince Hayes that soccer-style kickers were a sign of the future.

Corny's Prayer Is Answered

By the time the 1975 game arrived, it marked the third time in four trips to Ann Arbor that Ohio State arrived as the nation's number one–ranked team. They had lost in '69 and tied in '73.

As the '75 game progressed, it appeared the Buckeyes would suffer yet another heartbreaking loss at Michigan Stadium. At that point, they had not won there in eight years.

Michigan led 14–7 late in the game, and Ohio State faced a third-and-12 at its own 18-yard line.

"I got the group together and said, 'This prayer is for the believers,' and we got our hands together and prayed," quarterback Cornelius Greene said. "I didn't do it for us to win the ballgame. I did it to bring us back together as a unit. Then I called '84 Barb,' a play that called for a receiver wide right to run a streak pattern and for Brian [Baschnagel] to run an out pattern underneath."

The play was executed perfectly, as Baschnagel caught Greene's pass along the right sideline for the first down.

"Corny just looked at us in the huddle and said, 'Hold hands, and we are going to say a prayer.' It was the first time he had done that," Baschnagel said. "Now, I don't think the Lord really cares who wins a football game, but it worked—he threw long to me along the sideline for the first down."

The Buckeyes eventually converted that possession into a touchdown to tie the game 14–14. Moments later, Ray Griffin intercepted Michigan quarterback Rick Leach and returned it to the 3-yard line. Fullback Pete Johnson scored again, his third touchdown of the day, to give the Buckeyes a stirring 21–14 victory.

"That's the greatest comeback game I've ever coached," Hayes said.

The Broadnax Block

Vaughn Broadnax was a hulk of a fullback in the mode of many who played the position before him, but he did not get the opportunity for many carries over the course of his career, from 1980 to 1983. What he is known for, however, is throwing one of the greatest blocks in school history.

Trailing Michigan 9–7 late in the 1981 game at Ann Arbor, the Buckeyes faced a third-and-goal and, well, let's let Broadnax tell the rest of the story:

"In the huddle, Art [Schlichter] called 'Play Pass 28.' The play is designed to attack the outside and force the defense to either stop the run or defend the pass. Michigan chose to defend the pass."

Just when it looked as if Schlichter was surrounded by three would-be tacklers, Broadnax cleared the way.

"I was blocking Carlton Rose. I just held my block, and Carlton went down and tripped up the other two defenders, allowing Art to scamper into the end zone," Broadnax recalled. "At that time, I didn't realize the impact of the play, but I do all of these years later."

Broadnax's block of three Wolverines led to a 14–9 win that gave the Buckeyes a tri–Big Ten championship.

By the way, it's easy to say that Broadnax has fond feelings for his days as a Buckeye: he named his daughter Carmen, after Ohio State's alma mater.

Moments following that game, guard Scott Zalenski experienced one of the best moments he ever experienced with his father, Ted, a Penn State graduate who years earlier wanted his son to become a Nittany Lion.

Zalenski, from Pittsburgh, said, "As fabulous as the game was for the team and all of our fans, I remember the game for another, more personal reason as well. After we sang 'Across the Field' in the locker room after the game, my dad found his way in, came up to me, and with the firmest handshake I ever felt, told me, 'I'm finally glad you went to Ohio State.'

"It felt so good to hear him say that, especially in the exhilaration of that moment, as we celebrated our big win. To be able to share that excitement with my dad, as he expressed his satisfaction with my choice of schools, put the finishing touches on one of my best days as a Buckeye."

Before Scott's senior year, 1984, his parents moved to Chagrin Falls, Ohio. Recently, Ted was diagnosed with cancer and received treatments at OSU's Arthur G. James Cancer Hospital.

"He has had excellent results, and it is rewarding to know that OSU played an integral part," Scott said. "Perhaps fate had a hand in all of this, and perhaps not. All I know for sure is that OSU has impacted my life and those I love in ways we could never have envisioned—and I'll always be proud to say that I'm a Buckeye."

Music of the Week

As an annual ritual, Ohio State coaches had Michigan's fight song piped into the Buckeyes locker room, as early as the postgame celebration following the previous game. Then it continued all week during practice leading up to the game.

"They always played that Michigan fight song all week, and we had to listen to that," kicker Bob Atha (1978–1981) said. "They used to play that fight song until it got obnoxious. We just hated it. It was terrible."

Another ploy used by Buckeyes coaches: a sign will be placed above the player's locker, stating what was certainly a contrived quote from a Michigan player or coach.

"I had one above my locker that had a picture of Bo," Clark Backus said. "It read: 'Clark Backus couldn't have played in the Mid-American Conference!' I still have that poster."

Bumper-Sticker Obscenity

This may sound like a fable. It isn't. It actually happened.

On October 18, 1970, an OSU student was driving to campus when he was pulled over by the Columbus police. His crime? His car was adorned with a bumper sticker that read "F*ck Michigan."

Except there was an actual letter in place of that asterisk, if you know what I mean.

Thomas Harrington was charged with public obscenity.

Judge James A. Pearson wrote in his ruling of the case: "We must consider the material as a whole. It is interpreted that this means to have sexual intercourse with the state of Michigan. This is absurd. Most of the people of Ohio would say that Mr. Harrington's bumper sticker has redeeming social value."

The case was dismissed.

It could be added that Woody himself probably had said those two words often, except for the fact that he considered *Michigan* a swear word and never uttered it in public.

By the Numbers

- In the first 15 games in the series, Michigan outscored Ohio State 369–21. The Wolverines won 13 of them, and two ended in ties.

Ohio State fans cheer on the Buckeyes during the epic 2006 battle with Michigan.

- Before Woody Hayes arrived in 1951, the Buckeyes had a 12–31–4 record against Michigan. Since, they are 28–26–2.
- Hayes was 16–11–1 against UM. Bruce was 5–4. Cooper was 2–10–1, and following the 2006 season, Tressel was 5–1 in his first six meetings.
- Michigan's three-year record from 1972 to 1974 was 30–2–1, with all three blemishes at the hands of the Buckeyes. The Wolverines did not play in a Rose Bowl in that period.

Ohio State's Top-10 Victories Over Michigan

1. 1919 (13–3)—The first one, after 15 failures, had to be the sweetest. And it came in Ann Arbor.
2. 1968 (50–14)—The game was significant on many levels. First and foremost, because it led to Ohio State's national championship. It also indirectly resulted in Michigan's hiring of Bo Schembechler, which only intensified the rivalry.
3. 2002 (14–9)—Capped a 13–0 season in Jim Tressel's second year at Ohio State, leading to an upset win over Miami in the Fiesta Bowl and the school's first consensus national championship in 34 seasons.
4. 1954 (21–7)—At the end of a season which saved Hayes's job, it led to the legend's first national championship. It included Ohio State's first legendary goal-line stand.
5. 1975 (21–14)—Down 14–7 in the final minutes, a group of seniors led by Cornelius Greene, Archie Griffin, and Brian Baschnagel were determined not to lose.
6. 1942 (21–7)—In Paul Brown's second season, this win led to Ohio State's first national championship.
7. 1970 (20–9)—The revenge game. Woody started preparing his team for this game the day after the '69 loss to Michigan.
8. 1979 (18–15)—In Earle Bruce's first season as head coach, a late blocked punt led to the victory in Ann Arbor and an 11–0 season.
9. 2006 (42–39)—The game was set up as number one versus number two, a real Game of the Century, and Ohio State's victory would rank much higher on this list if not for the subsequent upset loss to Florida in the national championship game.
10. 1987 (23–20)—Bruce's final game as head coach, the Buckeyes were heavy underdogs heading into the game. It would be Ohio State's last win in the rivalry for seven long years.

chapter 12

So Close, So Many Times

Joe Germaine and the 1998 Buckeyes, probably John Cooper's best team, stumbled against Michigan State and finished with a number two ranking.

Ohio State has won five consensus national championships and counts seven overall, but if not for an upset here or there, the Buckeyes could have become the number one dynasty in college football history. At least 10 more OSU teams came within a game of winning the big prize.

Perhaps no college football program has come as close to winning as many national championships as Ohio State.

The school's media relations department counts seven national titles in all (1942, 1954, 1957, 1961, 1968, 1970, and 2002).

However, the 1957 team was named champion by UPI and finished ranked number two to Auburn in the Associated Press poll. The '61 team, which finished number two to Alabama in both wire-service polls, was declared champion only by the Football Writers Association of America and did not play in the Rose Bowl.

The '70 team also falls into a strange category. A perfect 10–0 at the time, the team was declared national champion only by the National Football Foundation *before* the Rose Bowl. Then they were shocked 27–17 by Stanford in the game, thus finishing second in one major poll and fifth in another.

Many players on that team contend the game was lost during preparation when Woody Hayes overworked them and was faced with a near-mutiny.

"I think we were so happy to beat Michigan that year, and we had put everything into that game," said Dave Cheney, the left tackle who was a senior that season. "We wanted to have some fun in California, and we went out there more than two weeks before the game. But as we flew over the Rocky Mountains, we were all getting taped for practice."

Several seniors got together in Pasadena and wrote a statement to Hayes, detailing their unhappiness with his strict approach during the bowl trip.

"They weren't my words, but I wrote it out," Cheney said. "We wanted to be able to stay out a little later and sleep in a little later, and I remember [assistant coach] Lou McCullough stood up and said, 'Well, let's send them all home if that's the way it is going to be.' Another senior then said, 'Okay with us.'

"Woody then realized how serious this was and said, 'Now, let's talk about these things.'"

It didn't soothe any feelings. The Buckeyes, a huge favorite that day, took a 17–13 lead into the fourth quarter before Heisman Trophy–winner Jim Plunkett rallied Stanford with two late touchdowns to win the game.

"A real disappointment," Rex Kern said. "That game and the '69 loss to the school up north will stay with me forever."

There are at least 10 other seasons in which the Buckeyes could have, or should have, won national championships if the football had bounced a certain way.

What is problematic and painful for the Buckeye Nation is that since 1968, the following teams won enough games and were ranked high enough to put themselves in position at the end of the season in which they were one game away from either playing for, or one win from, a national championship: 1969, 1973, 1975, 1979, 1996, 1998, 2002, and 2006.

Only one of those teams, the 2002 team, won a national championship.

That explains a 34-year drought between titles.

Here's a look at all of those great teams that fell a play or two short of the biggest prize in college football.

- The **1969** team, trying to defend its national championship of the year before, was ranked number one for all nine weeks of the season before being upset at Michigan 24–12.

   "It was the best team I ever played on," Kern said. "I had always heard that we had taken Michigan lightly. That is bullshit—Michigan played the greatest game in their school's history. I swear, it was like Bo was in our huddle. They knew exactly what we were going to do. It was an ugly day, and without question, the worst loss I ever experienced. When did I get over it?

   "I haven't."

   Kern added, "That '68 team was voted Team of the Decade by *The Sporting News* and one of the 10 greatest football teams of all time. I am here to tell you that the '69 team was much better."

   "We attacked people all season until that game," middle guard Jim Stillwagon said. "One of [Woody Hayes's] downfalls is that he would outthink himself, and I think he did that in that game. Woody was predictable when it was close. Bo knew Woody's mind-set, too. He knew he would run right and run left. He stacked those tackles in there on the line of scrimmage. That game set us back. It set Woody back."

- The **1973** team probably was the most dominating team in Ohio State history, even more so than any of the seven national championship teams. It is very likely the *best* team in more than 115 years of Buckeyes football. Consider that it outscored its opponents 413–64 that season and did not allow more than seven points in any one game until a 55–13 win over Iowa on November 17—the week before the Michigan game.

  "We steamrolled our way through that season," said All-American tackle John Hicks. "We knew we were a great team."

  By the time of the Michigan game, the Buckeyes had been ranked number one for eight consecutive weeks.

  "On paper, yes, that probably was our best team," Archie Griffin admitted recently. "How many points did that defense give up that season? Sixty-four? Wow! But then we had the 10–10 tie."

  Again, Bo Schembechler's Michigan team ruined OSU's national title hopes for the second time in four years with that tie in Ann Arbor, in a game in which Woody, again, went into an offensive shell after holding a 10–0 halftime lead.

  "I threw one pass that day," quarterback Cornelius Greene said. "During the Iowa game I had jammed my right thumb, and it was hurting during that 10–10 tie with Michigan."

  If not for Greene's injured thumb, Hayes surely would have been more open in his play calling and this team would have won it all.

- The **1975** team got by Michigan 21–14 in a classic game in Ann Arbor to become 11–0 and take its number one ranking of seven weeks into the Rose Bowl, a rematch with UCLA.

On October 4 of that season, a Saturday night at the Los Angeles Coliseum, the Buckeyes had dismantled the 13th ranked Bruins 41–20.

The next week, the Buckeyes were elevated to the top of the polls and remained there until New Year's Day. They faced the unenviable task of a rematch: they were a huge favorite facing UCLA in the Rose Bowl.

At the half, the Buckeyes had outgained UCLA 174–48 but led only 3–0.

"We moved the ball up and down the field, but we just didn't score," Griffin explained. "We let them hang around, and when you do that, they are going to think they can beat you. That's what happened."

The Bruins then erupted for 16 third-quarter points on their way to a 23–10 upset.

It was the final game for the great senior class of '75, which included Griffin, Brian Baschnagel, Greene, and Tim Fox.

"That was the most disappointing loss I ever experienced," Griffin said. "Period. That game really hurt."

Perhaps there never has been a collection of football talent on one campus in college football history to match what Ohio State possessed during the four seasons that concluded with that game. Consider that the Buckeyes won 40 games, lost five (three coming in Rose Bowls), and tied one. They were 3–0–1 against Michigan, won four consecutive Big Ten championships, and played in four consecutive Rose Bowls—the only school in college football ever to accomplish that feat.

In the three latter seasons of this span, the Buckeyes averaged 35.3 points per game, scoring 40 or more in 14 games. On defense, they allowed an even more impressive 8.4 points per game in those three seasons.

As far as pure talent, they produced college football's only two-time Heisman Trophy winner (Griffin), two three-time All-Americans (Griffin and punter/kicker Tom Skladany), three two-time All-Americans (Hicks, linebacker

Randy Gradishar, and defensive end Van Ness DeCree), and six All-Americans, as well as a whopping 35 All–Big Ten first-team players.

And yet, due to the '73 tie with Michigan and the upset loss to UCLA, the Buckeyes never secured a national championship in this period.

In fact, it could be stated that if a handful of plays had gone the other way, they could have won three consecutive national titles, just as they could have from 1968 to 1970. The two losses in '74 came on the controversial ending at Michigan State and a one-point loss to USC in the Rose Bowl.

"We were talented, very talented," Griffin said. "And I am judging from the results of that talent. We had All–Big Ten and All-Americans across the board. We were talent-rich. And my class [the freshman class of 1972] wasn't a big class. We had 17 guys, but they had names like Tim Fox, Cornelius Greene, Brian Baschnagel. And they were quality people, too."

"Let me tell you something," said tight end Greg Storer (1974–1977), "there have been tough players and great teams at Ohio State since, but they will never be like that again. Those guys that were seniors in 1974 and '75 were warriors. Pure warriors."

Storer will never forget his introduction to that train of thought. It happened during one game as he stood on the sideline as a freshman in 1974 next to fellow freshman Mark Lang.

"We noticed team captain [All-American center] Steve Myers sprinting off the field directly toward us," he said. "We were frozen like two deer staring into the headlights. Myers was bigger than life to us, and just one look at him and you knew he was not a person to be messed with. When he got to the sideline, he ran right between Mark and I, stopped, and bent over and puked on the AstroTurf. He then stood up, wiped his mouth on his sleeve, fastened his chin strap, and sprinted back to the huddle.

"Lang looked at me, and both of us were wide-eyed with our jaws on the turf. Myers and his class were the shit to us—they were the last of the great dinosaurs."

The other thing to remember is that winning a national championship wasn't a mentioned goal during Hayes's career.

"No, we never talked about that," Griffin said. "It was all about winning the Big Ten by beating Michigan and getting to play in the Rose Bowl. Remember, back then, most people looked at a bowl game as a bonus for a great season. It wasn't [the] national championship–type game that it is today."

"Arch is right," Baschnagel said. "We never even talked 'national championship,' because there wasn't the emphasis on it that there is now. We just said, 'We have to win the Big Ten.' My biggest regret now is that we never won a national championship, and the '73 and '75 teams were good enough to do it."

Those teams were the final chances for Woody to win another national championship, since the 1976 through 1978 teams were not as talented—it was a rebuilding period that concluded with a 25-9-2 record.

- The **1979** team, Earle Bruce's first at Ohio State, came as close as any Buckeyes team to winning a national title but didn't. It beat Michigan in Ann Arbor 18–15 to become 11–0 and jump to number one, heading into the Rose Bowl against number three USC.

The Buckeyes, led by sophomore quarterback Art Schlichter and an opportunistic defense, fought back from a 10–0 deficit to take a 16–10 lead over the Trojans into the final minutes of the game. Needing one last defensive stop to win the game and secure the national championship, the defense allowed the Trojans and Heisman Trophy–winning tailback Charles White to drive 83 yards to win the game 17–16.

"It is the first time I ever cried after a loss," defensive back Vince Skillings said. "Everyone was crying, from coaches to players. We knew we had that game won."

It was Bruce's only brush with greatness at Ohio State, as his next eight teams lost at least three games each.

Then came John Cooper.

- The **1993** team reached number three in the polls before being tied 14–14 at Wisconsin in the season's ninth game. This team lost to Michigan 28–0 two weeks later.

- The 1995 team reached 11–0 and number two, behind Nebraska, before being upset by number 12 Michigan 31–23 at Ann Arbor.

- The **1996** team rolled to 10–0 and a number two ranking, having already clinched the Big Ten championship and a Rose Bowl berth, before hosting number 21 Michigan. Again, the Wolverines ruined any national championship possibilities with a 13–9 shocker at Ohio Stadium. This OSU team then won the Rose Bowl, beating Arizona State 20–17 and allowing Florida to capture the national championship.

- The **1998** team took the top ranking into the season and held it impressively for eight weeks before blowing a 24–9 lead over Michigan State at Ohio Stadium. The 28–24 loss ended Cooper's final chance at a national championship. And that team, ironically, whipped Michigan 31–16 two weeks later and eventually finished number two after winning the Sugar Bowl over Texas A&M.

"That Michigan State game was the only real disappointment of my Ohio State career," quarterback Joe Germaine explained. "We were ranked number one and leading them 24–9, when…I still don't know what happened. I think we just tried to run out the clock and sit on the ball. It was just one of those things. That loss cost us a national championship."

- The **2006** team was the preseason number one–ranked team, rolling to a 12–0 record following a 42–39 win over Michigan. A touchdown-favorite to beat Florida in the BCS championship game, the Buckeyes suffered their second-worst bowl loss, losing 41–14.

Each of those 10 teams reached number three or higher in the major polls as late as mid-November, with five of them reaching the top of the polls, but only one (2002) could secure a national championship.

To summarize OSU's failures, Michigan took care of five of those teams. And in all five of those losses to the Wolverines, the Buckeyes were ranked higher and were favored. Michigan State eliminated one with an upset. And an upset loss in a bowl took care of three more.

How different would Ohio State's football history be if only a few of these teams had closed the deal?

"It is frustrating, I guess, if you look at it that way," Griffin said recently, "but what you come to realize is that we have wonderful tradition at Ohio State and we have played good enough to put us in a position to play for those national titles.

"We may have lost a game or two that knocked ourselves out of it, but we were right there to begin with. And a lot of schools can't say that."

Furthermore, when you put all of this into perspective, the legacies of Woody Hayes, Earle Bruce, and John Cooper would be much different today if those teams had not slipped late in the season.

Many close to him feel that Woody may have retired soon after winning his sixth national championship if the 1975 team had beaten UCLA in that rematch. The end of his career, and how he is regarded today nationally, could have been much different.

"I always thought that things would have been much different for Woody," said Craig Cassady, a defensive back from 1972 to 1975. "I bet he would have retired either after that game or within a year or two, and everything would have been different for him. All these years later, that game still hurts."

With a national championship in his first season, Bruce surely would have been respected by fans and the media in a different manner, and he would have had more job security in the end—if only Ohio State had held USC on the final drive of the 1980 Rose Bowl.

"I agree with that 100 percent," said Calvin Murray (1977–1980). "I saw Coach Bruce recently, and one of the things he said right away was, 'We were two minutes and three seconds away." It would have been different for him, I really believe that, if we had won. And guys on that team are still dealing with that loss, I know that."

And Cooper, for all his repeated failures against Michigan, likely would not have been fired if either his '96 or '98 team had won a national title.

History has shown that once a coach wins a national championship, he banks plenty of goodwill for the down seasons in years to come. His legacy is secure, and he can eventually retire in good graces.

For that matter, Jim Tressel's life would be much easier these days if his 2006 team had finished what it started by adding his second national title in his first six years at Ohio State. He would be on his way to legendary status. Instead, his reputation as a big-game coach plummeted in 60 terrible minutes.

"I don't know what to say, other than that game surprised everyone," said Griffin, now the president of Ohio State's Alumni Association. "It is disappointing, but we'll get over it—we always do. And the Bucks will be back."

Best OSU Teams Not to Win a National Title

1. 1973 (10–0–1)—Won nine games by an average of 36 points before season-ending 10–10 tie at Michigan. Whipped USC 42–21 in the Rose Bowl. Thought by many to be the best team in school history. All-Americans on team (three): John Hicks, Randy Gradishar, and Van Ness DeCree. National champion: Alabama.

2. 1969 (8–1)—Defending national champions were ranked number one throughout the season and did not have a close game before being shocked 24–12 at Michigan. All-Americans on team (three): Jim Otis, Jack Tatum, and Jim Stillwagon. National champion: Texas.

3. 1944 (9–0)—Played one close game, winning 18–14 over Michigan. All-Americans on team (three): Bill Willis, Les Horvath, and William Hackett. National champion: Army.

4. 1975 (11–1)—Senior-laden team which romped through an 11–0 season ranked number one before dropping rematch with UCLA 23–10. All-Americans on team (two): Archie Griffin and Ted Smith. National champion: Oklahoma.

5. 1998 (11–1)—Ranked number one for eight weeks until Michigan State rallied from a 24–9 second-half deficit in Ohio Stadium. Ended up beating Michigan 31–16 and winning the Sugar Bowl. All-Americans on team (two): Antoine Winfield and Rob Murphy. National champion: Tennessee.

6. 1996 (11–1)—Had already clinched Rose Bowl berth before Michigan upset then number two–ranked OSU 13–9 in Ohio Stadium. All-Americans on team (two): Mike Vrabel and Orlando Pace. National champion: Florida.

7. 2006 (12–1)—Rolled through season as number one before being shocked by Florida in the BCS Championship Game. All-Americans on team (three): Troy Smith, Quinn Pitcock, and James Laurinaitis. National champion: Florida.

8. 1979 (11–1)—Another 11–0 team that rose to number one after close win at Michigan. Came within one defensive stop of a national title. All-Americans on team (one): Ken Fritz. National champion: Alabama.

9. 1995 (11–2)—Stood 11–0 and ranked number two when upset 31–23 at Michigan, which was ranked number 12 and was a nine-point underdog. All-Americans on team (four): Terry Glenn, Eddie George, Mike Vrabel, and Orlando Pace. National champion: Nebraska.

10. 1974 (10–2)—A controversial three-point loss at Michigan State which ended with OSU on the 1-yard line and a one-point loss to USC in the Rose Bowl were the only blemishes. All-Americans on team (three): Steve Myers, Archie Griffin, and Van Ness DeCree. National champion: USC.

chapter 13

The First Time
at Ohio Stadium

*Coach Jim Tressel and
players wait to take the
field before a game in
2006. The first time a
player takes the field at
Ohio Stadium is an
unforgettable experience.*

For a Buckeyes fan, there is nothing like seeing a football game for the first time in massive Ohio Stadium. For a player, there is nothing like running out of the southeastern tunnel onto the playing field.

Sailors remember their first boat, and golfers remember their first hole in one. What do most Buckeyes remember? Their first time seeing a game at Ohio Stadium or their first time running out onto the field in uniform.

"I wish all fans could experience the feeling of running out of the tunnel in the Shoe after hearing the band come onto the field before a game," said Tom Skladany (1973–1976), an All-American punter. "You can't explain it with words. It is magical, intense, and overwhelming, and that is the exact moment when you know what being a Buckeye is all about."

Ohio State has had a tradition of starting each season with a win. The Buckeyes have lost only one home opener since 1967—a 19–0 shutout to fifth-ranked Penn State in 1978, which was Woody Hayes's final season.

From 1943 to 2006, Ohio State had a 49–4–1 record in opening games at Ohio Stadium.

"That is one of our great traditions that doesn't get mentioned much," Archie Griffin said. "Winning that opening game at Ohio Stadium."

Here are many others' thoughts about their first times:

Earle Bruce: "The first game I ever attended in the Horseshoe was against the Missouri Tigers in September of 1949. We won that day, 35–34. As all freshmen were ineligible to play, I was in the stands. I will never forget the band coming out of the tunnel onto the field, the drum major throwing the baton over the crossbar of the goalposts and catching it, and the enthusiasm of the fans. It made the hair on the back of my neck stick up. I became a Buckeye for life that day."

Dick Young (1953–1954): "The first game I ever saw at Ohio Stadium, I was six or seven years old and my dad took me to see Ohio State play Chicago in 1938. Chicago came out in those black-and-white uniforms, and Ohio State beat them badly [42–7]. I think Chicago soon dropped football [two years later]. The next game I saw was Michigan in '40, when Tommy Harmon just ran all over the place, tearing up the Buckeyes [40–0]. That was Francis Schmidt's final game. He got fired right after that game. The stadium held about 72,000 then, and it seemed huge to a kid like me. It was just a tremendous opportunity go to a game with my dad."

Cris Carter (1984–1986): "I had seen the team come out of that tunnel a dozen times...with Coach Bruce standing there in front and the police holding the team back. I just didn't know what it would be like to run onto that field. Literally, my feet didn't touch the ground that first time in my freshman season. It was so exciting. When I got into pro football, that feeling made me love Ohio State even more. You wind up chasing that feeling again for the rest of your life."

Bruce Elia (1972–1974): "It was a sunny day. I remember running out of that tunnel and looking up and seeing tons of thousands of people cheering. I thought, 'This is the most colorful place I have ever seen.' And it was the loudest place I had ever been in. It was electrifying. All of a sudden, I realized what they meant by home-field advantage. I realized this is what the Romans must have felt like all those centuries ago."

Bill Long (1966–1968): "I was seven years old when I saw my first game at Ohio Stadium. I was sitting in C-deck with my dad while Ohio State and the great Hop Cassady were playing Indiana [1954]. I remember waiting for the band to come out, and you know how the drummers always come out first before everyone else? When that happened, Dad said, 'Well that's it, that's the whole band.' I was so disappointed, but then the rest of the band came marching out. He was only joking with me. That day, I developed a dream to play quarterback at Ohio State.

"It's been more than 40 years now since that came true, and one of the things that sticks with me is that first time I ran out of the tunnel. It took my breath away, and I remember completing 12 of 14 passes with the two incompletions dropped. [Ohio State beat Texas Christian 14–7]."

Tom Backhus (1967–1969): "That first time...it was almost a numbing experience to run onto that field. Then I found that for every game, there was the excitement to run out of there. When I was on the field, being introduced before my first start, I had one thought: 'Wow.' "

Mike Sensibaugh (1968–1970): "I was from a class A high school, so I used to like to play away from home because there were more people there. The thing I remember the most about that first time at Ohio Stadium is that when we ran out there, it was so different from just 10 minutes earlier when we were warming up. I thought, 'Oh my God,' it was just chilling. It sends tingles down your spine. I was never nervous or affected by the fans or large crowds."

Bill Conley (1970–1971): "On a Saturday morning after a mid-season game during my senior year, 1967, [Pleasant View High] head coach Don Eby called the team together and said he had an extra ticket for that afternoon's Ohio State football game. He conducted an impromptu drawing to see who would accompany him, and I won. To this day, I still vividly remember the afternoon of that game like it was yesterday—the sweet aroma of charcoal, bratwurst, and beer as we walked amid a thundering sea of scarlet and gray–clad fans entering the archway of historical Ohio Stadium. Once inside, I could not absorb enough of the rumble caused by more than 80,000 people. My head was spinning in the spectacle of noise, which my pounding heart echoed. I've been to many stadiums in the past 35 years, but nothing compares to game day at Ohio State. I still get chills and goose bumps when the Best Damn Band in the Land marches out of the closed end of the stadium. Only those who have been here can truly appreciate it. I've had Michigan fans tell me that Wolverine games pale in comparison, even though Michigan Stadium now holds 111,000 people—now that's a compliment."

A.J. Hawk (2002–2005): "I remember seeing an Ohio State game for the first time during my sophomore year of high school when I went to a night game; the Buckeyes played UCLA. The atmosphere was great, and being a night game added to the whole experience. The only play I remember is [quarterback] Steve Bellisari getting a crack block on a defensive end. The crowd went crazy. Even though it did not seem possible at the time, I knew that I wanted to play there if I got the chance. It was a great game, and Ohio State won."

Rowland Tatum (1981–1983): "I was from Inglewood, California, so I never saw a game at Ohio Stadium until I played in one during my freshman year. That first time I ran out of the tunnel, it just took my air away. There were so many people there, I literally lost my wind. I kept running, but I couldn't breathe. Then I heard this noise behind me and Mark Hocevar had fallen and he was looking up, saying, 'Help me.' He had blown out his knee by tripping on the turf that comes after the track. He was looking at people and not what surface we were running on. He had to have surgery. That was my first game of my freshman year. I had never seen anything like it."

Thad Jemison (1981–1984): "We had played in front of about 25,000 at Cincinnati Princeton, and that's about what you are warming up in front of at Ohio Stadium, but they are scattered out. When you come back out of the locker room, the stadium is loaded. You come out of that tunnel, in front of all those people, and I remember, it just blew my mind. The upperclassmen had said, 'You will pee your pants.' Well, I didn't pee my pants, but I felt an awesome feeling. Then I remember the time that Coach Bruce pulled his hamstring and tripped and fell coming out of there."

Eddie George (1992–1995): "I played in several big games during my pro career, including the Super Bowl. Nothing compares to walking out in front of more than 100,000 fans in a sea of scarlet and gray. Playing in that Horseshoe in that atmosphere is the best experience any football player can imagine, even better than the Super Bowl. I miss those days."

Matt Finkes (1993–1996): "It was my senior year in high school and it was the Bowling Green game [a 17–6 Ohio State win]. We didn't beat them by much, but all I can remember is thinking how big the stadium was. It seemed so huge. I still remember the band, and it still is one of my favorite things about a game at Ohio Stadium. I was scared to death the next year, running out onto the field for the first time."

Bruce Ruhl (1973–1976): "Only OSU football alumni or current players can describe the experience of running through that tunnel and onto that field for the first time. To me, it was as if I was floating on a magic carpet out to the field, while the band

and the roar of the fans were our fuel. I don't recall feeling my feet hit the turf."

Jeff Logan (1974–1977): "Those memories of running out onto the field at Ohio Stadium for the first and for the last times are memories that no one else can own, unless they were one of the lucky few to wear that scarlet and gray uniform."

Barney Renard (1973–1976): "It was the opener of the '73 season, and what I remember is when Wood's pregame speech ended, the excitement and the energy that grew as we anticipated running out there. He was screaming, 'Seniors first! Seniors first! And if anybody tries to sneak in there first, I will tackle you myself.' And he meant it. Back then, there was a small archway and two doors to get through, and then it was a sprint to the 50-yard line. In those days, we stopped on the 50 and formed a big mass of players. You would see guys leaping and flying on top of the pile. I'll never forget coming out of those doors and hearing the roar of that crowd—it was just bigger than any one of us. Thinking of it still takes me back."

Ernie Andria (1975, 1977–1979): "I'll always remember my first time running out onto the field for a college football game. It was my freshman year, and I had made the traveling squad and we opened at Michigan State. There were seventy-some thousand in the stands, and I was in awe of all the people. We came out as a team and everybody was supposed to be stretching—and I am looking around at all the people. For our first home game the next week, Joe Robinson ran out in front of me and fell right on his face when he hit the turf."

Jim Otis Jr. (2000–2003): "The first time I ran out of the tunnel was in 2000, and I had no idea what to expect. My dad just told me he couldn't describe it for me because it was hard to describe. He said I had to live it for myself. Let me tell you, it just gives you goose bumps. It is one of the most gratifying experiences. I found out that it could be your first time or your last time, but it still sends chills up and down your body."

chapter 14
Buckeye Hilarity

Every football team likes to have a little fun, as long as it doesn't interfere with the 60-minute effort put forth on game day. Here, Coach Tressel gets a celebratory dousing at the end of the 2004 Alamo Bowl.

Winning football games is serious business at Ohio State. From pranks and poker games to unauthorized trips across the Mexico border, however, Buckeyes have had plenty of fun over the years.

Realize one thing about the Buckeyes football program: it is similar to a fraternity in its own right. No matter what year one played the game, being a Buckeye is like joining a brotherhood. That is why players from the 1950s and those from the 2000s consider themselves part of one family.

Just like in any fraternity, there have been plenty of legendary pranks and merriment off the field.

And sometimes on it...

A Quarterback "Gets Shot"

Stan Pincura was a quarterback who liked to joke around, but one time he carried his mischief too far. He pulled a prank in the midst of a game, leaving many fans at Ohio Stadium wondering what was happening.

In the 1930s officials would shoot blanks from a starter's gun to signal the end of each quarter. During one game, as Pincura was running from the sideline to the huddle, the official shot his gun and Pincura grabbed his heart, spun around, and fell to the ground. The crowd was stunned at first, with many fans believing their quarterback had been shot by a referee.

Tucker Smith, the Buckeyes' trainer, rushed out to the field and kneeled over Pincura.

"Are you okay?" he asked.

"I am okay," Pincura shot back, snickering, "but how's the crowd taking it?"

Who Has the Fastest Turtle?

After losing at Pittsburgh 12–0 in 1947, the team plane was delayed before its return trip to Columbus.

"We always had some fun while traveling in those days," said Joe Whisler, a running back/defensive back (1946–1948).

"We had this little prop job of an airplane, and we were delayed for some reason. Well, the boys went to the gift shop and bought all of these windup turtles. Here they were, having turtle races right out there near the runway by the airplane."

Broken Toe for Jacoby

Tackle George Jacoby (1951–1953) always kidded Buckeyes kicker and fraternity brother Tad Weed that "anybody could kick."

"So one day in front of the fraternity house, he said, 'Okay, Jacoby, you think it is so easy, let's go.'"

Jacoby tried kicking, promptly breaking his big toe. It resulted in his sitting out the Purdue game in 1952.

"There was a picture in the newspaper of me at the Purdue game, sitting on the bench with my big toe all bandaged," he said.

In the stands that day, some fans behind Nina Jacoby said, "I heard Jacoby got hurt by chasing his bride around the bedroom and he tripped on the vanity stool."

Mrs. Jacoby stood up and responded, "No, he didn't break it chasing his bride around the bedroom. How do I know? I am his bride!"

All–Big Ten tackle George Jacoby figured anyone could kick a little football, but his demonstration in front of his fraternity house proved costly.

Friday Night Poker Games

In the early days, players could get away with extracurricular activities that lasted late into the night before games much more than they can today.

In the 1950s Friday nights before games were fairly routine for Ohio State players: a light practice, a filling dinner, a movie that wasn't very interesting, and bed check at 10:00 PM.

"Then the fun would start for a certain group of guys," said Dick Young (1953–1954).

Once bed check was completed, a poker game was held in one player's room or another. Among the regular players were George Rosso, Fred Bruney, Hubie Bobo, and William Leggett.

"Those guys would play cards all night long, and they were playing for big stakes at the time," Young recalled. "I know one thing: it didn't affect their play the next day. They went out and played great, just as if they had slept all night."

Matte the Mischievous One

Tom Matte became a great NFL player for the Baltimore Colts, but before that, he drove Woody Hayes crazy with his tomfoolery and his disobedience.

"He once told me I was worse than Hubie Bobo and Vic Janowicz combined," Matte said. "I laughed and said, 'That puts me in a really good class.'"

In one of many examples of Matte's monkey business, he was arrested one night with a few others in his underwear, "writing" a Script Ohio in the snow.

"A lot of us had a party, and we were out there in our shorts, writing Script Ohio in the snow," he said. "At least I thought it was funny."

One time during practice, Matte, unhappy with what he felt was an injustice done to him by Woody Hayes, continued fumbling the snap from center—on purpose.

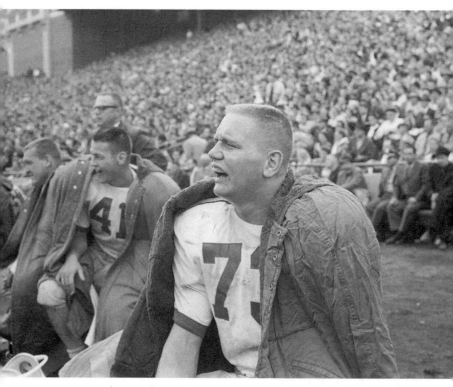

Tom Matte (No. 41), future NFL star, was one of the more relentless mischief makers in all of Woody's years. Here he's shown on the sideline laughing while the player in the foreground seems pretty concerned about the action on the field.

At the time, Bo Schembechler was coaching the quarterbacks.

"I told Bo Schembechler what I was going to do," Matte recalled.

"Tom, don't do it," the assistant warned.

"So I did it," Matte said. "I fumbled the ball from the snap six times in a row."

Hayes was so mad, he delivered a forearm to Matte's chest.

"I could have owned the school," Matte said. "Then he hit himself in the temple, and he went down like a sack of potatoes. Bo looked at me and said, 'When he wakes up, he's going to kill you.'

"It turned out he had to have five stitches in his head. I went back to the dorm and went into hiding."

"Just Checking for Lightning, Coach"

"Before the start of one game, we were in the locker room, and Woody asked von Allen Hardman to go outside and see what was happening with the weather, since there was the possibility of lightning and storms that day," recalled guard Wayne Betz (1960–1962). "The team was facing Woody, receiving our last-minute instructions, when Hardman reentered the room behind Woody. He had coat hangers sticking out of the ear holes of his helmet. The team sort of snickered, and Woody whirled around and saw Hardman.

"'What the hell are you doing?' Woody asked him.

"'Just checking for lightning, Coach,' Hardman replied.

"I thought Woody would die on the spot," Betz said.

On Mexico, Sideline Hot Dogs, and No Uniform

Backup quarterback Kevin Rusnak (1967–1969) was a real character who loved to have a good time. Of course, that didn't always go along with Hayes's serious manner of preparing his football team.

Rusnak's list of stories of getting into trouble, or trying to avoid getting caught, is a rather lengthy one.

There was the time he organized a sight-seeing trip to Mexico on Christmas Day, 1968, as the undefeated Buckeyes prepared to meet USC in the Rose Bowl. Ohio State players had a free day but had to be present at the team's Christmas party that night.

"Woody told us, you got a free day so you can go to the mountains, you can go here or there, just don't go to Mexico," Rusnak recalled. "A few of the guys looked at me and asked, 'Where are you going?'

"'Mexico,' I said."

While the local taxi drivers had been under strict orders not to take any Buckeyes across the border, Rusnak found an alternative method of transportation.

"I told the guys—I think it was Dave Foley, Ted Provost, Mike Sensibaugh, and Sam Elliott, who was a captain in '67 and now was a graduate assistant coach—to go down to the corner and I would meet them," Rusnak said. "I told one of the people at the hotel that I needed one of the official Rose Bowl cars for an emergency. It had a Rose Bowl sticker on the side of it and everything. They all got in, and we started driving to Mexico."

The group had conned Rex Kern, the starting quarterback, by saying they were headed to Disneyland.

"I was excited about that," Kern recalled. "About an hour into the trip, I said, 'Guys, we have been driving for a long time. Why aren't we at Disneyland yet?' There was no reply, and I knew then that I had been kidnapped."

Rusnak parked the car on the U.S. side of the border, and the group of Buckeyes walked into Mexico.

"We were buying things, I know I was having a drink here and there, we were just having a great time," Rusnak said. "When it came time to leave, everybody else gave me the stuff they bought to carry for them. Somebody gave me this big sombrero. As I am walking back to the U.S. side, nobody is around me, but I hear all of these guys yelling at me. Apparently, I walked right through the entrance lanes while they all went through the exit lanes to go through customs where I should have been."

By the time the group returned to the team hotel, Woody had been tipped off about their journey.

"His room was right at the top of the stairs, and he had his door open," Rusnak said. "Sam Elliott is the first one up, and he gets to the top step and trips and falls right in front of Woody's room. Woody walks out there, picks him up, takes him in his room, and slams the door.

"That is when the rest of us rushed in and made it to our rooms," Rusnak said.

"Woody saw me wearing a sombrero and asked how my day was," Kern said. "I don't know if he ever knew about the trip, but Anne Hayes mentioned it to me about 20 years later at a reunion. She told me, 'I don't know if he ever knew, but I knew.'"

Another time, during a game at Northwestern, as the Buckeyes entered the locker room at halftime, Rusnak told OSU cheerleader Susie Yung that he was hungry.

"As we came out of the locker room, she handed me a hot dog and I ate in on the sideline," he said.

"That is the game that we were ahead by about 30 points, and Woods wanted me to run the clock out. But I had relatives who lived near Northwestern's stadium and they rarely got to see me play. I changed the play, threw a touchdown pass, and when I got back to the sideline, he smacked me in the head."

Another time, at Wisconsin, "We had a huge lead, 40-something to 7, when Woods put me in the game. I stood there before the play and told those Wisconsin guys, 'You think you got your ass beat by the first team? Wait to see what we are going to do to you!' And all of the second-team linemen started laughing so hard, I had to call a timeout."

When Rusnak reached the sideline, Hayes asked, "What happened?"

"I told him, 'You don't want to know.' Then he smacked me in the head again."

The coup de grâce for Rusnak, however, came in his final game, the heartbreaking 24–12 loss at Michigan in 1969, in which the Buckeyes entered ranked number one and riding a 22-game winning streak.

Kern played most of the game injured before giving way to Ron Maciejowski, then a junior. As the final minutes ticked away, quarterbacks coach George Chaump walked up to Rusnak and told him, "Woody wants you to play in your last game."

There was a major problem, however. Rusnak had given his jersey and his helmet to his girlfriend, who had been sitting in the stands behind the bench.

"I started thinking late in the game that I wanted to keep my jersey and my helmet," he said. "I knew if I went into the locker room with them after the game, I wouldn't be able to keep them. So I saw my girlfriend, who was sitting about three rows from the field. I handed her my helmet and jersey and told her, 'Put this under your coat and make sure you get it out of the stadium.'"

Rusnak told Chaump, "George, if you would have been here about two minutes earlier, I would have been more than happy to go into this game."

He then opened up his parka and showed the assistant coach he couldn't possibly enter the game without a jersey or a helmet. Chaump then walked over to Woody and told him what Rusnak had done. Hayes turned around and yelled to Rusnak, "You dirty sons a bitch!"

"That's what he told me," Rusnak said. "He never said 'son of a bitch' to anyone, because that would be calling your mother a bad name. He always said 'sons a bitch.' He called me that a lot. Sometimes I think about that and I wonder if I could have gone in there and thrown a touchdown pass and then we could have got an onside kick…."

"Down the Middle, We Party"

One of the best lines about High Street, then the center of campus nightlife, came from Glen Mason, the former Buckeyes player under Hayes, assistant under Earle Bruce, and later head coach of Kansas and Minnesota.

Bruce Elia, an easterner who developed into a fine two-way player, was perhaps compelled to head west to Columbus because of Glen Mason's simple recruiting tip.

While New Jersey recruit Bruce Elia was visiting campus in 1970, Mason was his host.

"Glen had it down real simple," Elia said. "We stood outside Papa Joe's on High Street and looked north, and there were kids everywhere. He told me, 'On the left side, we go to school and we study and we live. On the right side, there are the sororities and fraternities and more housing. Down the middle, we party! Welcome to High Street."

It isn't a line that would make any one of Ohio State's presidents proud, but that's the way it once was.

Don't Drop the Future Mr. Heisman

As a freshman, Archie Griffin lived in Smith Hall, where many football players lived. One, named Ed Trepanier, was a huge lineman known for his mischief. He never lettered, but he was an All-American at getting on Woody's bad side.

Woody Hayes and Archie Griffin share a chuckle after Griffin was awarded the 1975 Heisman Trophy in New York City. Fortunately, Griffin survived a prank during his freshman season and lived to win not one, but two Heisman Trophies.

One day, Trepanier held Griffin out of the window of the dorm by the ankles, upside down.

"It was really only the third or fourth floor and not the 10th or the 11th as the story goes," Griffin recalled. "He had me by the ankles when I told him, 'Big Ed, whatever you do, don't drop me!'"

"Imagine if he would have dropped him," said Brian Baschnagel, a teammate at the time.

Fortunately, Trepanier had pretty good hands for a defensive lineman and Griffin lived to win two Heismans and become the president of OSU's Alumni Association.

A Jelly-Faced Punter

Tom Skladany (1973–1976) was an All-American punter with one of the strongest legs ever to wear a pair of Ohio State pants. He also was a natural cutup.

All-American punter Tom Skladany remembers at least one incident where he was left red-faced during a confrontation with Coach Hayes.

Sometimes during practices, especially if the weather was cold, Skladany would lead the punters and kickers into the locker room, where they would be doing just about anything: "Eating jelly doughnuts, drinking hot chocolate, playing cards, and sometimes even studying," he admitted.

"This one time the trainer ran in, and he was yelling my name," Skladany recalled. "'Woody can't find you!'

"I went out of there running as fast as I could. I could hear Woody: 'Where the hell is the punter?' Everybody was laughing because I had jelly all over my face. I stayed outside after that."

Look Out Below!

Barney Renard, a tackle from 1973 to 1976, remembers when the idea of sneaking a late nighttime snack turned awry one night.

"One night inside Baker Commons, a few of us snuck off and went back to the cafeteria. The refrigerators were not locked, and inside one was a full watermelon. I think I was with Mike Datish, Bill Lukens, and [Tom] Skladany," he said. "We thought that watermelon would be a good snack before bedtime, but when we got up to our room on the 10th or 11th floor, nobody had a knife.

"Then one of us had the bright idea to throw it out the window. So two of us chuck this big watermelon out the window and, as we are watching it fall, we noticed it was headed toward an El Camino. Now everybody knew who that car belonged to. Fortunately, it missed the car, but it landed right next to it, splattering watermelon seeds, juice, and parts of that watermelon all down the side of Woody's El Camino. There was a little stir the next day about it, but he never found out who did it."

Can I Change the Snap Count?

Ed Thompson (1973–1976) signed at Ohio State as a quarterback but later switched to linebacker. Cornelius Greene may be one reason, but Renard thinks he knows the cause of the switch. (And his story is R-rated if you want to stop here.)

"We always got new, clean pants for practice," Renard said. "But one day, mine had a hole in the crotch. As I was practicing that day, the hole kept getting bigger and bigger. I was at center, and Ed was the quarterback. I thought I would have some fun with him and I just moved my jock to the side and all my stuff fell out of the hole.

"Ed gets to the line, and I could feel him put his hands under me to get the snap. He starts with 'Down, ready, set, set, set,' and then he said, 'Damn, what the f*ck is that?' He soon wanted to become a linebacker, and some people really think that is what changed his mind about playing quarterback."

"That was one of the funniest things that ever happened at practice," defensive back Bruce Ruhl said. "Ed was from Portsmouth and he had that southern twang, and as he called out that snap count in his twang, he started to swear and then backed away from center. Even all the assistant coaches were laughing."

Calling Larry Molls

Larry Molls was a backup running back in the mid-1970s who rarely saw playing time. But this story illustrates how well Hayes knew every detail about every player.

In one game, star tailback Archie Griffin jogged to the sideline because of a problem with his helmet.

"Larry Molls!" Woody screamed. "Larry Molls! Larry Molls, get up here fast!"

Molls scrambled from the back of the bench.

"He called my name, so I knew I was getting in the game," Molls recalled.

When he reached Woody, the coach said, "Larry, take your helmet off and give it to Archie."

The coach knew the two players had the same head size.

Where's the Horn?

In Woody's regime, the Buckeyes' practices were broken up into 15-minute segments. A student manager would declare the end of one segment by blowing an air horn.

One of Elia's and running back Billy Ezzo's favorite gags was to hide the air horn from the student manager.

"We did it all the time," Elia said.

One day during a practice at Ohio Stadium, "I distracted him, and Billy snatched it," Elia recalled. "We hid it under the [blocking] dummies."

"At times, Woody would say, 'Okay, son, it's time to blow the horn,'" Ruhl explained. "So this time, he looks over and orders that kid to blow the horn. All you can see are towels flying everywhere on the bench as this kid is trying to find the horn.

"Then Woody stood at midfield, looked up at the sky and said, 'Lord, there are 50,000 students at The Ohio State University, and I can't find one to blow a f*cking horn!'"

Sensibaugh's Venison Gets Swiped

Safety Mike Sensibaugh (1968–1970) was a real character with a great personality. But he had sticky fingers on the field (OSU's all-time leading interceptor with 22) and off of it as well.

"Our practice balls had 'Ohio State University' inscribed in them, and I decided they made great gifts for family members and friends," he said. "I lived right behind the football facility at Buckeye Village. So if I ever got a real good ball when I was punting in practice, I would shank one purposely over the fence and come back and get it later. I would stick them in bushes where we entered and exited practice. You know those orange cones that block off parking lots? I would stuff a football right up there and come get it later."

Then on one cold December day, Sensibaugh, fresh from a hunting trip, hung a deer carcass on a blocking dummy.

"I had skinned it, and it was ready for the butcher," he said. "I had planned to come back and get it later, but somebody stole it. The joke was, 'Somebody stole the meat from the thief.' It had to be a teammate, but I still don't know who did it."

Short-Sheeting Earle

One night during summer camp, centers Tom DeLeone (1969–1971) and Jim Conroy (1968–1970) set out to short-sheet assistant coach Earle Bruce's bed at Park Hall.

"Earle had to do bed check, and we had the double room next to him," Conroy recalled. "DeLeone was the lookout, and I just started in on Earle's bed and he yelled, 'Here he comes!'

"For some reason, Earle had come back to his room early. DeLeone got back in the room and Earle didn't see him, but he caught me. All his sheets were lying on the floor. He never swore, but he was muttering, 'You guys! I know who did this!' The next day, he had us running all day."

Safety Mike Sensibaugh makes a theft here against Purdue in 1969, but he ultimately learned that crime doesn't pay.

Michigan Coed Lets Loose

One of the funniest stories involving Hayes—and there are millions of them—came from a recruiting trip at a Michigan high school while he was recruiting Ruhl.

It is well-known that Woody, known for his love of America's wholesome values, hated long hair, free love, torn jeans, and the whole hippy-influenced ways of the late '60s and early '70s. So one day while recruiting Ruhl, he noticed a well-dressed high school girl walking his way outside the school.

"She had on this pretty dress, had her hair done in a bow and all that," Ruhl said. "Woody was walking toward her, and he said something like, 'Now see there, I guarantee you that girl comes from a good, wholesome family with good values. That's what we need more of in this country.'

"But just as he walked by her, a car drove by and hit a mud puddle. Mud and water flew all over that girl...and she suddenly let out a litany of profanity, screaming every bad word in the book.

"Woody just continued walking and never said a word."

A Rumble in the Cafeteria

Ruhl says that his getting beat deep in the opening game of the 1976 season resulted in a rumble between the coaches in a dormitory cafeteria. Here's how it transpired:

"We are beating Michigan State pretty good late in the game, and they move me to the other side," Ruhl explained. "Now I see this receiver come into the game that I haven't seen before, and I am not too worried about him beating me deep. The quarterback takes one step back and throws it as far as he could. I am thinking, 'Who is he throwing that to?' Well, this kid goes flying by me like a flash, catches it in front of Woody on our sideline, and scores. It was the only time I was ever beaten deep in my four years.

"The next day while we are watching film, I ask the coaches, 'Who was that kid?'

"His name was Kirk Gibson, and they said he was supposed to be a pretty good baseball player, but he was a freshman and we had no scouting report on him."

A day or two later, the defensive coaches were sitting in the cafeteria of the dorm, using the salt-and-pepper shakers to describe pass coverage schemes.

"Woody walks up, and he is watching and listening," Ruhl recalled. "The coaches are telling him, 'Now this is Ray Griffin here and Bruce Ruhl here...'

"All of a sudden, Woody grabs one of the salt shakers and screams, 'Yes, and he will get beat deep just like he did in the Michigan State game!' Next thing you know, bacon and eggs and salt and pepper are flying everywhere. It turned into a real rumble. The coaches were fighting, and there was food all over the floor."

Michigan native Bruce Ruhl received a recruiting visit from the coach that included an embarrassing encounter with one of Ruhl's female high school classmates.

Don't Sleep during Study Table

Following practice, Woody often dropped by the players' study table, where there were two basic rules: no talking and no sleeping.

"One time we were at study table and Ben Lee (1978–1981) fell asleep," running back Cal Murray recalled. "He had his hands folded as if he was praying, but we knew he was really sleeping. As Coach Hayes was walking in, we couldn't get over to Ben to wake him up in time. Then just as Coach Hayes walks by him, Ben wakes up and says, 'Amen!'

"Coach was completely fooled by it, because later we heard he got in the coaches' meeting and was telling the others, 'Boy, I didn't know that Ben is a pretty religious guy.'"

Elvis Has Left the Facility

Longtime team trainer Billy Hill, who died in 1994, controlled the stereo in the team's locker room and training room. He kept it, literally, under lock and key, secured in a wooden box so nobody would change the radio station.

"He liked it on some local radio station," said linebacker Bill Harvey (1981–1984). "But I was an Elvis fanatic."

Harvey had learned his love for Presley's music from quarterback Art Schlichter. So one day, Harvey convinced one of the assistant trainers to give him the key to the stereo box. He then popped an Elvis tape into the cassette, turned it on, locked it, and hid the key.

"Billy was running all over the training room looking for that key," Harvey recalled. "Elvis must have played for at least an hour as Billy searched for this key. Finally, on my way out the door, I quietly put the key back on his desk."

Pagac's Weak Stomach

One of Earle Bruce's practice routines was to require the Buckeyes to run two miles during every Sunday practice following a game. It was by design, preventive medicine in case players had planned to, let's say, indulge too much on Saturday nights. If they did happen to have too much of a good time, then it served as a natural punishment.

Coaches could always tell who was out late drinking something other than soft drinks. Those were the players vomiting.

And they soon learned that assistant coach Fred Pagac could not see or hear someone else upchuck without then doing it himself.

"We always would go out after the games," center Jim DeLeone (1977–1981) said. "So when it came time for two-mile run on Sundays, if I felt like I was going to throw up as I was running, I would hold it until I got close to Fred Pagac. I made him barf a few times."

A real throwback, Pagac often coached in Hayes's own style. He was fiery, he had a temper, and he didn't care much for the frills of the coaching business.

"I love this place," he said. "I played here; I coached here. Ohio State has been good to me."

Linebacker Greg Bellisari realized how much Pagac loved Ohio State following a 28–0 loss at Michigan in 1993, when a few players were joking around on the bus ride home.

"He got in their face and let 'em have it," Bellisari recalled. "He was real hot that day. He loves the tradition of this place, and he brings the past to the present here. You had better not take a game or a practice lightly around him if you wear an Ohio State uniform."

It is no coincidence that the Buckeyes defense improved dramatically and relied more on an attacking, blitzing style when Pagac was promoted from linebackers coach to defensive coordinator in 1996.

"Coach Pug turned us loose and let us go play," defensive end Mike Vrabel said. "We loved that guy."

chapter 15

Buckeye Bling

Some Buckeye bling: a championship ring, a leaf-encrusted helmet, and the coveted gold pants.

Rose Bowl rings. National championship rings. Bowl watches. Gold pants. If you played football for the Buckeyes, these are no doubt some of your most prized possessions, at least as far as jewelry is concerned.

Let's face it, anybody with enough money can wear a Rolex, but only a few ever get to wear a championship ring with that Block O in the middle of the stone or own a pair of gold pants, signifying a win in the greatest rivalry in sports.

These items mean more than your average diamond ring. They are symbols of achievement, and in some cases, a love and bond that stretches well beyond football.

Jim Conroy was a member of Ohio State's 1968 championship team. A few years later, when his older brother Mike was departing for Vietnam, he gave him something to help him through what surely would be the most difficult time of his life.

"He is six years younger than me, but my brother and I always were very, very close," Mike explained recently. "On the day I was headed for the airport, he told me that he wanted me to take something with me to Vietnam.

"He reached down and started wriggling his finger and handed me his national championship ring."

"This is for my assurance that you will come back," Jim told him. "We were fortunate enough to have good luck in '68 to get this ring, and I want you to have good luck over there."

"Jim, this is your most prized possession…I can't take that ring," Mike told him.

"No, Mike," Jim interrupted. "*You* are my most prized possession, and I want you to come back."

Mike took the ring, slipped it onto his finger, and hugged his brother. He had tears in his eyes and "a huge knot in my stomach."

"It was so touching," he said. "It still is."

Mike Conroy arrived in Vietnam June 25, 1971. He was assigned to Chu Lai, about 20 miles from the China Sea. Through the worst of times as a surgeon on a firebase in the heart of the battlefields of a war-torn country, Mike Conroy would look down at his hand and stare at that gold ring with the inscription "OHIO" set in block letters on a scarlet stone. He would think about home, Ohio State football, and his brother.

The ring took him away from the horrors of war, if only in his mind for a few moments.

"It was a rough time. I was scared to death, but that ring was very comforting to me. It seemed I could remember the times my brother and I had together," he explained. "I worked on a golf course in college, and he would be my caddy. I would think of the times we played golf together, and I would think, 'We are going to play golf again.'

"When they beat Michigan 50–14 in '68, I took a picture of Jim on the sidelines, smiling, with the crowd behind him. I would look at that ring, with the stadium engraved on one side of it, and think of those times. You never had a wallet or personal possessions with you over there. That ring was all I had, and I never took it off. Not for one day."

Since the Conroys had grown up in Bay Village, Ohio, Mike had a Cleveland *Plain Dealer* subscription mailed to him. Every 10 days or so, he would receive a bundle of newspapers.

"When I got time inside of my hooch, I would be reading. The medics would always ask me about my ring, and I would tell them how my brother gave it to me, and we would talk about the football games," he said. "There was a big interest in football among the guys.

"They would say something like, 'Hey, Doc, I hear that Ohio State coach is pretty rough on his players.'

"No," he told them, "Coach Hayes is a good man. He was good to my brother, and all of his players love him. He would be like a good colonel—right there with you in battle...not one of these colonels who avoids the front lines."

Too many times, Mike saw death up close. He often saw young men who had stepped on booby traps, losing limbs, if not their lives. He saw the results of M-16s and AK-47s.

"They had such high velocity that they would leave a hole about the size of a CD," he said. "For the guys who took one somewhere in the upper body, there was nothing you could do for them."

One night, during a shelling of the base, Mike climbed into a foxhole.

"They were more like tubes," he said. "You would get down in there and make sure your head was below ground level. When the mortar shells would come in, you could really feel the concussion if they were close to you. The ground just shook.

"One time I felt one that was real, real close."

When the shelling stopped, Mike climbed out of the tube to discover that a medic in a nearby foxhole had taken a direct hit.

"He was a good man who had been there 10 months," he said. "Between the smoke and the darkness, we couldn't find enough of him to put into a body bag. I don't even think we could find his dog tags. I wrote a letter to his family that stated how brave he was, but it made me realize how vulnerable we were. We were scared."

On October 20 that year, Mike took his leave and returned to Columbus to see Jim, who was then in his first year of law school at Ohio State. One day earlier that week, Hayes had called Jim, wanting him to show a potential law student from his hometown of Newcomerstown around campus.

"I can't, Coach," Jim told him, "my brother is coming home on leave from Vietnam, and I want to spend time with him."

"Jim, I want you to bring that young man to see me after the game," Woody told Conroy.

Mike already had lost 40 pounds from his four months in Vietnam by the time he arrived at Port Columbus, wearing Bermuda shorts and sporting a military haircut during a period when college men's hair usually flowed beneath their collars.

"I didn't have any regular clothes that fit me, and Jim told me not to get off the plane in my military clothes because there had been some demonstrations on campus," he said. "It was cold that week, and he brought some heavier clothing to the airport for me."

Following the 31–6 win over the Badgers, Jim and Mike Conroy worked their way to a room above the OSU locker room to find Hayes.

"The guy guarding the room let me in, and there was Coach Hayes and a fellow dressed in a marine uniform," Mike recalled. "I said to Coach, 'Hello, sir, nice to see you again.' Right away, he noticed I was wearing my brother's ring."

Hayes introduced two-star general Lewis Walt.

"Son, sit down," Hayes said. "I want you to talk to us about Vietnam."

As the three men talked, with Jim listening, his brother informed Hayes of the ongoing problem with heroin and the toll it was taking on the troops. He told them of their fears of dying and the boredom that led them to it. Once they tried it, they became addicted, he told Hayes.

"I could tell that he was very concerned about the drug problem," Mike recalled. "He wanted to know if the boys were being fed well, if we had enough supplies, if we were being taken care of, had ammunition and all those type of things."

Every five minutes or so, OSU sports information director Marv Homan would stick his head in the door and tell the coach it was time he addressed the media, as is custom following every game.

"Not now!" Hayes would say. "Not now!"

Another five minutes would go by, and Homan would try again.

"Tell those sons a bitches they'll just have to wait," Woody barked.

Finally, Hayes relented and excused himself, as Mike stood up to salute the general.

"No, no, son," the general said. "Don't salute me. I just want to shake your hand."

Hayes then grabbed Conroy's hand and told him, "If you ever need anything that I can help you with, you write to me personally. On the outside of the envelope in the left corner at the bottom, you write 'Vietnam' and underline it. That is the code I use for my secretary to know that I need to read the letter. If you need anything for the boys, I won't let you down."

"By God," Conroy said, "I will tell you it was a marvelous feeling when I walked out of there. What a great man."

When he returned to Vietnam, he worked in a hospital helping the GIs who were hooked on heroin to detoxify and recover.

He left Vietnam for California for debriefing in late April 1972. He arrived in South Bend, Indiana, two months later, and Jim was at the airport to greet him. Immediately, he started to pull the ring off his finger to give it back to his brother.

"I promised you I would take care of it," Mike said, handing it back to Jim.

"I have a feeling it will always mean more to you than it will to me," Jim said. "You've done well with it. You keep it. If I want it back, I know where it is."

Recently, Jim said, "I was just thrilled he came home."

While Mike still wears the '68 national championship ring, Jim has worn a Big Ten championship ring from 1970 and a Varsity O ring through the years.

"When the time comes, we will be handing these rings down to our sons," Mike explained. "This ring has been such a huge part of my life…it has started a lot of interesting conversations. And it helped me think of the good things during the most difficult times of my life. However, I want to say that the glory of this story really goes to my brother."

Mike set up a family medical practice in South Bend following the war and retired in 2004. Jim still lives in Bay Village, and his son John was an offensive lineman who lettered for Ohio State (2004–2005). The brothers email or speak with each other frequently and often meet in Columbus on fall Saturdays to watch the Buckeyes play.

Through the years, Mike received many letters of appreciation from those veterans whom he treated in the heroin-recovery hospital.

"They would all say something like, 'I was hooked and didn't know what I was doing back then, so I didn't have the sense to thank you,'" Mike explained.

These days, he still deals with the daily pain from his one-year tour in Vietnam, resulting from his exposure to Agent Orange. Around 1999, a burning sensation in his feet developed. As the years go by, he said, the pain has progressed, preventing him from walking distances.

"Sometimes I can't feel my feet, and sometimes they burn so much the pain is excruciating," he said. "I try to minimize this because I saw so many things that were hideous, from amputations to the loss of facial parts. I just feel fortunate that I came back alive and I had 35 years practicing medicine and helping people once I returned."

Mike never wrote to Woody Hayes but did talk to him a few other times during spring scrimmages over the years. Recently, he walked through the Woody Hayes Athletic Center and remembered that meeting with the legend and the general.

When he wants to reminisce, he pulls out an Ohio State program or two from the late '60s and flips through the pages.

"Looking at those pictures," he said. "It just seems like a different age, a different time. I remember the times when I came home and went to a game...the band would come out of that tunnel and play the national anthem, the raising of the flag, I would get choked up and teary-eyed...

"I am glad to have lived to come home to see it again."

The Gold Pants

In what is one of the most unique traditions in college football, every Buckeyes player and coach earns a charm of gold pants following each victory over Michigan. Each pair of pants is inscribed with the person's initials, the score, and the date of the game.

To understand how it started, you must realize that Ohio State rarely fared well against the University of Michigan in the early years of the series.

The Wolverines program was much older, and thus got a head start on the Buckeyes. It was 1919 before OSU beat Michigan, starting in a 0–13–2 hole in the series before that upset win, which accounts for most of UM's 57–40–6 lead following the 2006 game.

By 1934 Ohio State was on a two-game losing streak to Michigan when Francis Schmidt replaced Sam Willaman as head coach. The 13–0 loss to the Wolverines was the Buckeyes' only loss of 1933.

Nobody or no team intimidated Schmidt. When someone asked him how his team would fare against Michigan, he answered, "They put their pants on one leg at a time just like everybody else."

The gold pants charm originated from that statement.

"I'll tell you how it started," said Charlie Ream, who played for OSU from 1934 to 1937. "People around here were tired of losing to Michigan. Simon Lazarus, the president of the Lazarus store, and Herb Levy, president of the Union Company, were big, big football fans. They put their heads together and came up with the Gold Pants Club. They created this charm made of gold that would be given to every letterman who played on a team that beat Michigan."

Schmidt's first team did just that, walloping the Wolverines 34–0 and thus earning the first set of gold pants.

"I am proud to say that I have three pairs, all from the first three years they were given away," Ream said.

A few years ago, one pair popped up on eBay and was promptly bid up to $1,000 until Ohio State officials inquired about the seller. The item was quickly removed from the website, which would not reveal the seller's name.

Jim Tressel called the attempted sale of a pair of gold pants a "slap in the face" for all Buckeyes.

"I don't care how much they are worth," said linebacker Ryan Miller (1993–1996), who earned one pair. "To me, they are priceless. They're a significant part of the history of Ohio State. They mean the world to me. I just wish I had a couple more."

"When I first heard about them, I thought you got a real pair of pants," Troy Smith said. "Then I saw them and thought how small they were. They were like a Christmas ornament. Now I love them. I treasure them. They are priceless to me."

And like Ream, he also has three pairs.

"I get calls every once in a while from somebody who wants to buy a pair," Ream explained. "I don't even ask, 'How much?' because why would I ever want to sell a pair of them? They mean too much to me."

"Those gold pants were and still are a favorite of mine," said defensive back Bruce Ruhl (1973–1976). "Being from Michigan, beating Michigan was always special to me. They called me a traitor when I left the state."

While standing next to his three sons, when the late Ken Kuhn (1972–1975) spoke to the '95 team before The Game, he said, "They mean as much to me as my three little guys standing right here. I had three pairs of gold pants, but I guess one of my girlfriends got away with one pair."

A Treasured Buckeyes Helmet

Clark Backus was an Ohio State linebacker from 1981 to 1983. He has spent the past 19 years in the U.S. Army and has relocated

12 times. With the rank of lieutenant colonel, he is a professor of military science at Marquette University in Milwaukee.

"When you move, you always misplace or lose a thing or two," he said. "You have moving trucks and all that, and there is only so much you can stick in your car."

One of the first things he always secures and places in the car during a move is his helmet from his playing days.

"The mouthpiece is in the upper, right-hand part of my face-mask where I last put it in there," he said. "There is still some maize and blue paint on it from that final game against Michigan. It still has the Buckeye leaves on it, although they are starting to peel off.

"When I taught at West Point, I asked my students to bring in one thing that details them as a person. I would bring in my helmet and explain that there would be no place to affix those individual leaves if it wasn't for the helmet, which represents the state of Ohio and the team as a whole. It was a lesson to teach them that the whole, or the team in this case, is more important than the individual's achievement.

"I will never go anywhere without that helmet. They can bury me with it."

chapter 16

Buckeyes and Presidents

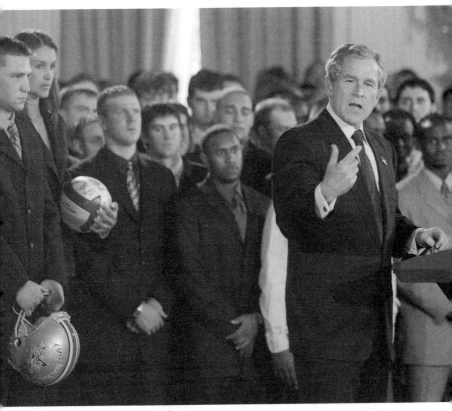

President Bush meets with members of the Ohio State national championship team on February 24, 2003. Punter/presenter Andy Groom is at the far left with helmet.

From Nixon and Ford to Clinton and George W., U.S. presidents have become friends with the Buckeyes over the years.

Ohio State players and coaches have mixed and mingled with residents of the White House often over the years.

It was no secret that Woody Hayes was a die-hard Republican who not only followed politics but was involved in them as well. He was also a longtime, loyal friend to Presidents Richard Nixon and Gerald Ford…which led to one of the funniest miscommunications in locker room history.

Following the 14–11 win over Michigan in 1972, team manager Tom Mannix picked up a ringing telephone in the lower level of the locker room. Upstairs, Woody was congratulating the Buckeyes and handing out team balls.

"The thing is, our equipment manager, John Bozick, was always so good with practical jokes," Mannix remembered. "So I am sitting by the phone and it rings and John looked at me and said, 'Get that, will you? That's the White House calling.'

"I pick up the phone, and the voice on the other line says, 'The White House is calling, the president would like to speak to Woody Hayes.'"

Just then Mannix figured Bozick had set him up to be the butt of yet another practical joke. Therefore, he said into the phone, "Well, this is the Vatican and I am the Pope."

"Young man, this *is* the White House," the caller said. "Can the president speak to Woody Hayes?"

Mannix, still not a believer, answered, "Not right now. He is upstairs giving away game balls, and I think I may have heard a keg being tapped, and Woody will be pouring beers for the press. You know how well he gets along with them!"

The caller responded, "Sir, *this is* the White House, and *this is* the number that was given to us."

"You'll just have to call back," Mannix said. "Give us about 15 minutes."

And he hung up.

"Mannix!" Bozick shouted. "That was the White House! We had this call set up for a week."

While this was happening, Woody was still in the midst of his postgame talk, which always lasted longer after a win over Michigan.

"Woody was standing on the bench and was so excited," Tom Battista (1970–1972) recalled. "He could not say enough how proud he was and the importance of beating 'that team from up north.'

"As he continued talking, someone yelled 'Hey, Coach, President Nixon on the telephone!' He continued talking, and about a half of a minute later, 'Hey, Coach, President Nixon is on the telephone!'

"Then he looked over and said, 'Tell that sons a bitch to wait—I am talking to *my team!*'

"We all screamed and hollered! Only Woody could call the president of the United States an SOB!"

Moments later, the coach walked downstairs to take the call, but Mannix's blunder had delayed the connection.

"I had no [sooner] hung up when Woody came around the corner and asked, 'Is the president on the line yet?'" Mannix added. "I couldn't find a place to hide. Bozick came around and said, 'Yes, he just hung up, but we had some trouble on the line.'"

The White House called the locker room again a few minutes later, and as Nixon and Hayes talked—mostly about the game and about their families—Mannix cowered in the corner of the locker room.

And the coach was never told of Mannix's gaffe.

"The thing is, as I said those things on the phone line, I would hear an 'umph' now and then on the other end of the call, but I don't think it was coming from the man I was speaking to," Mannix said. "I've always wondered if President Nixon was on the other end, listening in, but I'll never know.

"I always felt like I let the university down and I let Woody down. It was always such an honor and a privilege to be associated with that football team. I was only 21 years old, but there was no way I was going to let Bozick get me on a practical joke."

As a footnote, one of the few calls Nixon took following his resignation from office was from Hayes. And likewise, one of the few calls Hayes took following his firing a few years later was from Nixon, who delivered the eulogy at the coach's funeral in 1987.

Twenty-three years later, on October 20, 1995, John Cooper and a few assistants were milling around the Woody Hayes Athletic

Center when a member of the Secret Service called. President Clinton was due to give a speech on campus soon, and his limo would be headed south on Olentangy River Road in a few minutes, they were told.

Cooper grabbed a few scarlet jerseys to give to the president, and a few backup players walked out with him. Most of the starters were in meetings.

When the motorcade rolled down Olentangy, Clinton hopped out of his limo to shake hands with Cooper and a few Buckeyes.

"I've seen you on TV a few times—you've got a real fine team," the president said.

As Clinton walked down the line shaking hands, a Secret Service agent shouted, "No autographs, please!"

That didn't stop scout-team quarterback Joe Germaine from pulling a new football from underneath his sweatshirt as Clinton asked, "Oh, you want me to sign that?" before happily doing so.

"Joe was smarter than all of us," Cooper said.

A few years later, Germaine thought back on that moment.

"My big regret is that one of my roommates ended up with that football," he said. "Man, I wish I had it now."

Germaine would have his own trophy soon enough. A junior-college transfer from Scottsdale Community College, Germaine would go on to set several Ohio State passing records from 1996 to 1998, as well as be named the MVP of the 1997 Rose Bowl.

Following the 2002 championship season, when the Buckeyes visited the White House, Jim Tressel faced an important decision. Which player should present President Bush with a special gift, an Ohio State national championship helmet?

"About 30 minutes before we were to meet President Bush, Coach Tressel pulled me aside and said, 'Groomy, you're my man,'" punter Andy Groom recalled.

"I said, 'What do you mean?'"

"You're our guy who will present the helmet to the president," Tressel told him. "Don't screw it up. Don't talk politics. Just call him 'Mr. President.'"

Groom handled the job as he did his punting chores during the championship season (averaging 45.0 yards per punt)—flawlessly.

"Now, I knew I had come a long way from being a walk-on...but talking to the president of the United States was something I could never have imagined in my wildest dreams," he said. "I could not believe he picked me to do this, and I have to admit I was a little nervous—it's nothing like before a crucial punt."

Before the Buckeyes exited President Bush's property, however, they did get in a little trouble. Tight end Ben Hartsock decided to make a snow angel on the White House lawn.

"As he was doing this, the Secret Service popped out and screamed at the top of their lungs at Ben," Groom recalled. "Well, he didn't hear them and continued in his mission on the lawn. While this was happening, Coach Tressel was dying with laughter, but Ben didn't understand what the fuss was about. He got scolded by the Secret Service and was a little red in the face. It capped off the day, making it one to remember for the rest of our lives."

chapter 17

The Pregame Flick

John Wayne and his many Westerns were favorite pregame movie selections of Coach Hayes's.

Woody Hayes was not a fan of the movers and shakers in Hollywood, other than Bob Hope, that is. They made too many sex-driven, liberal-themed movies for his taste. But the Buckeyes had to watch something on Friday nights...

The night before every game, the Buckeyes' routine is to eat dinner and then watch a movie together, a tradition dating back to Woody Hayes's early days.

But Woody had strict rules: he wanted a movie that would motivate his team. There were to be no love stories, no sex, no comedies, and certainly nothing with a liberal political theme. That made for slim pickings when it was time for Woody's "movie coach" to pick the flick.

Most of the time, especially during the 1950s and '60s, Woody would be back at the team hotel watching a film of his own—film of the next day's opponent.

"I looked at our movies as a time to relax and maybe sleep," said Earle Bruce, an assistant to Hayes from 1966 to 1971. "I was so relieved to get away from Woody, I hardly watched the movie."

Hayes was especially fond of Westerns, including anything in which John Wayne was the star, but the players soon grew bored with Westerns.

"He loved John Wayne," said Erwin Thal, a team manager from 1954 to 1957, who later became close friends with Woody. "And he loved Patton and Abe Lincoln, too. You can say Woody was as American as apple pie."

And he liked his movies just as wholesome. Hence, the controversial ending of *The Sergeant,* the night before a game in 1968, left Woody seething.

"Rod Steiger played one of these tough drill sergeants," said quarterback Bill Long. "But in the end it turns out he is gay. Now remember this is in 1968, so that was not very common to have a movie theme like that at the time. In one of the final scenes, he kisses this guy flush on the mouth, and every player about fell out of his chair. I think Woody blew a gasket when he heard about the end of that movie."

Here's one of linebacker Rick Middleton's favorite stories:

"We were up in Michigan for the biggest game of our careers because we were undefeated going into that [1973] game and so was Michigan. During our Friday night dinner, several of the players came over and talked to me about the movie that we might see. Rumor had it that the assistants couldn't find a new movie that fit the rules that Woody had. The movie had to be a 'macho' movie with lots of physical action and violence that still had a decent moral value attached to it.

"In our time at OSU we, the seniors, had seen the movie *Billy Jack* so many times that we literally had many of the lines memorized. On that night in Ann Arbor, it looked like *Billy Jack* would ride again. The players were literally begging me to make sure that we saw something else. During the dinner, I went over to Woody's table and said, 'We heard that we might be seeing *Billy Jack* again, and honestly, Coach, we would rather see almost anything else.'

"Woody almost exploded at me. 'There *isn't* anything else! The only thing that is also available is that lousy *Executive Action* movie!' he shouted.

"For those who can't remember that movie, it was a fictional account of how some people essentially had JFK assassinated, and it was generally a scathing look at our society. I actually wanted to see the movie and told Woody so. I also told him that many other players would like to see it, too.

"'No!' he yelled at me. 'You guys will come out of the movie depressed, thinking that your government turns on its own, that we kill our own presidents!'

"I was getting ticked off at that point. Right in front of the team, I told him, 'That's crap, Coach! I've seen *Bambi* a dozen times, and I still don't believe that deer can talk!'

"Soon after that, the entire football team was singing the song 'One Tin Soldier' as we watched *Billy Jack* for about the 10th time under Woody's regime."

Dave Cheney (1968–1970) can relate, saying, "I am not sure which season it was, but we watched *The Dirty Dozen* multiple times one season."

It is true that Woody often fired his "movie coach," including once terminating Bruce, who had made the mistake of picking *Easy Rider,* a film which included a flag-burning scene.

"Woody wasn't at the movie that night, but when he found out about it and its content, he went berserk," Rex Kern recalled. "If Woody stayed at the hotel to watch film, when you came back from the movie, he would always ask you what you liked about it and did not like about it.

"The thing about it was, he always would transfer the movie into the performance the next day. If we didn't play well, his reason was because of that movie we saw the previous night."

It is something Bruce will never forget.

"Yep, *Easy Rider* got me fired," he said recently. "You were limited, anyway. There was to be no sex and no love and mushy stuff and no comedies. The kids all wanted to go see *Easy Rider,* but I didn't know what the hell it was about. So then we are coming back after the movie and Woody asked, 'How was the movie?'

"Well, [assistant coach] Dave McClain just buried me. He told Woody, 'It was the worst thing I ever seen!' Then we didn't play well the next day, couldn't stop a screen pass all day, and Woody finally declared, 'I know what it was! It was that damn movie!' And he fired me and gave the job to Rudy Hubbard."

The truth is, nobody on the Ohio State staff wanted the job to pick the team movies.

During the 1968 season, Lou Holtz's only season on the staff, Bill Long and Don Polaski set him up for the scare of his life. The movie that night was the popular thriller *Wait Until Dark,* starring Audrey Hepburn, who plays a blind woman terrorized by three thugs.

"There is a scene where she gets a knife and stabs one of the intruders in her basement apartment," Long explained. "You think the bad guy is dead, and after all of this tension from this fight, he suddenly leaps out of this closet and attacks Audrey Hepburn. When that happened, Lou Holtz jumped right out of his chair."

"Lou was always saying things, 'I can do this. I can do that. I can take this. I can take that,'" Kern recalled. "So those guys bet him he couldn't stay in his seat throughout that movie. Then they set him up. One scary part comes and goes and Lou is still there. They tell him, 'Coach, you made it through it,' knowing there was a worse part to come. I think at the end, Lou wanted to run out of that movie theater. Those guys were howling that night."

At the end of that season, the night before the Buckeyes were to play USC in the Rose Bowl for the national championship, the movie being shown was *Hellfighters,* a flick about firefighters who battled oil-well blazes. It consisted of four reels of film, and when Woody discovered the length of the movie to be longer than two hours, he ordered the third reel removed.

"It was a bad movie anyway," guard Tom Backhus said, "but when Woody had that third reel left out of it, it made no sense to us. We had to watch that thing and return to those stark single-bed rooms at the seminary up in the mountains. It was terrible."

Once, in 1977, the team went to see *Slap Shot,* the hilarious but raunchy hockey movie starring Paul Newman. Unfortunately, Hayes attended the movie that night.

"They get to the part where they mentioned [a slang word for *lesbian*], and Woody just stood up and walked out," said Lenny Davis, a team manager. "Then everybody left with him. Let's just say that he didn't like that movie."

Another movie Woody claimed took a few liberties was *Patton.* There probably wasn't a better student of General George Patton than Woody Hayes. He had read every book about the man, so when Hollywood played with a few facts in the screenplay, the coach didn't like it.

"At one point, he shouted, 'That is not true! That did not happen that way!'" guard Ernie Andria (1975, 1977–1979) said. "He knew Patton inside and out."

Another time, during the viewing of *The Gambler,* the lead character, named Axel Freed and played by James Caan, was a literature professor. During a lecture on bravery, Caan's character stated his case that many heroes become heroes simply because of cowardice as opposed to sheer bravery. At that point, a loud "Bullshit!" was shouted from the audience. As Caan continued his lecture and took a verbal swipe at Abraham Lincoln, there was another "Bullshit!"

Later, Woody apologized to his team for his critical outbursts, but he wanted to let his players know that Freed's viewpoint was not necessarily his own.

For picking *The Gambler,* Rudy Hubbard was fired as movie coach.

Surely, whoever selected a Jane Fonda movie in 1978 was fired by Woody within minutes after the final credits ran down the screen, if not earlier. If you know anything about Woody and his feelings for the antiwar protestors, you would know that Fonda would be at the top of his objectionable list.

"I walked out to get some popcorn," guard Jim Savoca said, "and Woody was out there in the lobby."

"What do you think of the movie?" Woody asked Savoca.

"I knew how to answer that one," Savoca said. "I knew how he felt about Jane Fonda before that movie ever began. After I told him I didn't much care for it, I think he called her every name in the book."

Robert Redford gave the Buckeyes cause to have some fun at fullback Pete Johnson's expense one Friday night.

Johnson (1973–1976) had just purchased a large fur coat before the team viewed *Jeremiah Johnson,* in which Redford starred as a mountain man living off the land in the West during the Civil War. When Redford was first shown on screen wearing a heavy coat made of fox furs, several players yelled, "Pete!" simultaneously.

Bruce, too, continued Woody's discretionary ways of picking movies. He remembered the night he was fired as movie coach, but in the end, he didn't allow comedies or movies with controversial messages, either.

"Movies during the Earle years tended to be somewhat non-controversial and mainstream," said receiver Mike Lanese (1982–1985). "There were lots of action and suspense. Not a whole bunch of the Fonda kids or Fellini. That's not to say we didn't get the occasional *Five Easy Pieces* or *Blade Runner,* but those were exceptions to the rule. Comedies were forbidden because they violated one of Earle's sacrosanct principles: 'You can't make a tackle with a smile on your face.' Sylvester Stallone was definitely and repeatedly acceptable. Woody Allen was out. Not even *Sleeper.*

"Friday night films were especially memorable for me because I had somehow assumed the role of the team's de facto Roger

Ebert. I can't remember exactly how it started, but over time it just kind of evolved into an obligation. After the credits rolled, every film had to be dissected and critiqued. Then I had to assign a final grade. I gave *Cool Hand Luke* a B+, *Rambo* a C+, *Dirty Harry* a B-, *The Longest Yard* a B. Sometimes my teammates agreed with my assessment, but mostly they didn't.

"Over the years, I've often wondered how much better we could have been if *Gladiator* and *The Matrix* had been out back then. I'd also like to think that *Pulp Fiction,* one of my all-time favorites, could've provided some interesting inspiration as well, but I doubt that an assistant coach would've risked his job over any Quentin Tarantino film."

Under Jim Tressel, each player is given a choice: watch the team movie together or watch a movie in your hotel room. That led to a tradition started by linebackers A.J. Hawk, Bobby Carpenter, and Anthony Schlegel, as well as defensive back Rob Harley, who tells it this way:

"We had this routine on Friday nights, whether we were at home in the Blackwell Hotel or on the road where we would take our own DVD player. It had to be an '80s movie. We loved anything campy, like a Tom Cruise movie. Or *Roadhouse* or *Dirty Dancing.* I think during one season, we watched *Top Gun* every Friday night but one.

"The team would be downstairs with a first-run promotional movie, something not yet in theaters, and we would be watching some idiot B movie. But we loved it."

Before the movie, everything had to be in order. Never mind that the players had already eaten the team meal, usually consisting of steak and chicken and all the trimmings, by 6:00 PM. During the movie, Harley and Schlegel would snack on a few double cheeseburgers while Carpenter and Hawk would snack on protein bars.

"For Schlegs and me, it had to be Wendy's," Harley explained. "Bobby and A.J. were too healthy for that. They wouldn't eat a greasy cheeseburger. Some nights, Schlegs would eat three."

Schlegel also had to be wearing his lucky Blackwell-issued robe, while the other three players usually wore warm-up suits.

Hawk and Harley would be in one bed; Schlegel and Carpenter in the other.

"Imagine guys our size piled into those small double beds that you get at some of the hotels we stay in on the road," Harley said. "There wasn't much room.

"Then we would break down the movie just like we broke down film. Every scene, every line…if it couldn't happen, we would jump all over it. Like the time when the martial arts expert uses a pool cue to do a flip in *Roadhouse*. You know that the pool cue wouldn't hold his weight."

Carpenter and Harley became so enamored with *Top Gun* that Harley often dressed up as Maverick, Tom Cruise's character, for Halloween, while Carpenter imitated Ice Man, Val Kilmer's character.

And they always requested that "Danger Zone," one of the hit songs from the film's soundtrack, be played during Thursday's practice, when loud music was piped in to prepare the Buckeyes for the expected crowd noise they would face two days later.

"I can't explain why we loved those '80s movies, considering we all grew up later, but those Friday nights are what we looked forward to," Harley said. "Even today, when we talk to each other, we talk about how much fun we had on nights like that. We don't talk much about football.

"Those are the memories that I'll never forget, and I know Bobby, A.J., and Schlegs feel the same way."

chapter 18

Buckeyes and the Heisman Trophy

Archie Griffin holds up two fingers after he wins his second consecutive Heisman Trophy, in 1975.

From Les to Troy, Ohio State players have made regular trips to New York City to bring home college football's most prestigious individual award. Mr. Two-Time himself, Archie Griffin, is one of the university's most recognizable names.

Ohio State and the prized 13½" high, 25-pound, leather-helmeted, bronzed, stiff-arming trophy have had a long and lasting relationship.

A Buckeye has won the Heisman Trophy seven times, including the only two-time winner in its 72-year history: Archie Griffin.

The Buckeyes are tied with USC and Notre Dame for the most Heisman winners.

"I expect that sometime, somewhere along the line, somebody is going to win it twice," Griffin said. "That award, and winning it twice, is very, very special to me. And with Les, Vic, and Hop before me, and Eddie and Troy following me, it has been very special to Ohio State."

Heisman winners from Ohio State span 63 seasons—from 1944 to 2006—the longest streak in the history of the award that began in 1935.

Les Horvath (1944)

In his words: "At first I wasn't even sure I wanted to play football in college. Dental school was quite taxing. But Coach [Carroll] Widdoes agreed I could miss a practice or two for school."

From a teammate: "Les and I grew up together in Parma, Ohio, two streets apart from each other. Les was a great guy, but he really was just an average runner…an average passer. But there was nothing average about that man's smarts. He was always the smartest guy playing football. He was a great tactician who could outthink the opponent." —Bob Brugge

The stats: Finished his career with 2,055 yards of total offense. Rushed for 924 yards and 12 touchdowns and passed for 344 yards in Heisman-winning season. Also played safety on defense.

The runner-up: Glenn Davis, Army.

After Ohio State: Played with the Los Angeles Rams and the Cleveland Browns before becoming a successful dentist in California. He died on November 14, 1995.

The best story: It is legendary, hilarious, and true. It seems Les's wife was not much of a football fan and, while living in

California, he grew closer to Tom Harmon (who won the Heisman in 1940 with Michigan) and Felix "Doc" Blanchard (who won it in 1945 with Army). First of all, Les's wife thought the trophy was not that attractive and discouraged him from displaying it in the living room. He tried over and over again to convince her that it was a special and unique award and that few athletes get the chance to win it. After visiting the Harmons one night and then visiting the Blanchards another, Mrs. Horvath noticed each of Les's friends had a Heisman proudly displayed.

"Les," she told her husband, "you told me that football trophy of yours was really special, but it turns out that everyone we know has one!"

Vic Janowicz (1950)

In his words: "I liked to have fun away from football. I guess it was too much fun for some people, mainly the coaches."

From teammates: "Vic could do anything. He just ran like a deer." —tackle George Jacoby

"I played with many great players, like Hop Cassady and others, and Vic was the best there ever was." —end Robert "Rock" Joslin

From his coach: "Vic excelled in every phase of the game. He not only was a great runner, passer, and blocker, but he also did all of our kicking, punting, field goals." —Wes Fesler

The stats: Won the award as a junior, totaling 875 yards of offense, passed for 12 touchdowns, and scored 65 points.

The runner-up: Kyle Rote, Southern Methodist.

After Ohio State: Played two years for the Pittsburgh Pirates and switched back to football. Became an NFL star until a near-fatal automobile accident left him with career-ending injuries in 1956. He died February 27, 1996, at the age of 66.

The best story: Woody Hayes arrived at Ohio State in 1951 and promptly changed the offense, which in turn prevented Janowicz from having a big statistical season as a senior. The

Buckeyes struggled to a 4–3–2 record, and Hayes was soundly criticized for not using Janowicz enough. Six years later, while Janowicz was being treated in a Chicago hospital following his accident, Woody visited him before the game at Northwestern. Not satisfied with the treatment Janowicz was receiving, he had him transported to the team plane and brought back to Columbus to be admitted to University Hospital, where he completed his recovery. "It was the turning point for me," Janowicz said later, "the start of a new life."

Howard "Hopalong" Cassady (1955)

In his words: "Growing up in Columbus, I visited Ohio Stadium often as a kid, sneaking into the giant Horseshoe to watch the games with other kids. We would climb over the fence a few hours before the games and hide somewhere in the stadium until they opened the gates. I never even figured I would go to college, because nobody in my family ever went to college. Why would I go to college? I weighed about 135 pounds, and everybody in college was so much bigger than I was."

From his coach: "He was the greatest player of this century." —Woody Hayes, in the late 1950s

The stats: A great two-way player, Hop, as he is known to friends, scored 37 touchdowns in 36 career games. Rushed for 958 yards and 15 touchdowns in his Heisman-winning season. A great defensive back, he recorded 230 career return yards on 10 interceptions, the second-best in school history (behind Mike Sensibaugh's 248).

The runner-up: Jim Swink, Texas Christian.

After Ohio State: A first-round pick of the Detroit Lions, he also played with Cleveland and Philadelphia in the NFL before working for George Steinbrenner's companies. Eventually Cassady became a scout and director of player personnel with the New York Yankees. His son Craig was a defensive back for the Buckeyes from 1972 to 1975.

Howard "Hopalong" Cassady won the Heisman Trophy in 1955.

The best story: Hop is mentioned in the song "Massive Coiling Boss" by the Fratellis, with the line: "Cassady was the hopalong man, but I am the singer of the band, hand to hand, oh man, come back Howie, we miss you *you* big galoot."

Archie Griffin (1974, 1975)

In his words: "The first time, I went to New York on a Tuesday and I was the only one there and they made the announcement that I won. The second year, they called and told me on a Monday that I had won but to keep it a secret.

"They told me how emotional the presentation can be. Malcolm McCloud of the Downtown Athletic Club said, 'Don't worry if you get up there and cry. It will be all right.' Well, I wasn't that type. I just couldn't see myself crying up there. So I got up to give my speech and what did I do? I couldn't get 10 words out before I started crying. I was sort of embarrassed, but I got through it."

From a teammate: "After a few days, I was thinking about transferring. Then after practice, Archie came up to me and looked me right in the eye. 'Look, you are from Pittsburgh, I am from Columbus. If it were the other way around, they would have asked you to go into the game and you would have done the same thing.' I wanted to hug him right there. I decided on the spot that I would be proud to play behind Archie Griffin for four years." —Brian Baschnagel, after Griffin set a then-school record of 239 rushing yards against North Carolina as a freshman

From his coach: "The greatest, most unselfish player I have ever known. Archie Griffin could be the first black president." —Woody Hayes

The stats: Rushed for 1,695 yards and 12 touchdowns as a junior and 1,450 and four touchdowns as a senior. Finished career with 5,589 rushing yards and 26 touchdowns. Compiled a remarkable 31 consecutive games in which he rushed for 100 yards or more. Played on four Big Ten championship teams.

The runners-up: Anthony Davis, USC, 1974; Chuck Muncie, California, 1975.

After Ohio State: A first-round pick of the Cincinnati Bengals, he played seven seasons in the NFL and then joined the Ohio State athletic administration staff. Griffin is the director of the OSU Alumni Association.

The best story: He fumbled on his very first carry as a freshman against Iowa. "I was thinking about breaking a long run and scoring a touchdown. They called '18 Sweep' to the right side. As the play developed, I was shocked because there was this gaping hole in front of me. I kept my eyes on that hole and never looked back at the football, which hit me right on the hands and bounced off. I had fumbled on my first play."

Eddie George (1995)

In his words: "A lot of people had told me that I would never reach this level, but I did. It's funny, but when I came to Ohio State, I wanted to wear No. 20 or No. 6, but they were both taken, so they asked me to choose between 38 and 27, and now my No. 27 is retired."

From his coach: "I never saw Archie Griffin, but [Eddie's] the best I have ever seen a running back run on this level of football. His determination to be the best is unbelievable." —Tim Spencer, then–OSU running backs coach

The stats: Rushed for 1,927 yards and 24 touchdowns in Heisman-winning season. Highlight was his 314-yard game against Illinois, an OSU single-game record. A big, bruising tailback, he finished his career with 3,768 rushing yards and 44 touchdowns.

The runner-up: Tommie Frazier, Nebraska.

After Ohio State: Became a star with the Tennessee Titans (formerly the Houston Oilers), being named the 1996 NFL Rookie of the Year. He went on to play in four Pro Bowls and one Super Bowl. He rushed for 10,441 yards and scored 78 touchdowns in his career before retiring in 2004.

The best story: George's mother, Donna, raised her son by herself. She had changed her schedule as a flight attendant with TWA to be in San Antonio when Eddie signed his first NFL contract on July 19, 1986. If she hadn't, she would have been working aboard TWA Flight 800, which crashed in the Atlantic Ocean shortly after takeoff two days earlier, killing all aboard.

Troy Smith (2006)

In his words: "My earliest memories of Ohio State are of Eddie George and Terry Glenn and those great players. The Michigan games. When I look back and think of the history of Ohio State, two quarterbacks come to mind: Cornelius Greene because he was the first black to play the position and Craig Krenzel because of the way he worked and helped others behind him. I

Troy Smith holds up his Heisman Trophy after winning the prestigious award in 2006.

still remember sitting in the recruiting office and this little short guy, [quarterbacks coach] Joe Daniels, told me I could be the quarterback for this university."

From a teammate: "Troy is Troy. He deserves everything he has earned, because he worked hard to get it. And he became a great leader." —Ted Ginn Jr.

From his coach: "When you think of Troy, the first thing that comes to my mind is leadership. The second is competitiveness, and maybe the third thing about Troy is his hunger to be in command." —Jim Tressel

The stats: Passed for 2,507 yards and 30 touchdowns and was intercepted only five times as Ohio State rolled to 12–0 regular season. Finished career with 54 touchdown passes and only 13 interceptions, by far the best touchdown-to-interception ratio in OSU history. First to have a 3–0 record as a starting quarterback against Michigan.

The runner-up: Darren McFadden, Arkansas.

The best story: Smith received 86.7 percent of the votes, a record for the 72-year-old award. His 1,662-point victory over McFadden is second only to O.J. Simpson's 1,750-point victory over Purdue's Leroy Keyes in 1968. Remarkably, Smith is the only Heisman winner to wear No. 10. Not highly recruited as a quarterback, he signed at Ohio State under the position "athlete."

The Buckeye Who Should Have One

The Buckeyes could have and perhaps should have had one more winner: Keith Byars.

Byars's junior season in 1984 was spectacular enough to win the Heisman Trophy. He gained 1,764 yards, highlighted by a 274-yard (second-best in school history), five-touchdown performance against Illinois (a school record).

His famous 67-yard, shoeless touchdown run against the Illini is one of the most replayed in Buckeyes history.

"As I was going upfield, I made my last cut to the left," Byars explained, "and my shoe started to come loose. I was about to lose it anyway, so I just kicked it off. Then I thought, 'I had better run faster, because I don't want anybody to step on my foot.'"

It was one of his 24 touchdowns he scored that season—he averaged more than two per game. But the Buckeyes' season concluded November 17—six days before Boston College would play at Miami the day after Thanksgiving.

The Eagles had a quarterback short on stature but long on heroics. His name? Doug Flutie. And as Flutie's final play Hail Mary settled into Boston College receiver Gerard Phelan's hands in the Miami end zone early that night, giving the Eagles an improbable 47–45 victory, the Heisman slipped right out of Byars's massive hands. While watching the game on national television, many voters made up their minds right there and then to vote for Flutie.

"I will always believe that the TV people wanted Flutie to win that award because they played that Hail Mary over and over and over again until the Heisman ceremony," Earle Bruce said. "They never played Keith's shoeless run against Illinois."

Flutie ended up with 2,240 points to Byars's 1,251.

"I thought I really should have won the Heisman Trophy," Byars admitted. "Later in the NFL, I would ask Doug Flutie, 'How's my trophy doing?' I should have won it, but things don't always work out the way you want them to."

"The biggest frustration of my career," receiver Mike Lanese said, "was seeing him robbed of the Heisman Trophy in 1984."

Byars's chance for a Heisman as a senior was ruined when he broke his right foot during preseason camp.

Others Who Received Votes

In addition to Ohio State's six winners, dozens more have received votes.

In fact, John Hicks, who finished second to Penn State's John Cappelletti in 1973, is the highest-finishing lineman in the history of the Heisman. Also that year, Griffin and linebacker Randy Gradishar finished fifth and sixth, respectively—one of two times that a team has placed three on the top-six of Heisman vote-getters (Army also did it in 1946).

"That shows you how talented that '73 team was," Griffin said.

Hicks, Byars, and Bob Ferguson (1961) are the three Buckeyes who have finished second. Also, Art Schlichter is the only Buckeye to finish in the top 10 three times.

Here's a look at Ohio State finishers who placed: Gene Fekete, eighth, 1942; Warren Amling, seventh, 1945; Jim Parker, eighth, 1956; Bob White, fourth, 1958; Tom Matte, seventh, 1960; Rex Kern, third, 1969, fifth, 1970; Jim Otis, seventh, 1969; Jack Tatum, 10th, 1969, seventh, 1970; Art Schlichter, fourth, 1979, sixth, 1980, fifth, 1981; Chris Spielman, 10th, 1986, sixth, 1987; Orlando Pace, fourth, 1996; Joe Germaine, ninth, 1998; and A.J. Hawk, sixth, 2005.

Flying Elvises, Columbus Chapter

One of former assistant coach Bill Conley's favorite stories is the time all the assistant coaches were invited to New York at the last minute for Eddie George's Heisman Trophy presentation.

The award announcement has been made annually on a Saturday night on live television, but the actual presentation always has been in Manhattan during a black-tie reception on the following Monday night.

The assistant coaches were invited to attend the banquet on that Monday morning, two days after the announcement.

"None of us owned a tuxedo at that time, so we rushed down to a tux shop in downtown Columbus and rented matching black tuxedos," Conley wrote in his book, *Buckeye Bumper Crops*.

"We decided to wear them on the plane to save time. What a sight it must have been to see eight rather large, athletically built men in black tuxedos running through airports in Columbus and then Philadelphia, where we had a brief layover before flying into LaGuardia. As we boarded our plane in Philadelphia, a flight attendant quipped that we looked like a singing group. Well, that's all it took for Fred Pagac to tell her we were the 'Flying Elvises, Columbus Chapter.'

"As the airplane taxied on the runway, the pilot announced to the passengers, 'Please enjoy your flight to New York City. And by the way, I'd like to extend warm wishes to the "Flying Elvises" from Columbus, Ohio.'"

The Jinx Wears Scarlet and Gray

Much has been made of the Heisman Trophy jinx, since many winners of the trophy have failed miserably in their subsequent bowl games and/or not become NFL stars.

It certainly has applied to Buckeyes.

No Ohio State player has ever won the award and then played on a team that won a bowl game.

Hopalong Cassady had a huge day, gaining 92 yards in the 20–7 win over USC, but that was in the 1955 Rose Bowl, 11 months *before* he won the award.

Ditto for Griffin, who darted for 149 yards on 22 carries in the 42–21 trouncing of the Trojans in the 1974 Rose Bowl, also before he went on to win two Heismans. In the 1975 Rose Bowl, he was held to 75 yards in an 18–17 loss to USC. And in the 1976 Rose Bowl, he gained 93, but the Buckeyes suffered a national championship–crushing 23–10 loss to UCLA.

"That day, we moved the ball up and down the field, but we just didn't score," he said. "That was my final game and the most disappointing loss I ever experienced. Period. We all thought we were good enough to be national champions that year, but we never got one. That game really hurt. It still does."

In the 1996 Citrus Bowl, Eddie George lost a crucial fumble in a 20–14 loss to Tennessee.

Recently, Troy Smith played terribly in the 2006 BCS Championship Game. "I don't really buy into superstitions," Smith said just three days before the game, "and I can't control what other Heisman winners did or didn't do before me. I think that stuff is an excuse, a cop-out. If you focus on what you have to do and take your time to get ready [for the bowl game], you can play at the same level that got you there. I can't speak for those past players. I can only speak for myself. I am not going into this game thinking I am the Heisman Trophy winner, so I have to do this or that."

In by far the worst game of his career, Smith, while running for his life most of the game, passed for only 35 yards on four completions in the Buckeyes' stunning 41–14 loss to once-beaten Florida. He threw an interception, lost a fumble, and was sacked five times.

It's as if the weight of the trophy suddenly provides its holders a path to failure. The reasons are many and varied, if they do exist, but evidence suggests the jinx is very real.

One could point to the physical aspect. There are two weeks of solid banquets that a Heisman winner endures, starting with the college football awards televised show in Orlando the preceding week. A player's diet, for instance, likely isn't the same as it was when he was living on campus. And perhaps he doesn't take the time to work out while on the road. Thus, he may gain a few pounds from the period of the final regular-season game until the first day of practice leading up to the bowl game.

Then there's the mental part. The adulation that comes with the buildup to the award, the actual winning of the award, and subsequent ceremonies in New York are sometimes too much for even the nation's best college football player to handle.

The demand on a Heisman winner's time also affects him as well as everyone around him. Woody Hayes realized that back in 1974.

"He told me, 'You can't do everything for everybody, and if you keep going around doing everything for everybody, you are going to affect the team and you are going to affect your season next year,'" Griffin said.

Times have changed over the past 20 years, with awards shows preceding the Heisman ceremony and with a higher media demand on today's players.

"The ceremonies down in Orlando are pretty exhausting in themselves, all the anticipation of who wins the awards," George said. "And [the day of the Heisman presentation] is probably going to be the longest day. You've got to wait all day just to find out [the winner]."

A Heisman winner is still a 22- or 23-year-old college student and not yet a person who has endured the rough knocks of a lifetime of ups and downs. So when everyone tells him for weeks that he is the greatest player on earth, he tends to believe it.

"Stay humble," Smith said. "That's all Coach Tressel said to me before the [Heisman ceremony]. The only thing that upset me the whole time was being away from my teammates. I felt like I was cheating those guys."

If Smith was not humble before the bowl game, Florida's defense humbled him in a three-hour beating.

"If that's the worst thing that ever happens to me in my life," Smith said after the game, "then I am cool with it."

chapter 19

A Who's Who of Assistant Coaches

Even die-hard Buckeyes fans may be surprised to know that Pete Carroll, Lovie Smith, and Nick Saban are among the many successful coaches who have served on Ohio State's coaching staff during their careers.

They never received much money or fame. But assistant football coaches at Ohio State generally had bright futures in the profession. The list of assistants is full of well-known names, such as Gillman, Schembechler, Holtz, Bruce, and Tressel.

The list of the names of Ohio State's assistant coaches who have passed through the Buckeyes program on their way to fame and, in some cases, fortune to become head coaches is quite impressive.

From future NFL head coaches who would lead their teams to Super Bowls to college head coaches who later won national championships at other universities, and one in particular at Ohio State, several coaching icons were one-time Buckeyes assistants.

No less than 32 former Ohio State assistant coaches have gone on to become head coaches in either college football or in the NFL.

Did you know that USC coach Pete Carroll was an Ohio State assistant in 1979?

Or that Alabama coach Nick Saban was Ohio State's defensive backs coach in the 1980–1981 season? (When then–head coach Earle Bruce, a Buckeyes assistant himself from 1966 to 1972, fired him following an awful year for the Buckeyes secondary, it was the only time Saban had ever been fired, before or since.)

Also, Sid Gillman (1938–1940), Joe Bugel (1974), Carroll, Saban, Dom Capers (1982–1983), and Lovie Smith (1995) later became NFL head coaches.

Smith took his Chicago Bears (and former Buckeyes running back and assistant Tim Spencer as the Bears running backs coach) to Super Bowl XLI.

Current Michigan State coach Mark Dantonio (2001–2003), Marshall coach Mark Snyder (2001–2004), and Illinois coach Ron Zook (1988–1990) were one-time OSU assistants, as were future head coaches Glen Mason (1978–1985), Walt Harris (1995–1996), and Larry Coker (1993–1994), who were fired from Minnesota, Stanford, and Miami, respectively.

Not to mention the current Buckeyes boss himself, Jim Tressel, who was one of Bruce's assistants (1983–1985).

Remarkably, five Buckeyes assistants went on to win national championships as head coaches: Tressel (Ohio State, 2002), Coker (Miami, 2001), Lou Holtz (Notre Dame, 1989), Saban (LSU, 2003), and Carroll (USC, 2003, 2004). Saban's and Carroll's teams split the two major polls during the '03 season.

"I learned more about coaching from working one year at Ohio State under Woody Hayes, than I learned in any other year of my career," Holtz once said. "And I still know all of the words to 'Across the Field.'"

And of course, there was one Glenn E. Schembechler. Yes, Bo was one of Woody's top assistants from 1958 to 1962.

"Look at that list of assistant coaches...it is quite impressive," said former OSU assistant Bill Conley. "And I am proud to be on that list."

When most assistants pass through Columbus, adding Ohio State's name to their résumés, they are in search of head-coaching jobs or their next move upward. That's just the nature of the business. However, there were two assistants that made Ohio State their home....

Esco and Ernie

Ernie Godfrey joined the Ohio State staff in 1929 and retired in 1961—a remarkable run of 33 straight seasons under seven head coaches, from Sam Willaman to Woody Hayes.

"When I think of Ohio Stadium, sometimes I think of Ernie," said Wayne Betz (1960–1962). "At practice every day, he would point to Ohio Stadium and tell us: 'It was not built in a day.'"

Godfrey also was known for his unique ways of butchering the English language or for his confusing sayings that made little sense to his players.

"Ernie would say things such as, 'Pair off in groups of three and scatter out in little bunches,'" Betz said. "I always wondered, but never asked Ernie, what did scattering out in little bunches really mean?"

Following a game at Wisconsin in which the offense couldn't gain many yards, a reporter talked to Godfrey. He was quoted in the newspaper the next day as saying, "The reason we couldn't move the ball against Wisconsin is that they were using all of those 10-men, 11-men, and 12-men lines."

Perhaps he was one reason Hayes didn't want his assistants talking to the media.

Even after Godfrey retired, however, Woody talked him into working with the Buckeyes' kickers for 11 more years—on his own time.

"The thing I loved about Ernie was that he got us to singing all the great songs that belong to Ohio State, such as the 'Buckeye Battle Cry' and 'Carmen Ohio,'" said Dick Young (1953–1954). "Ernie would come into the locker room and get it started, and everybody would follow along."

Godfrey also coached the signs-and-props committee of the motivational department, if there was such a thing, creating the "Beat Michigan" messages that would be seen in the bottoms of all the team cups or on the floor mats or locker-room walls. At times, they were even seen in the bottom of the urinals.

"Those were the type of things Ernie contributed later in his career," Young said. "He loved Ohio State."

Ernie is a member of the National Football Foundation Hall of Fame, and the Columbus chapter is named after him.

*   *   *

Esco Sarkkinen was an All-American end at Ohio State in 1939 and later an assistant coach for the Buckeyes from 1946 to 1977.

When Esco decided to enter coaching after World War II, he recalled much later, "I told my wife, Freda, that she could expect to move a minimum of 10 times before I was through. But that never happened, because I got the Ohio State job, with all the tradition and great players and coaches that go with it, and nothing else ever really appealed to me."

Of Finnish descent, Sarkkinen was known as Hayes's finest scout.

"He had no equal in scouting ability," Hayes said when Esco retired. "He had this uncanny knack of analyzing game situations."

Godfrey, who died in 1980, and Sarkkinen, who died in 1998, dedicated their lives to coaching Ohio State football players, without the attention, fame, or money given to head coaches.

"One of my favorites was Esco," defensive back Bruce Ruhl (1973–1976) said. "Esco would hold daily trivia contests on the team bus when we bused down to the stadium for practices. He would say, 'Anyone with the right answers wins my orange drink.'

"Esco also was a traditionalist. He once interrupted our ring committee meeting, composed of juniors and seniors who were designing the ring to commemorate the 1975 season and the trip to the Rose Bowl. We were breaking tradition by having a gold rose on top of the stone, instead of the 'O' or 'OHIO' that was usually inscribed. Esco yelled at us for messing with tradition."

Years later at Anne Hayes's funeral, Ruhl noticed Esco's fingers.

"He was wearing two rings—the 1968 national championship ring and the '76 Rose Bowl ring, which we had designed and had broken tradition," Ruhl said.

"It was one of my favorites," Esco told him.

"During his funeral," Ruhl said, "he was received while wearing those two rings and a pair of gold pants on his lapel."

Longest Tenure as an OSU Assistant

1. Ernie Godfrey, 32 years.
2. Esco Sarkkinen, 31 years.
3. Fred Pagac, 19 years.
4. Bill Conley, 16 years *(t)*.
   Lyal Clark, 16 years *(t)*.

chapter 20

The Greatest Buckeyes

*Troy Smith will go down
in history as one of the
greatest Buckeyes
quarterbacks of all time.*

Ohio State has had 174 first-team All-Americans through the 2006 season, including seven three-time All-Americans, seven Heisman Trophy winners, and 15 Big Ten Most Valuable Players. The letterman's list is full of legends, with names like Tatum, Willis, Gradishar, Fesler, Stillwagon, and Hicks. Ranking them is nearly impossible.

But I did it anyway.

Who's the greatest this or the best that of all time is always a very subjective way to categorize football players. There really is no definitive way to rank them. The difficult part is the categorization. Is it judged by personal awards, statistics, performance, talent, or, even, if the player was a part of a championship team?

For example, was a running back who played in the 1950s and who was a two-time All-American and a Heisman Trophy winner a greater player than a running back who played in the 1980s and didn't win the Heisman and missed most of his senior season with an injury?

That's the case of Howard "Hopalong" Cassady and Keith Byars, who finished his career with 734 more yards than Cassady.

If you check the north end of the Ohio Stadium façade, you will notice Hop's No. 40 is retired, but there is no mention of Byars, who finished as the runner-up in the 1984 Heisman Trophy race.

It illustrates how subjective and how unfair picking teams and making lists is. I have never liked to compare players and teams of one era with another. The game has changed so much over the years, the numbers don't equate well. Furthermore, the rankings here are not affected by the player's success, or lack of it, during his NFL career.

However, for the sake of an argument, here's my list of the best in Ohio State history at each position:

Quarterbacks

1. Troy Smith (2003–2006).
2. Art Schlichter (1978–1981).
3. Rex Kern (1968–1970).
4. Joe Germaine (1996–1998).
5. Bobby Hoying (1992–1995).
   Honorable mention: Greg Frey (1987–1990), Mike Tomczak (1981–1984), and Cornelius Greene (1972–1975).

I know. I know. Vic Janowicz won the Heisman in 1950, but Vic completed only 41 passes...in his career! Consider that Hoying holds the OSU career record with 498 completions, or more than 10 times that of Janowicz.

If Smith had completed his career with a solid performance and a win over Florida in the 2006 BCS Championship Game, putting him at the top of this list would be much easier. But he failed miserably in his final game, even if he spent most of the night being chased. However, you cannot take away that he is the first quarterback in school history to start in three consecutive wins over Michigan (Tippy Dye did not start all three games from 1934 to 1936), and he played brilliantly in all three games. Smith's touchdown-to-interception ratio (54-to-13) also is by far the best in school history. And after all, he is the first true quarterback in school history to win the Heisman Trophy.

Schlichter's legacy among fans and media is tainted greatly by the legal trouble he encountered following his career, but I would not hold that against him here. He probably was the most-talented quarterback ever to wear a Buckeyes uniform but came up short in big games. He was 2–2 against Michigan and 1–3 in bowl games. He was a great drop-back passer, and he also was very effective running the option. He still holds most of OSU's career passing records and probably will for a long time. "I saw him get hit with the best of them," said linebacker Glen Cobb. "He was one tough amigo on the field."

One of my favorites, Kern, doesn't belong on the list statistically, but he was limited by Woody's conservative offense, especially during his senior season. Rex attempted only 364 passes in his career—less than what Germaine attempted during the '98 season! Rex also had more interceptions than touchdown passes—but he did lead OSU to the 1968 national championship and had a 27–2 record in his three years. And he followed that up by marrying the Rose Bowl queen!

Germaine holds most of the Buckeyes single-season records for his '98 season, in which he passed for 3,330 yards and 25 touchdowns on 230 of 384 attempts. If not for that shocking home loss to Michigan State that year, he would have led Ohio State to a national championship. And remember, he did lead the Buckeyes to their first Rose Bowl win (1997) in 23 years. Why

John Cooper did not play him more over Stanley Jackson in the 1996–1997 season, I will never understand.

Running Backs

1. Archie Griffin (1972–1975).
2. Eddie George (1992–1995).
3. Keith Byars (1982–1985).
4. Howard "Hopalong" Cassady (1952–1955).
5. Tim Spencer (1979–1982).

Honorable mention: Bob Ferguson (1959–1961), Jim Otis (1967–1969), Pete Johnson (1973–1976), Pepe Pearson (1994–1997), and Carlos Snow (1987–1989, 1991).

There are four Heisman Trophies on this list.

Nobody can argue with putting Mr. Two-Time first. Archie was the best player in the game from 1973 to 1975 and rolled up one 100-yard game after another, even when defenses were stacked to stop him. Remember, the Buckeyes didn't exactly have a balanced attack in those days, and the deep pass was not a threat to keep linebackers honest. That makes his 5,589 career rushing yards even more remarkable.

I can't think of anyone who worked harder to accomplish what he did in 1995 than George. He was big, powerful, and tough to tackle in rushing for a school-record 1,927 yards and 24 touchdowns that season. It made fans forget his two fumbles in a tough home loss to Illinois as a freshman. Ironically, when George set the single-school rushing record of 314 yards, it was against the Illini.

Byars is simply Ohio State's most deserving winner of the Heisman Trophy who didn't win the Heisman Trophy (Boston College's Doug Flutie won it in 1984). Consider that Byars rushed for 1,764 yards and scored 22 touchdowns that season. (He finished his career with 46 rushing touchdowns, second only to Pete Johnson's 56.) At least that was good enough to earn the Big Ten's MVP award and become a first-team All-American. His 1985 season was lost to a broken foot.

Spencer seems forgotten by most fans, but his 3,553 career rushing yards rank third in school history.

Receivers

1. Cris Carter (1984–1986).
2. David Boston (1996–1998).
3. Gary Williams (1979–1982).
4. Joey Galloway (1991–1994).
5. Michael Jenkins (1999–2002).

Honorable mention: Doug Donley (1978–1980), John Frank (1980–1983)*, Dee Miller (1995–1998), and Brian Baschnagel (1972–1975). *Tight end.

Nobody, and I mean nobody, had better hands than Carter. He could catch anything near him. His one-handed catch near the sideline in the 10–7 win over BYU in the 1985 Citrus Bowl defies description. But he tainted his own career by accepting money from an agent and was declared ineligible before what would have been his senior season in 1987. That season, the Buckeyes stumbled to a 6-4-1 record, and Earle Bruce was fired the week before the Michigan game.

Boston is the career leader with 34 touchdown receptions.

Jenkins, surprisingly, ranks third on the all-time list in receptions with 165. And you cannot forget his over-the-shoulder touchdown reception on fourth down that beat Purdue in 2002, thus keeping Ohio State's national championship hopes alive. He was one of Ohio State's most clutch receivers.

Terry Glenn would have made this list, but he was a one-year wonder. He had 64 of his 79 career receptions during his senior season.

Offensive Linemen

1. Orlando Pace (1994–1996).
2. Jim Parker (1954–1956).
3. John Hicks (1970, 1972–1973).
4. Chris Ward (1974–1977).
5. Bill Willis (1942–1944).

Honorable mention: Jim Lachey (1981–1984), Korey Stringer (1992–1994), Dave Foley (1966–1968), Steve Myers (1972–1974), Ken Fritz (1976–1979), Jim Houston (1957–1959), and LeCharles Bentley (1998–2001).

All five on this list were two-time All-Americans, and all were dominating blockers.

Orlando Pace may be the greatest offensive lineman ever to wear a Buckeyes uniform.

Willis was probably the best two-way lineman ever to play at Ohio State, a punishing blocker and a great tackler. So, let's give him that honor right from the beginning.

You want to know how football has changed?

Willis stood 6'2" and weighed 215 pounds, or about the size of most tailbacks in today's game. Parker was 6'2", 200, about the size of a free safety today.

Pace, a dominating left tackle, was among the most decorated even though he left for pro football before his senior season, becoming the top pick in the 1997 NFL draft. He won the Lombardi Award twice and the Outland Trophy once.

Hicks finished second in the Heisman Trophy voting in 1973 but did win the Lombardi and the Outland that year.

Defensive Linemen

1. Jim Stillwagon (1968–1970).
2. Mike Vrabel (1993–1996).
3. Van Ness DeCree (1971–1974).
4. Jim Marshall (1957–1958).
5. Dan Wilkinson (1992–1993).

Honorable mention: Bob Brudzinski (1973–1976), and Quinn Pitcock (2003–2006).

Stillwagon, a middle guard, is a no-brainer choice for the top of the list. In 1970 he became the first player in college football to win the Outland and the Lombardi in the same season.

Most people think of Vrabel as one of the NFL's best linebackers. But at Ohio State, he was one of college football's best rush ends. A two-time All-American, he recorded a remarkable 66 tackles for loss and 36 quarterback sacks—both school records.

DeCree, a dominating defensive end, was a two-time All-American.

Wilkinson's legacy would have been more secure if he had played more than two seasons. But during those two, he was virtually unblockable, recording 23½ tackles behind the line of scrimmage. He was the first pick of the 1994 NFL draft.

Linebackers

1. Tom Cousineau (1975–1978).
2. Chris Spielman (1984–1987).
3. Randy Gradishar (1971–1973).
4. A.J. Hawk (2002–2005).
5. Marcus Marek (1979–1982).

Honorable mention: Steve Tovar (1989–1992), Andy Katzenmoyer (1996–1998), Thomas "Pepper" Johnson (1982–1985), Dwight "Ike" Kelley (1963–1965), and Glen Cobb (1979–1982).

This category is the toughest to rank because Ohio State probably has produced more top linebackers than any school, including Penn State. All of these linebackers were great. I mean, how could you rank Gradishar third on any list? The guy was an excellent linebacker, finishing his career with 320 career tackles.

I believe that nobody dominated the game like Cousineau. From sideline to sideline, he usually made the tackle, finishing with 569 in his career. Consider that he had 16 *solo* tackles in one game in 1978 and holds the single-season record with 211 total tackles (17.6 per game).

Spielman ranks number one on the career list with 283 solo tackles.

Hawk, a two-time All-American, won the Lombardi Award and should have won the Butkus Award as a senior. He had 394 tackles, including 41 for loss, and also intercepted seven passes during his career.

Marek is Ohio State's all-time leading tackler with 572.

Tovar was very underrated during his career. He ranks fourth all-time in tackles with 408. You may wonder why Katzenmoyer, the 1997 Butkus Award winner, isn't higher on this list. He did not lead the team in tackles in any of his three seasons. But he did make huge plays, finishing his career with 18 sacks and six interceptions.

Defensive Backs

1. Jack Tatum (1968–1970).
2. Mike Doss (1999–2002).
3. Mike Sensibaugh (1968–1970).
4. Neal Colzie (1972–1974).
5. Antoine Winfield (1995–1998).

Honorable mention: Fred Bruney (1950–1952), Shawn Springs (1994–1996), Ted Provost (1967–1969), Arnie Chonko (1962–1964), and Tim Fox (1972–1975).

Tatum was far and away Ohio State's finest defensive back. He could have been an All-American running back with his speed and ability or an All-American linebacker with his size. As it was, he was named an All-American twice and was the nation's Defensive Player of the Year as a senior.

Doss, a strong safety, is only one of seven Buckeyes ever to become a three-time All-American and the only defensive back to do so. He also was the Big Ten's Defensive Player of the Year in 2002.

Sensibaugh had a nose for the ball and glue for hands. He is the Buckeyes' all-time interception leader with 22.

Colzie, who finished with 15 career interceptions, held Ohio State's punt-return record for career average (14.3 yards) for 32 years until Ted Ginn Jr. broke it recently.

Winfield was a two-time All-American and the first Buckeye to win the Thorpe Award. He was a fierce hitter who played the run as well as any cornerback in Ohio State history, finishing with 278 tackles.

Kickers

1. Mike Nugent (2001–2004).
2. Dan Stultz (1997–2000).
3. Tim Williams (1990–1993).
4. Vlade Janakievski (1977–1980).
5. Josh Jackson (1994–1996).

Mostly a category for statistics, Nugent ranks above everyone else in accuracy and distance. He finished his career with 72 field goals—13 more than number two on the list, Dan Stultz. Nugent holds the school record with 24 consecutive field goals made and also has the top two seasons in school history in field goals made—25 in 2002 and 24 in 2004. For his career, he made 72 of 88 field-goal attempts, which is also good for the best percentage (81.8) in school history.

Jackson is second on that list at 73.5 percent and holds the record for consecutive PATs made in a season (46 in 1995).

Williams leads in career PAT percentage: 98.6 percent (143 of 145).

Punters

1. Tom Tupa (1984–1987).
2. Tom Skladany (1973–1976).
3. Andy Groom (2001–2002).
4. Brent Bartholomew (1995–1998).
5. B.J. Sander (1999–2003).
Honorable mention: Tom Orosz (1977–1980).

Tupa averaged 47.1 yards in 1984 as a freshman and 47.0 yards in 1987—the top two punting averages in Ohio State history.

Skladany also shared some place-kicking duties but was known more for his booming punts. He finished his career with a

42.7-yard average. Groom is at the top of the Buckeyes' career list in average at 45.0, but that is based on only 109 punts in two seasons as the starter.

chapter 21

"When One Buckeye Is Down, We're All Down"

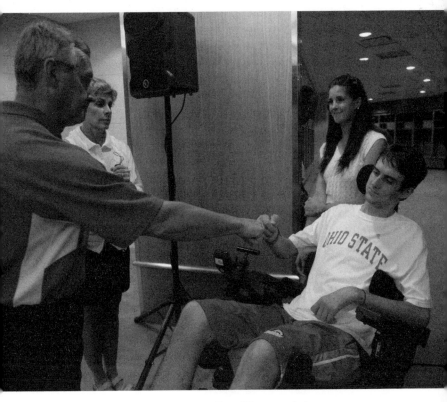

Jim Tressel bumps knuckles with Tyson Gentry after a July 27, 2006, news conference. Gentry suffered a broken neck during an April scrimmage.

Injuries such as torn knee ligaments and broken wrists are as much a part of the game of football as blocking and tackling. But one Buckeye sustained a serious injury that won't soon be forgotten. For now, it has taken all his ability to stand and to walk. Tyson Gentry's heart and determination, however, is operating at full strength.

It was Good Friday, April 14, 2006, when the Buckeyes conducted a spring scrimmage at Ohio Stadium.

As the scout-team offense was about to run a play, Tyson Gentry, a third-year walk-on punter/receiver from Sandusky, lined up to the right. At the snap of the ball, he ran downfield and cut inside, catching a pass. As he turned to run up the field, defensive back Kurt Coleman caught him from behind and tackled him. Gentry landed awkwardly on the right side of his head, breaking his C4 vertebra in his neck. After he was stabilized, he was rushed to the emergency room at the Ohio State medical center. Head coach Jim Tressel promptly ended the team's practice and rushed to the hospital to be with Tyson's parents, Bob and Gloria Gentry, who were watching the scrimmage when the injury occurred.

Tyson underwent surgery that night and again three days later.

Within a few months, his weight dropped to 133 pounds as his appetite subsided and his body fought off infections. Tyson has regained some movement in his upper body as well as more than 30 pounds. He continues his daily rehabilitation therapy sessions to gain strength and movement and also carries a heavy class load at Ohio State.

As with most serious spinal cord injuries, doctors will not make any predictions when, or if, Tyson will walk again.

If his resolve, determination, and attitude have any say in the matter, his father says, Tyson Gentry will take steps on God's green earth again one day.

"His attitude is very good," said Bob Gentry, who played for the Buckeyes in the mid-1970s. "That's the scary thing about it— his attitude is unbelievable. He never asked, 'Why me?' He has handled this much better than I would have. He is such a good kid. It's hard to say that you could ever love your children more than you once did, but I really do. It really is a story made for TV."

During the 2006 season, every Buckeyes player wore his No. 24 in a decal on the back of their helmets to honor their fallen teammate.

In this chapter, Tyson tells his story and thanks Buckeyes fans for their outpouring of support.

From a real young age, growing up in Norwalk, I dreamed of playing football at Ohio State. I wore my dad's jersey, No. 25, at Halloween. It seemed I would always be an Ohio State player during Halloween. Dad was in coaching, and he would get me some real small shoulder pads that fit me, and I would put his jersey over them. That was cool.

One time when I was in middle school, Dad took me into the Ohio State locker room to meet some of the players. I just remember how neat it was. Later, at Sandusky Perkins High School, I started off as a quarterback and then moved to receiver. I punted, and I also played basketball as a freshman and as a senior, and I also ran track.

Cincinnati and Ohio University recruited me, but I was going to head to Capital because my sister Ashley was going there—until Ohio State started talking to me about their walk-on program. Brandon Schnittker was from my high school, and he talked to me about coming down and taking a look. I thought to myself, "Well, if it doesn't work out, I can always transfer to Capital."

When I got there, I knew I would be behind some of the returning upperclassmen in trying to win the punting job, but I wanted to compete for the second-string job. The punting job was open, but it was a battle between Kyle Turano and Josh Huston that year. It was definitely intimidating for me because they were upperclassmen and I just wanted to go out there and kill the ball right away. Let's just say it didn't go that well.

Running out onto that field at Ohio Stadium for the 2004 opener [a 27–6 win over Cincinnati] was amazing for me. I remember when we got to camp that summer, the seniors all got up and talked about different things. They talked of their favorite memories—and they talked about running out onto the field for the first time. Until you do it, they said, it is tough to describe to others. When I did it, it was unreal. I remember how bright it was and how loud it was. It is something I will never forget.

The spring of '05 was a lot better for me in the punting department. I started in the spring game, but it was a cold and rainy game and the ball was snapped over my head one time. I ran back there to get it and got tackled. All things considered, it wasn't that bad.

Since my freshman year, I had started doing some scout-team receiving during drills, and I had wanted to get more involved in it. I loved it. I knew I had a better chance at playing at punter, but I liked the aspect of going out on a route and making a catch.

This brings me to spring practice in 2006 and what happened to me. It was a 12- to 14-yard dig route, and I was lined up on the right. I came across the middle, caught the ball, and turned up the field. The ball started to slip a little. Kurt Coleman caught up to me and dragged me down to the ground. I had been hit a lot harder than that. I mean, guys get hit 10 times harder than that all the time, but as I went down, my head went to the side. I realize it was just a freak accident.

I haven't watched the tape of the play. Mark Quisenberry, Ohio State's audio/video coordinator, put it on a DVD for me if I ever want to see it, but I haven't yet. It will be tough watching it, but I definitely want to see it, eventually.

Doctors told me from the beginning not to count on much. They don't want you to get your hopes up. I think they pretty much prepare you not to get your hopes up to ever walk again. The rehab people have been great. They prepare you to work with what you have, and they keep it all open that you will walk again. I just stay positive. I keep working to do what I can to walk again someday. My ultimate goal is to make a complete recovery and walk again.

Of course, my more immediate goals are smaller. I want to get more use with my upper body, and I would be satisfied with that for now. I definitely have noticed progress. I want to take this one small goal at a time, and they say I am way ahead of the game at the level of the injury that I had.

I never have asked, "Why me?" I never feel it's a question of that—it's more a question of "Why did it happen so easily?" The way it happened, I know it could have happened to anybody. But there's no sense getting down about it.

I have received somewhere between 1,500 and 2,000 cards and letters. For my birthday, last July 20, 2006, I received about

500 birthday cards. It has been unbelievable. That just shows how great the Buckeyes family is. It shows how close everybody is, that we are there for each other. I know that good people exist and that a lot of good has come from this. I was in awe of how much everybody really cares.

One of the cards that came a couple of weeks after the injury is one that I will never forget. It read: "When one Buckeye is down, we're all down."

The coaches have been great to me, too. They have visited me quite a bit. I didn't know the team was going to do that beforehand [wear the No. 24 decal on their helmets]. I saw it during the first game last season [against Northern Illinois], and it was really neat—and seeing it on TV for the away games.

I am still taking classes, and I am about at a junior level in credits, majoring in speech pathology. My sister Ashley goes to class with me and takes notes for me. She graduated from Capital and took a year off to come live with me and work with me, to make sure things get done for me. My other sister, Natalie, drives down often, too. They have really helped me in every way.

My family was close before this, but we are closer now. My mom and my dad have been a huge support for me. We all depend on each other.

The main thing I want to do is thank everyone out there for their support. Their cards, donations, and moral support have meant so much to me and my family. I knew it before, but I know it now more than ever that the Buckeyes family is a great group of people.

*   *   *

Contributions for Tyson Gentry's medical expenses can be made to: The Tyson Gentry Medicaid Payback Trust, c/o National City Bank, 9 East Main Street, Norwalk, Ohio 44857.

chapter 22

Traditions

The Best Damn Band in the Land is just one of the many proud traditions Buckeyes fans look forward to each season.

From those famous helmets full of Buckeye leaves to the incomparable Script Ohio, Ohio State football is surrounded by an array of traditions that make being a Buckeye a lifelong experience.

Those Cherished Buckeye Leaves

Following the 1967 season, Woody Hayes wanted to change the appearance of the Buckeyes' uniforms, and he also wanted a way to reward his players for making plays that led to his favorite thing in the whole word—winning football games.

Thus, Ohio State scrapped the old helmets known for that wide scarlet pad down the middle, and the team started wearing silver helmets. The names of each player were added to the back of the scarlet jerseys that year, and wide gray-and-white stripes were added to the sleeves.

That was just window dressing, however.

In creating what has become one of the most-recognizable signatures of any college football helmet, Hayes and longtime trainer Ernie Biggs brainstormed the idea of creating Buckeye leaf decals. The purpose was to reward players for such plays as interceptions, touchdowns, and fumble recoveries. Milton Caniff, an Ohio State alumnus and a well-known political cartoonist, designed the leaf decal.

And during that season, ironically enough, Ohio State won its sixth national football championship.

"Ernie and Woody put their heads together and came up with the new look," said John Bozick, Ohio State's equipment manager from 1955 to 1991. "It was kind of an abrupt thing, and it was all done in a two- or three-month period in the off-season."

In the late 1960s and '70s, the decals were the approximate size of a silver dollar and approximately 13 fit on each side of a helmet.

"You got a portion of a leaf with a big play, so it took three or four big plays to get a whole one," Bozick said. "They used to call [defensive back] Ted Provost 'Tree' because he once had 13 on his helmet. That was unheard of at that time."

These days, the leaves are the size of a quarter and approximately 48 will fit per side. The first leaves earned are adorned on the left side of the helmet. If a player should be so lucky to have the left side filled, then they are placed on the right side, always starting at the back of the helmet and moving to the front.

Ted Ginn Jr. finished the 2006 season with 99 leaves on his helmet, a far cry from the days in which Provost led the team with 13.

Each head coach has changed the requirements for receiver leaves over the years. Under Jim Tressel, they are awarded for touchdowns, interceptions, quarterback sacks, achieving special teams goals, offensive and defensive goals, and when a player grades a winning performance.

And as has always been the custom, dictated by Hayes himself, no player receives a single leaf following a loss.

"What's always really cool is that as soon as our players walk into the locker room before a game on Saturdays, they check to make sure they were given their Buckeye leaves and that their helmet has the right amount," said Rob Lachey, the team's equipment manager.

"If they don't, they will bitch up a storm. That's how important they are. At the end of each season, most players take the time to peel each one off their helmets and take them as keepsakes."

Buckeye Grove

One of the first things Jim Marshall visited on his recruiting trip, this patch of trees has become a must-visit for recruits who dream big.

Just south of Ohio Stadium, in front of Morrill Tower, is a grove of Buckeye trees, planted in the honor of each All-American. At the base of each tree, a plaque is inscribed with the player's name and years played.

"I always wanted to see my name there," Marshall said.

The first tree in the grove was planted in 1934 to honor Buckeyes legend Charles "Chic" Harley.

Script Ohio

One of the greatest traditions in all of college football started on October 10, 1936, before a game at Ohio Stadium against Pittsburgh (a 6–0 loss), only five years before the country was pulled into World War II.

Today, Script Ohio by the Ohio State University Marching Band is the most identifiable and unique signature of any marching band in the world.

Band director Eugene Weigel, while visiting New York City in the 1930s, created the idea of having his band march into a formation to spell *Ohio,* according to university archives.

"Searching for ideas, I remembered the rotating sign around the Times Square Building in New York City, and during my student days at Columbus, I always remembered the skywriting advertisements at the state fair," he said.

From that origin, he developed a marching formation that began with the revolving block O and evolved into *Ohio,* completed by the dotting of the *i* by a selected sousaphone player.

Today, the band performs three different sets of Script Ohio: a single, a double, and, when the Alumni Band attends a September game each football season before fall quarter begins, a quadruple script.

Only five non-band members have ever dotted the *i* performed by TBDBITL: Bob Hope, Woody Hayes, Bob Ries, Novice Fawcett, and the latest, golfer Jack Nicklaus on October 28, 2006. Several others have dotted the *i* during a script done by the Alumni Band.

When Buckeyes football players are asked what they enjoy most about watching a game for the first time at Ohio Stadium once their playing careers are finished, they mention seeing Script Ohio performed.

"We didn't get to see Script Ohio much as players, but now I get chills when I see it," said Greg Frey, the Buckeyes quarterback from 1988 to 1990. "I have so much respect for our band. One of my favorite times of each game was the end of the third quarter because you could look up in the stands and listen to 'Hang On Sloopy.' The stadium would always be rocking when it was played."

"That is why most players really realize how great our band is once they graduate," Rex Kern said. "I will never forget the time when I went back to Ohio Stadium for the first time after my playing days were done. I saw that band come down the ramp, march onto the field, and that drum major touching his head to the ground behind him, the stands were erupting, cheering.

"The next thing I know, tears are rolling down my face. That is such an emotional experience."

Kern recalled a moment when he was an incoming freshman, checking into his dormitory in the fall of 1967.

"It was my first day on campus," he explained. "A slender young man was in our elevator, and he had the most discouraging, depressing look on his face. I asked him what was wrong.

"'I just got cut from the band for the very last time,' he told me. 'It had always been a goal of mine my whole life to make that marching band.'

"That planted a seed in my mind that there must be something pretty special about our marching band," Kern said. "Then I realized how special it was later on."

The band has developed a close, symbiotic relationship with the football team over the decades. The week before the Michigan game, the band attends one practice and performs Script Ohio so the football players can participate or watch, something they do not get to experience on game days.

"Coach Hayes loved our band," running back Cal Murray (1977–1980) explained. "When we got to see the band come out that week before the Michigan game and perform Script Ohio, I thought, 'Wow, this is what everybody gets excited about.'

"Coach Hayes told us, 'Look at these band members. They are the greatest fans you have, right here.'"

"That is one of the reasons I want our players to attend the Skull Session before the games [at St. John Arena]," Jim Tressel said. "We can't go out and watch Script Ohio at halftime, because we are busy."

Linebacker Clark Backus (1980–1983) added, "Pretty quickly, I came to appreciate how close the band is to the Ohio State team. When the band came to practice during Michigan week, they played Script Ohio on the field, and I'll never forget [tight end] John Frank jumping up and down while watching it. He was like a kid in a candy store. That band draws Buckeyes together."

Scott Terna, a walk-on punter for the Buckeyes, got especially close to one of the greatest Script Ohio performances of all time, before the Fiesta Bowl national championship game against Miami on January 3, 2003.

As a crew member of ESPN's *College GameDay*, he assisted the cameraman, standing in the middle of the field that night in Tempe, Arizona.

"By this time, I had seen Script Ohio many times since my playing career was over, and I knew it is one of the *greatest* things ever!" Terna said. "TBDBITL is something that will make the hair on the back of your neck stand up as they take the field. Sometimes, I admit a few tears well up as the memories would run through my mind like a movie reel.

"On this night, however, it was our job to film the *i*-dotter. My heart started pounding as we waited on the Ohio State sideline. Then about one-third of the way through 'Le Regiment,' we started walking out toward the middle of the field. I looked up around me as the band continued marching, and it was the most incredible feeling—all I could see was a sea of scarlet in the stands and 'Le Regiment' pounding in my ears as the band members marched by me. I thought to myself, *I'm in the middle of the field during Script Ohio at the national championship game—it can't get much better than this!* As the drum major led the sousaphone player out to dot the *i,* the crowd erupted and cameras were flashing throughout the stadium. It was amazing! As a fan or non-band member, you can't get any closer to dotting the *i* without actually doing it! That forever will be my greatest Script Ohio story. I'll remember it for as long as I live."

By the way, a trumpet player by the name of John Brungart dotted the *i* in the first Script Ohio. By the next year, 1937, and for the next 70 years and beyond, only a sousaphone player has been allowed to perform the honor.

"Across the Field"

Varsity manager William A. Dougherty, a fraternity brother and close friend of Chic Harley's, wrote the Buckeyes' first fight song in 1915 as a dedication to Coach John Wilce. It was performed for the first time October 16 of that season—a 3–3 tie against Illinois.

"Across the Field" was ranked in the top 10 fight songs by Bill Studwell, a Northern Illinois University librarian and expert on America's fight songs.

To this day, the Buckeyes gather in the locker room and sing the words following each victory:

Fight the team across the field,
Show them Ohio's here
Set the earth reverberating with a mighty cheer
Rah! Rah! Rah!
Hit them hard and see how they fall;
Never let that team get the ball,
Hail! Hail! The gang's all here,
So let's win that old conference now.

"Carmen Ohio"

On October 25, 1902, Fred Cornell rode a train from Ann Arbor to Columbus, disappointed and yet proud. A member of the Ohio State Glee Club and an amateur poet, Cornell was returning from the Buckeyes' football game at Michigan, an 86–0 loss to the Wolverines.

That is when he composed the lyrics to Ohio State's alma mater:

Oh come let's sing Ohio's praise,
And songs to Alma Mater raise.
While our hearts rebounding thrill,
With joy which death alone can still.
Summer's heat or winter's cold,
The seasons pass, the years will roll,
Time and change will surely show,
How firm thy friendship O-hi-O.

"Carmen Ohio" was first performed the following year and has developed into one of the university's most beloved traditions and trademarks.

Ohio State fans and alumni have sung the school's alma mater at sporting events for more than a century, but Tressel's arrival in 2001 brought a new awareness to the cherished song.

In one of his first orders of business, he made sure that all of his players knew the words, and the team immediately started singing it with the marching band at the south end of Ohio Stadium at the conclusion of each game.

"Before, we always sang the fight song after games, and I knew we had an alma mater, but I never heard it until Coach Tressel came here," defensive lineman Kenny Peterson said. "I never knew the words. Do you know what goes through my mind now when I hear 'Carmen Ohio'? It almost brings tears to my eyes."